Middle School 2-2

기말고사 완벽대비

적중 100

영어 기출 문제집

중 **2**

천재 | 정사열

Best Collection

구성과 특징

교과서의 주요 학습 내용을 중심으로 학습 영역별 특성에 맞춰 단계별로 다양한 학습 기회를 제공하여 단원별 학습능력 평가는 물론 중간 및 기말고사 시험 등에 완벽하게 대비할 수 있도록 내용을 구성

Words & Expressions

Step1 Key Words 단원별 핵심 단어 설명 및 풀이
Key Expression 단원별 핵심 숙어 및 관용어 설명
Word Power 반대 또는 비슷한 뜻 단어 배우기
English Dictionary 영어로 배우는 영어 단어

Step2 실력평가 단원별 수시평가 대비 주관식, 객관식 문제풀이

Step3 서술형 대비 학업성취도 및 수행능력평가 대비 서술형 문제풀이

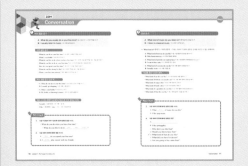

Conversation

Step1 핵심 의사소통 의사소통에 필요한 주요 표현 방법 요약
핵심 Check 기본적인 표현 방법 및 활용능력 확인

Step2 대화문 익히기 상황에 따른 대화문 활용 및 연습

Step3 기본평가 시험대비 기초 학습 능력 평가

Step4 실력평가 단원별 수시평가 대비 주관식, 객관식 문제풀이

Step5 서술형 대비 학업성취도 및 수행능력평가 대비 서술형 문제풀이

Grammar

Step1 주요 문법 단원별 주요 문법 사항과 예문을 알기 쉽게 설명
핵심 Check 기본 문법사항에 대한 이해 여부 확인

Step2 기본평가 시험대비 기초 학습 능력 평가

Step3 실력평가 단원별 수시평가 대비 주관식, 객관식 문제풀이

Step4 서술형 대비 학업성취도 및 수행능력평가 대비 서술형 문제풀이

Reading

Step1 구문 분석 단원별로 제시된 문장에 대한 구문별 분석과 내용 설명
확인문제 문장에 대한 기본적인 이해와 인지능력 확인

Step2 확인학습A 빈칸 채우기를 통한 문장 완성 능력 확인

Step3 확인학습B 제시된 우리말을 영어로 완성하여 작문 능력 키우기

Step4 실력평가 단원별 수시평가 대비 주관식, 객관식 문제풀이

Step5 서술형 대비 학업성취도 및 수행능력평가 대비 서술형 문제풀이
교과서 구석구석 교과서에 나오는 기타 문장까지 완벽 학습

Composition

|영역별 핵심문제|

단어 및 어휘, 대화문, 문법, 독해 등 각 영역별 기출문제의 출제 유형을 분석하여 실전에 대비하고 연습할 수 있도록 문제를 배열

|서술형 실전 및 창의사고력 문제|

학교 시험에서 점차 늘어나는 서술형 시험에 집중 대비하고 고득점을 취득하는데 만전을 기하기 위한 학습 코너

|단원별 예상문제|

기출문제를 분석한 후 새로운 시험 출제 경향을 더하여 새롭게 출제될 수 있는 문제를 포함하여 시험에 완벽하게 대비할 수 있도록 준비

|단원별 모의고사|

영역별, 단계별 학습을 모두 마친 후 실전 연습을 위한 모의고사

on the textbook····················· 교과서 파헤치기

- **단어Test1~2** 영어 단어 우리말 쓰기와 우리말을 영어 단어로 쓰기
- **대화문Test1~2** 대화문 빈칸 완성 및 전체 대화문 쓰기
- **본문Test1~5** 빈칸 완성, 우리말 쓰기, 문장 배열연습, 영어 작문하기 복습 등 단계별 반복 학습을 통해 교과서 지문에 대한 완벽한 습득
- **구석구석지문Test1~2** 지문 빈칸 완성 및 전문 영어로 쓰기

Contents

Lesson 7

A Step Inside the Culture

 의사소통 기능

- 관심에 대해 묻기
  Are you interested in taking pictures?

- 칭찬하기
  Good job!

 언어 형식

- 현재분사
  It looks like a happy woman **walking** down a road with autumn leaves.

- It ... to부정사
  It is not easy **to write** by hand well at first.

Words & Expressions

Key Words

- **actually** [ǽktʃuəli] 부 실제로, 사실
- **artistic** [ɑːrtístik] 형 예술의, 예술적인
- **autumn** [ɔ́ːtəm] 명 가을
- **awesome** [ɔ́ːsəm] 형 멋있는, 대단한, 굉장한
- **beatbox** [bíːtbɑks] 동 비트 박스를 하다
- **below** [bilóu] 전 …의 아래에
- **between** [bitwíːn] 전 …의 사이에
- **both** [bouθ] 대 둘 다
- **calligraphy** [kəlígrəfi] 명 캘리그래피
- **character** [kǽriktər] 명 글자, 성격
- **classical** [klǽsikəl] 형 고전의
- **craft** [kræft] 명 공예
- **creative** [kriéitiv] 형 창의적인
- **collect** [kəlékt] 동 모으다
- **culture** [kʌ́ltʃər] 명 문화
- **detective** [ditéktiv] 명 탐정 형 탐정의
- **difference** [dífərəns] 명 차이
- **dish** [diʃ] 명 음식, 접시
- **draw** [drɔː] 동 그리다
- **dynasty** [dáinəsti] 명 왕조, 왕가
- **enjoy** [indʒɔ́i] 동 즐기다
- **example** [igzǽmpl] 명 예, 사례
- **excellent** [éksələnt] 형 훌륭한, 뛰어난
- **express** [iksprés] 동 표현하다
- **fantasy** [fǽntəsi] 명 판타지, 환상, 공상
- **figure** [fígjər] 명 (사람, 동물의) 상, 모형
- **foreign** [fɔ́ːrən] 형 외국의
- **handwriting** [hǽndraitiŋ] 명 손 글씨, 필적
- **hold** [hould] 동 잡다
- **horror** [hɔ́ːrər] 명 공포
- **imagine** [imǽdʒin] 동 상상하다
- **include** [inklúːd] 동 포함하다
- **inside** [insáid] 전 …의 안에, …의 안으로
- **learn** [ləːrn] 동 배우다
- **lightning** [láitniŋ] 명 번개
- **monster** [mʌ́nstər] 명 괴물
- **nowadays** [náuədèiz] 부 요즘에는, 오늘날에는
- **online** [ɔ́nlain] 형 온라인의, 인터넷의
- **period** [píːriəd] 명 시대, 기간
- **perfect** [pə́rfikt] 형 완벽한
- **performance** [pərfɔ́ːrməns] 명 공연
- **person** [pə́ːrsn] 명 사람
- **poem** [póuəm] 명 시
- **popular** [pápjulər] 형 인기 있는
- **practice** [prǽktis] 동 연습하다 명 연습
- **season** [síːzn] 명 계절
- **selfie** [sélfi] 명 셀피, 자신의 사진 찍기
- **sharp** [ʃɑːrp] 형 날카로운
- **step** [step] 명 (발)걸음
- **tail** [teil] 명 꼬리
- **tale** [teil] 명 이야기
- **title** [táitl] 명 제목
- **try** [trai] 동 시도하다, 노력하다
- **tool** [tuːl] 명 도구, 수단
- **unique** [juːníːk] 형 독특한, 특별한
- **widely** [wáidli] 부 널리
- **wizard** [wízərd] 명 마법사
- **works of art** 예술 작품

Key Expressions

- **at first** 처음에(= **at the beginning**)
- **be interested in** …에 관심이 있다
- **be made of** …로 만들어지다
- **build up** 만들다(= **develop**)
- **dance to** …에 맞춰 춤추다
- **do taekwondo** 태권도를 하다
- **for free** 무료로
- **go shopping** 쇼핑하러 가다
- **keep -ing** …을 계속하다(= **continue**)
- **lead to** …로 이끌다, …로 이어지다
- **look like+명사** …처럼 보이다
- **ride a bike** 자전거를 타다
- **take+시간+to V** …하는 데 시간이 걸리다
- **take a class** 수업을 듣다
- **take a picture** 사진을 찍다
- **What do you think?** 너는 어떻게 생각하니?
- **You got it.** 바로 그거야.

Word Power

※ 서로 반대되는 뜻을 가진 어휘

☐ **include**(포함하다) ↔ **exclude**(제외하다)

☐ **difference**(차이) ↔ **similarity**(유사, 비슷함)

☐ **popular**(인기 있는) ↔ **unpopular**(인기 없는)

☐ **outside** (밖에) ↔ **inside** (안에)

☐ **perfect**(완벽한) ↔ **imperfect**(불완전한)

☐ **foreign**(외국의) ↔ **domestic**(국내의)

※ 서로 비슷한 뜻을 가진 어휘

☐ **autumn** : **fall** (가을)

☐ **awesome** : **amazing** (굉장한)

☐ **wizard** : **sorcerer** (마법사)

☐ **at first** : **at the beginning** (처음에)

☐ **sharp** : **keen** (날카로운)

☐ **unique** : **distinct** (독특한)

☐ **excellent** : **outstanding** (우수한)

☐ **tool** : **implement** (도구)

English Dictionary

☐ **artistic** 예술의
→ relating to any form of art 어떤 예술의 형태와 관련된

☐ **autumn** 가을
→ the season between summer and winter
여름과 겨울 사이의 계절

☐ **below** …의 아래에
→ in a lower place or position 더 낮은 장소나 위치에

☐ **calligraphy** 캘리그래피
→ the art of producing beautiful handwriting using a brush or a special pen
브러시나 특수 펜을 이용한 아름다운 필체를 제작하는 기술

☐ **dynasty** 왕조
→ a series of rulers of a country who all belong to the same family
모두 같은 가문에 속한 한 나라의 일련의 통치자들

☐ **express** 표현하다
→ to show feeling or opinion 감정이나 의견을 나타내다

☐ **include** 포함하다
→ to make someone or something part of a group
누군가나 어떤 것을 그룹의 일부로 만들다

☐ **lightning** 번개
→ the bright flashes of light that you see in the sky during a storm
폭풍우가 몰아치는 동안 하늘에서 보이는 밝은 빛의 섬광

☐ **nowadays** 요즘에는, 오늘날
→ at the present time
현재의 시간에

☐ **period** 시기
→ a particular time in history 역사에서의 특별한 시기

☐ **poem** 시
→ a piece of writing using beautiful or unusual language arranged in fixed lines that have a particular beat and often rhyme
특정한 박자와 종종 운율을 가진 고정된 행으로 배열된 아름답거나 독특한 언어를 사용하는 한편의 글

☐ **popular** 인기 있는
→ liked by most people
대부분의 사람들이 좋아하는

☐ **season** 계절
→ one of four periods of year that is based on the earth's position toward the sun
태양을 향한 지구의 위치를 바탕으로 한 1년의 네 시기 중 하나

☐ **tale** 이야기
→ a story about imaginary events or people
상상의 사건이나 사람들에 관한 이야기

☐ **title** 제목
→ the name of a book, poem, movie, play, or other work of art
책, 시, 영화, 연극 또는 다른 예술 작품의 이름

☐ **tool** 도구
→ a piece of equipment, usually one you hold in your hand, that is designed to do a particular type of work
특정한 유형의 일을 하기 위해 고안된 보통 손에 드는 장비

☐ **unique** 독특한
→ not the same as anything or anyone else
다른 어떤 것 또는 누구와도 같지 않은

☐ **wizard** 마법사
→ a man in stories who has magic powers
마법의 힘을 가지고 있는 이야기 속의 남자

중요

01 다음 문장의 빈칸에 들어갈 말로 알맞은 것은?

> How do you _____ your feelings? Do you sing or dance?

① divide ② include
③ express ④ imagine
⑤ save

서답형

02 다음 빈칸에 영영풀이에 해당하는 말을 주어진 철자로 쓰시오.

> • Nowadays, it is p_____ to express feelings through handwriting.
> <영영풀이> liked by most people

➡ _____

03 다음 중 밑줄 친 단어의 우리말 뜻이 잘못된 것은?

① Are you <u>interested</u> in Korean culture? (관심 있는)
② The <u>wizard</u> waved his magic stick back and forth. (마법사)
③ Computers are <u>widely</u> used these days. (널리)
④ Every person has a <u>unique</u> fingerprint. (독특한)
⑤ He told a <u>tale</u> about magical animals. (꼬리)

서답형

04 우리말에 맞게 빈칸에 알맞은 말을 두 단어로 쓰시오.

> 사실, 나는 무료로 온라인 강좌를 듣고 있어.
> ➡ Actually, I'm taking an online class _____.

➡ _____

[05~06] 다음 영영풀이에 해당하는 단어를 고르시오.

05

> to make someone or something part of a group

① mix ② imagine
③ ride ④ include
⑤ collect

중요

06

> in a lower place or position

① beyond ② below
③ among ④ above
⑤ between

서답형

[07~08] 다음 빈칸에 공통으로 들어갈 단어를 쓰시오.

07

> • *Hangeul* is a lot easier to learn than Chinese _____s.
> • In Korea, the green dinosaur Dooly is a beloved _____.
> • Generosity is part of the Korean _____.
>
> *generosity 관대함

➡ _____

08

> • All calligraphers had to _____ hard to make their unique styles.
> • It's not easy to write by hand well at first, but _____ makes perfect.

➡ _____

01 대화의 빈칸에 들어갈 단어를 주어진 철자로 시작하여 쓰시오.

> A: I enjoyed your p_____. You did a good job.
> B: Thank you. Are you interested in playing the ukulele?
> A: Sure.

02 다음 빈칸에 영어 설명을 참고하여 주어진 철자로 시작하여 쓰시오.

> • It looks like a happy woman walking down a road with a _____ leaves.
> <영어 설명> the season between summer and winter

03 우리말과 같은 뜻이 되도록 빈칸에 알맞은 단어를 쓰시오.

(1) 아래에 있는 한국과 영국의 두 사례를 보아라.
 ➡ Look at the two _____ from Korea and the UK _____.

(2) 여러분은 그 차이를 구별할 수 있는가?
 ➡ Can you tell the _____?

(3) 여러분은 영화 포스터, 책 표지, 음악 CD, 그리고 의류에서 디자이너들의 예술적인 손길을 발견할 수 있다.
 ➡ You can find designers' _____ _____es on movie posters, book covers, music CDs, and clothes.

(4) 괴물의 커다란 입, 날카로운 이빨, 그리고 추하고 긴 꼬리를 상상할 수 있는가?
 ➡ Can you _____ the _____'s big mouth, sharp teeth, and ugly, long tail?

04 영영풀이에 해당하는 단어를 <보기>에서 찾아 첫 번째 칸에 쓰고, 두 번째 칸에는 우리말 뜻을 쓰시오.

> ┤ 보기 ├
> monster / vegetable / dynasty / traditional / fantasy

(1) _____: a pleasant, exciting, or unusual experience that you imagine is happening to you: _____

(2) _____: an imaginary creature that is large and frightening: _____

(3) _____: a series of rulers of a country who all belong to the same family: _____

05 우리말에 맞게 주어진 단어를 이용하여 문장의 빈칸을 채우시오. (어형 변화 필수)

(1) 캘리그래피는 요즘 우리 주변에서 널리 쓰이고 있다.
 ➡ Today calligraphy is _____ used around us. (wide)

(2) Harry의 번개나 마술사 모자가 보이는가?
 ➡ Do you see Harry's _____ and the wizard hat? (light)

(3) 요즈음에는 손 글씨를 통해 감정을 표현하는 것이 인기다.
 ➡ Nowadays, it is popular _____ feelings through handwriting. (expression)

(4) 오래 전의 다양한 종류의 많은 캘리그래피 작품들이 세계 곳곳에서 발견되고 있다.
 ➡ Many _____ kinds of calligraphy _____ from long ago can be _____ all around the world. (differ / work / find)

Conversation

---

1 관심에 대해 묻기

Are you interested in taking pictures? 사진 찍는 것에 관심이 있니?

■ "Are you interested in …?"은 상대방에게 무언가에 관심이 있는지 묻는 표현이다. 'in' 다음에는 명사 또는 동명사 형태가 온다. 이에 대한 대답은 "Yes, I am." 혹은 "No, I'm not. I'm interested in …"으로 한다.

> *e.g.* A: Are you interested in cooking?
> B: Yes, I am. / No, I'm not. I'm interested in swimming.

관심에 대해 묻는 표현

- What are you interested in?
- Do you find something interesting?
- Are you interested in science?
- Are you interested in taking pictures?
- What are you into?
- What are your main interests?

■ **관심 표현과 관련된 유사한 표현**

I am interested in ~., I have an interest in ~., I am fascinated by ~. 등이 있다.

> *ex)* I am interested in K-pop.
> = I have an interest in K-pop.
> = I am fascinated by K-pop. 저는 K-pop에 관심 있습니다.

핵심 Check

1. 다음 대화의 빈칸에 들어갈 말로 알맞은 것은?

A: _____

B: I'm interested in musicals.

① Do you find musicals interesting?
② What are you going to do?
③ Do you want to learn a musical?
④ What makes you think so?
⑤ What are you interested in?

② 칭찬하기

Good job! 잘했어!

■ "You did a good job." 혹은 "Good job."은 상대방의 어떤 행동에 대해 칭찬하는 표현이다.

e.g. A: I got a good grade on the math exam.
　　　B: Good job!

칭찬하기

- (Very) Good!
- Great! / Excellent!
- What a nice dress!
- (You did a) Good job!
- Good work!
- Well done!
- Good for you!
- How kind she is!

칭찬에 답하기

- Thanks. / Thank you (very much).
- I'm glad you like(d) ~.

핵심 Check

2. 다음 대화의 빈칸에 들어갈 말로 알맞지 <u>않은</u> 것은?

B: _____ Someone is holding a cloud? How creative!

G: Thank you.

① Good work!
② How nice!
③ Good job!
④ Don't get stressed.
⑤ Excellent!

Get Ready 2

(1) B: Do you like K-pop?

G: Yes. ❶I enjoy listening to SJ's songs. I can ❷dance to his songs.

B: ❸Great!

(2) B: ❹Are you interested in cooking Korean dishes?

W: Yes. I sometimes cook *bulgogi* for my family and they love it.

(3) B: ❺Are you interested in learning *Hangeul*?

G: Yes. Actually, I'm learning it in my calligraphy class. Look! This is my work.

B: Excellent!

(1) B: 너는 K-pop을 좋아하니?
G: 응. 나는 SJ의 노래를 듣는 것을 즐겨. 그의 노래에 맞춰 춤을 출 수 있어.
B: 멋지다!
(2) B: 당신은 한국 음식을 요리하는 것에 관심이 있나요?
W: 네. 때때로 저는 가족을 위해 불고기를 요리하고 그들은 그것을 좋아해요.
(3) B: 너는 한글 배우는 것에 관심이 있니?
G: 응. 실제로, 나는 캘리그래피 수업에서 한글을 배우고 있어. 봐! 이게 나의 작품이야.
B: 훌륭하다!

❶ enjoy는 동명사를 목적어로 취하면서 '~을 즐기다'는 의미로 사용된다.
❷ 'dance to ...'는 '…에 맞춰 춤추다'는 의미로 여기서 to는 전치사이다.
❸ 상대방을 칭찬할 때 사용하는 표현이다.
❹, ❺ 상대방이 어느 것에 관심을 가지고 있는지 물어볼 때 사용하는 표현으로 'be interested in ...'은 '…에 관심이 있다'는 뜻이다.

Check(√) True or False

(1) G can dance to SJ's songs. T ☐ F ☐

(2) W isn't interested in cooking Korean dishes, but sometimes cook *bulgogi*. T ☐ F ☐

(3) G is learning *Hangeul* in her calligraphy class. T ☐ F ☐

Start Off Listen & Talk A

(1) B: ❶Good job! Someone is holding a cloud? How creative!

G: Thank you. Are you interested in taking pictures?

B: Yes, I am. Actually, ❷I'm taking an online class for free.

G: Oh, ❸good for you.

(2) G: ❹Good work! I think your painting expresses the feeling of autumn well.

B: Thank you. ❺Are you interested in painting?

G: Yes, I am. I started taking a class on weekends.

B: Oh, I didn't know that.

(1) B: 잘했다! 누군가 구름을 잡고 있는 거야? 정말 창의적이구나!
G: 고마워. 너는 사진 찍는 것에 관심이 있니?
B: 응. 그래. 사실, 나는 무료로 온라인 강좌를 듣고 있어.
G: 오, 잘됐구나.
(2) G: 잘했다! 네 그림은 가을의 느낌을 잘 표현하고 있는 것 같아.
B: 고마워. 너는 그림에 관심이 있니?
G: 응. 그래. 나는 주말마다 수업을 듣기 시작했어.
B: 오, 몰랐어.

❶, ❸, ❹ 상대방을 칭찬할 때 사용하는 표현으로 'Excellent!, Well done!' 등으로 바꾸어 쓸 수 있다.
❷ 'take a class'는 '수업을 듣다'는 뜻이고, 'for free'는 '무료로'의 뜻이다.
❺ 상대방이 관심을 가지고 있는지 물어볼 때 사용하는 표현이다.

Check(√) True or False

(4) G is interested in taking pictures. T ☐ F ☐

(5) We can guess both G and B are interested in painting. T ☐ F ☐

Start Off Listen & Talk B

B: ❶You did a good job! It's awesome.
G: Thanks.
B: What is it made of? Glass?
G: Yes, it is. ❷Are you interested in glass art?
B: Yes, very much. ❸How long did it take to make it?
G: It took one month.

❶ 상대방을 칭찬할 때 사용하는 표현으로 'Excellent!, Well done!' 등으로 바꾸어 쓸 수 있다.
❷ 상대방이 어디에 관심을 가지고 있는지 물어볼 때 사용하는 표현이다.
❸ 시간이 얼마나 걸리는지 물어볼 때 사용하는 표현이다..

Speak Up Look and talk

B: I enjoyed your performance. You did a good job.
G: Thank you. Are you interested in playing the ukulele?
B: Sure. Can you teach me?
G: ❶No problem.

❶ 상대방의 부탁에 승낙하는 표현이다.

Speak Up Mission

A: Are you interested in watching horror movies?
B: ❶Yes, I am. I watch horror movies very often. / ❷No, I'm not. I'm interested in reading detective stories.

❶ 관심이 있는지 묻는 말에 대한 긍정의 답이다.
❷ 관심이 있는지 묻는 말에 대한 부정의 답이다.

Real-life Scene

James: What are you doing, Mina?
Mina: I'm practicing calligraphy.
James: You're writing with a brush. ❶It looks fun.
Mina: Are you interested in calligraphy?
James: Yes, very much.
Mina: Look at this! I just wrote it. ❷What do you think?
James: It ❸looks like a person dancing with open arms.

Mina: You got it. This Korean word means "dance."
James: ❹You did a good job! Can I try it?
Mina: ❺Why not? Take this brush.

❶ 'look+형용사'로 '재미있어 보인다'라는 의미이다.
❷ 상대방의 의견을 구하는 표현으로 '어떻게 생각하니?'의 뜻이다.
❸ 'look like+명사'는 '…처럼 보이다'라는 뜻이다.
❹ 상대방을 칭찬할 때 사용하는 표현이다.
❺ 'Why not?'은 '왜 안 되겠니?'의 뜻으로 상대방의 제안에 승낙하는 표현이다.

Your Turn

A: You're writing something. What's this?
B: It's my art homework. Do you like it?
A: Sure. ❶I think you did a good job!

❶ 상대방을 칭찬할 때 사용하는 표현으로 'Good for you., Excellent!, Well done.' 등으로 바꾸어 쓸 수 있다.

Express Yourself

(1) B: Look! Two girls are learning *Hangeul*.
    G: Are you interested in *Hangeul*, Kevin?
    B: Yes, very much. I want to join them and learn it.
(2) B: Julie, are you interested in *hanbok*?
    G: ❶Not really.
    B: Then, what are you interested in?
    G: Well, I'm interested in *taekwondo*. It is a traditional Korean sport. It's awesome.
(3) G: ❷Look at the two men learning *pansori*.
    B: Are you interested in *pansori*, Nancy?
    G: Sure. I like the sound of it. I want to learn it.

❶ 관심이 있는지 묻는 말에 '별로 관심없어.'라는 부정의 뜻이다.
❷ learning=who are learning

Learning Diary Listen & Speak

B: Minji, are you interested in animals?
G: Yes, I am. ❶I'm good at taking care of them.
B: ❷How about plants? Are you interested in them, too?
G: No, I'm not. I can't grow them well.

❶ 'be good at ~'은 '~을 잘하다'라는 의미이다.
❷ How about ~?: ~은 어때?

● 다음 우리말과 일치하도록 빈칸에 알맞은 말을 쓰시오.

Get Ready 2

(1) B: Do you like K-pop?
G: Yes. I _____ _____ to SJ's songs. I can _____ _____ his songs.
B: _____!

(2) B: Are you _____ _____ _____ Korean dishes?
W: Yes. I _____ cook *bulgogi* _____ my family and they love it.

(3) B: _____ _____ _____ in learning *Hangeul*?
G: Yes. _____, I'm learning it in my _____ class. Look! This is my work.
B: _____!

Start Off Listen & Talk A

(1) B: _____ _____! Someone is _____ a cloud? _____ _____!
G: Thank you. Are you interested _____ _____ _____?
B: Yes, I am. Actually, I'm _____ an online class _____ _____.
G: Oh, _____ _____ you.

(2) G: _____ work! I think your painting _____ the _____ of _____ well.
B: Thank you. _____ you _____ in painting?
G: Yes, I am. I started _____ a class on weekends.
B: Oh, I didn't know _____.

Start Off Listen & Talk B

B: You _____ a good job! It's _____.
G: Thanks.
B: What is it _____ _____? Glass?
G: Yes, it is. _____ you _____ _____ glass art?
B: Yes, very much. _____ _____ did it _____ _____ _____ it?
G: _____ _____ one month.

Speak Up Look and talk

B: I _____ your _____. You did _____ _____ _____.
G: Thank you. Are you _____ in _____ _____ ukulele?
B: Sure. _____ _____ teach me?
G: No problem.

(1) B: 너는 K-pop을 좋아하니?
G: 응. 나는 SJ의 노래를 듣는 것을 즐겨. 그의 노래에 맞춰 춤을 출 수 있어.
B: 멋지다!

(2) B: 당신은 한국 음식을 요리하는 것에 관심이 있나요?
W: 네. 때때로 저는 가족을 위해 불고기를 요리하고 그들은 그것을 좋아해요.

(3) B: 너는 한글 배우는 것에 관심이 있니?
G: 응. 실제로, 나는 캘리그래피 수업에서 한글을 배우고 있어. 봐! 이게 나의 작품이야.
B: 훌륭하다!

(1) B: 잘했다! 누군가 구름을 잡고 있는 거야? 정말 창의적이구나!
G: 고마워. 너는 사진 찍는 것에 관심이 있니?
B: 응, 그래. 사실, 나는 무료 온라인 강좌를 듣고 있어.
G: 오, 잘됐구나.

(2) G: 잘했다! 네 그림은 가을 느낌을 잘 표현하고 있는 것 같아.
B: 고마워. 너는 그림에 관심이 있니?
G: 응, 그래. 나는 주말마다 수업을 듣기 시작했어.
B: 오, 몰랐네.

B: 너 정말 잘했구나! 정말 멋져.
G: 고마워.
B: 무엇으로 만든 거니? 유리?
G: 응, 그래. 너는 유리 공예에 관심이 있니?
B: 응, 많이 관심 있어. 그거 만드는 데 시간이 얼마나 걸렸니?
G: 한 달 걸렸어.

B: 너의 공연 즐거웠어. 정말 잘했어.
G: 고마워. 너는 우쿨렐레 연주하는 것에 관심이 있니?
B: 물론이야. 날 가르쳐 줄 수 있니?
G: 그럼.

Speak Up Mission

A: Are you _____ in watching _____ movies?

B: Yes, I _____. I watch horror movies very often. / No, _____ _____. I'm _____ _____ reading _____ stories.

Real-life Scene

James: What are you doing, Mina?

Mina: I'm _____ _____.

James: You're _____ with a brush. It _____ _____.

Mina: Are you _____ in _____?

James: Yes, very much.

Mina: Look at this! I just wrote it. _____ do you _____?

James: It _____ _____ a person _____ with _____ arms.

Mina: You _____ it. This Korean word _____ "dance."

James: You _____ a good _____! Can I _____ it?

Mina: _____ _____? Take this brush.

Your Turn

A: You're writing _____. What's this?

B: It's my art homework. Do you like it?

A: Sure. I think you _____ a _____ job!

Express Yourself

(1) B: Look! Two girls are _____ Hangeul.

G: Are you _____ _____ Hangeul, Kevin?

B: Yes, very much. I want to _____ them and _____ it.

(2) B: Julie, are you interested _____ hanbok?

G: _____ really.

B: Then, _____ are you _____ in?

G: Well, I'm _____ in taekwondo. It is a _____ Korean sport. It's _____.

(3) G: Look at the two men _____ pansori.

B: Are you _____ in pansori, Nancy?

G: Sure. I like the _____ of it. I _____ _____ _____ it.

Learning Diary Listen & Speak

B: Minji, are you _____ in animals?

G: Yes, I am. I'm _____ _____ _____ _____ them.

B: _____ _____ plants? Are you _____ in them, too?

G: No, I'm not. I can't _____ them well.

01 다음 대화의 빈칸에 들어갈 말로 알맞은 것은?

> A: Are you interested in *Hangeul*?
> B: Yes, I am. _____

① I want to wear it.   ② I want to play it.
③ I'm not interested in learning it.   ④ I want to learn it.
⑤ I want to eat it.

02 다음 대화의 빈칸에 들어갈 말로 알맞은 것은?

> G: Look at the two men learning *pansori*.
> B: _____, Nancy?
> G: Sure. I like the sound of it. I want to learn it.

① Are you interested in *pansori*
② Are you good at *pansori*
③ What happened
④ Do you learn *pansori*
⑤ What are you interested in?

03 다음 대화의 우리말에 맞게 주어진 단어를 이용하여 영어로 쓰시오.

> A: You're writing something. What's this?
> B: It's my art homework. Do you like it?
> A: Sure. 잘한 것 같아! (think / do / good job)

➡ _____

04 다음 대화를 알맞은 순서대로 배열하시오.

> (A) No problem.
> (B) I enjoyed your performance. Good job!
> (C) Thanks. Are you interested in *taekwondo*?
> (D) Sure. Can you teach me?

➡ _____

[01~02] 다음 대화를 읽고 물음에 답하시오.

> B: Do you like K-pop?
> G: Yes. I enjoy listening to SJ's songs. I can dance ___(A)___ his songs.
> B: _____(B)_____

01 위 대화의 빈칸 (A)에 들어갈 말로 알맞은 것은?

① with　② of　③ to　④ in　⑤ for

02 위 대화의 빈칸 (B)에 들어갈 말로 나머지와 성격이 <u>다른</u> 하나는?

① Great!　　　② Excellent!
③ Good job!　　④ Well done!
⑤ I'm into K-pop, too.

서답형

03 다음 대화에서 빈칸에 주어진 단어를 활용하여 관심을 묻는 말을 완성하시오.

> A: _____ (be / interest / ride)
> B: Yes, I am. I ride a bike very often.

➡ _____

[04~06] 다음 대화를 읽고 물음에 답하시오.

> B: You did a good job! It's awesome.
> G: Thanks.
> B: What is it made of? Glass?
> G: Yes, it is. _____(A)_____
> B: Yes, very much. _____(B)_____
> G: It took one month.

04 위 대화의 빈칸 (A)에 들어갈 말로 가장 적절한 것은?

① Are you interested in cooking?
② Are you interested in glass art?

③ I enjoyed your performance.
④ Can you teach me?
⑤ Are you interested in music?

05 위 대화의 빈칸 (B)에 들어갈 말로 알맞은 것은?

① How often did you make it?
② How far is it?
③ What date is it today?
④ How long did it take to make it?
⑤ How old is it?

서답형

06 다음 영영풀이가 설명하는 단어를 위 대화에서 찾아 쓰시오.

> • extremely impressive, serious, or difficult so that you feel great respect, worry, or fear
> • very good

➡ _____

[07~08] 다음 대화를 읽고 물음에 답하시오.

> James: What are you doing, Mina?
> Mina: I'm ①<u>practicing</u> calligraphy.
> James: You're writing with a brush. It ②<u>looks</u> fun.
> Mina: ③<u>Are you interested in</u> calligraphy?
> James: Yes, very much.
> Mina: Look at this! I just wrote it. What do you think?
> James: It ④<u>looks</u> a person dancing with open arms.
> Mina: You got it. This Korean word means "dance."
> James: You ⑤<u>did a good job</u>! Can I try it?
> Mina: Why not? Take this brush.

07 위 대화를 읽고 답할 수 없는 것은?

① What is Mina doing?

② Is Mina writing with a pen?

③ Is James interested in calligraphy?

④ Is it easy to start writing calligraphy?

⑤ How does James think of Mina's work?

08 위 대화의 밑줄 친 ①~⑤ 중 어법상 어색한 것은?

①   ②   ③   ④   ⑤

[09~10] 다음 대화의 빈칸에 들어갈 말로 알맞은 것은?

09

> G: Good work! I think your painting expresses the feeling of autumn well.
> B: Thank you. _____
> G: Yes, I am. I started taking a class on weekends.
> B: Oh, I didn't know that.

① What are you interested in?

② What is special about it?

③ Are you interested in painting?

④ Are you interested in Korean culture?

⑤ What do you think?

10

> B: Julie, are you interested in *hanbok*?
> G: _____
> B: Then, what are you interested in?
> G: Well, I'm interested in *taekwondo*. It is a traditional Korean sport. It's awesome.

① Not really.   ② I like *hanbok*.

③ Why not?   ④ Yes, I am.

⑤ How about you?

11 다음 중 짝지어진 대화가 어색한 것을 고르시오.

① A: Are you interested in taking pictures?

   B: Good job!

② A: Who is the man playing the piano?

   B: He's Jake.

③ A: Are you interested in music?

   B: Yes, I am.

④ A: Are you interested in cartoons?

   B: No, I'm not. I'm interested in sports.

⑤ A: I enjoyed your performance. You did a good job.

   B: Thank you.

[12~13] 다음 대화를 읽고 물음에 답하시오.

> B: Minji, are you interested in animals? (①)
> G: Yes, I am. _____
> B: (②) Are you interested in them, too? (③)
> G: No, I'm not. (④) I can't grow them well. (⑤)

12 대화의 빈칸에 들어갈 말은?

① I'm interested in collecting insects.

② I'm good at taking care of them.

③ I play soccer very often.

④ I'm interested in Chinese culture.

⑤ You aren't interested in animals.

서답형

13 다음 주어진 문장이 들어갈 위치로 알맞은 것은?

> How about plants?

①   ②   ③   ④   ⑤

[01~03] 다음 대화를 읽고 물음에 답하시오.

James: What are you doing, Mina?

Mina: I'm practicing calligraphy.

James: You're writing with a brush. It looks fun.

Mina: _____ (A)

James: Yes, very much.

Mina: Look at this! I just wrote it. (a)어떻게 생각해?

James: It looks like a person dancing with open arms.

Mina: You got it. _____ (B) _____

James: You did a good job! Can I try it?

Mina: Why not? Take this brush.

01 위 대화의 빈칸 (A)에 들어갈 표현을 주어진 〈조건〉에 맞게 쓰시오.

┌── 조건 ──┐
• 상대방이 캘리그래피에 관심이 있는지 묻는 표현을 쓸 것.
• 'interest'와 'calligraphy'를 활용할 것.
• 5단어의 문장을 사용할 것.
└─────────┘

➡ _____

02 다음 그림을 참고하여 Mina가 만든 캘리그래피가 무엇을 나타내는지 빈칸 (B)를 완성하시오. (주어진 단어를 이용할 것)

(this / Korean word / mean)

➡ _____

03 위 대화의 밑줄 친 (a)의 우리말에 맞게 'what'으로 시작하는 4단어로 영작하시오.

➡ _____

04 다음 그림을 보고 상대방이 무엇에 관심이 있는지 묻고 답하는 대화문을 완성하시오.

take selfies
(not interested)

cook
(interested)

A: Are you _____ (A) _____ ?
B: No, I'm not. _____ (B) _____

➡ (A) _____
(B) _____

05 대화의 흐름상 빈칸에 들어갈 표현을 주어진 〈조건〉에 맞게 쓰시오.

B: You did a good job! It's awesome.
G: Thanks.
B: What is it made of? Glass?
G: Yes, it is. Are you interested in glass art?
B: Yes, very much. _____
G: It took one month.

┌── 조건 ──┐
• 시간이 얼마나 걸리는 지 묻는 표현을 쓸 것.
• 대명사 'it'을 2번 사용할 것.
• 과거시제를 사용할 것.
└─────────┘

➡ _____

Grammar

① 현재분사

> • It looks like a happy woman **walking** down a road with autumn leaves.
> 그것은 마치 단풍잎이 깔린 길을 따라 걷고 있는 행복한 여인처럼 보인다.

- **형태와 의미**

  형태: '동사원형+-ing'이며, 동명사의 형태와 같다.

  의미: '…하고 있는, …하는'의 의미이다.

- **쓰임**: 분사는 동사와 형용사의 성질을 나누어 가지고 있다고 해서 붙여진 이름으로, 현재분사가 동사의 역할을 할 때는 주로 진행형인 'be동사+현재분사'의 형태로 쓰이고, 형용사의 역할을 할 때는 명사를 수식하거나 보충 설명할 때 쓰인다.

- **현재분사의 위치**

  형용사 역할을 하는 현재분사는 일반적으로 명사 앞에 와서 명사를 수식하는데, 대개 분사가 단독으로 쓰일 경우이다. 반면, 분사가 목적어나 어구를 수반할 때에는 명사 뒤에 와서 앞의 명사를 수식한다. 이를 현재분사의 '후치 수식'이라고 한다.

- **'관계대명사+be동사'의 생략**

  현재분사가 뒤에서 명사를 수식하는 경우, 명사와 현재분사 사이에 보통 '관계대명사+be동사'가 생략되어 있다고 볼 수 있다.

  - The boy **playing** soccer is my brother. 축구를 하고 있는 저 소년은 나의 동생이다.
    = The boy **who is playing** soccer is my brother.

- **현재분사 vs. 과거분사**

  현재분사는 '능동이나 진행'을 나타내는 반면 과거분사는 '수동이나 완료'를 나타낸다.

  - The man **playing** the piano is Jake. 피아노를 치고 있는 남자는 Jake이다.

  - Look at the **broken** window. 깨어진 창문을 보아라.

- **현재분사와 동명사**

  현재분사와 동명사는 같은 형태를 갖지만 현재분사는 형용사처럼 명사를 수식하거나 진행 시제를 나타내며 동명사는 '…하는 것, …하기'의 의미로 명사처럼 '주어, (동사나 전치사의) 목적어 및 보어 역할'을 한다.

  - Look at the **sleeping** baby. 잠자고 있는 아기를 보아라. 〈현재분사〉

  - **Sleeping** is important. 잠자는 것은 중요하다. 〈동명사〉

핵심 Check

1. 주어진 어휘를 빈칸에 어법에 맞게 쓰시오.

   (1) Look at the two men _____ *pansori*. (learn)

   (2) I was awakened by a _____ bell. (ring)

② It ... to부정사

• **It** is not easy **to write** by hand well at first. 처음부터 손으로 글씨를 잘 쓰기는 쉽지 않다.

■ **형태와 의미**

형태: It is+형용사+to+동사원형 ….

의미: …하는 것은 ~하다

■ **쓰임**: 비교적 긴 to부정사 부분이 문장의 주어로 쓰일 때 대부분 주어 자리에 형식상의 주어(가주어) 'it'을 쓰고 원래 주어(진주어)인 to부정사(구)는 문장의 끝으로 보낸다. 가주어 'It'은 아무 의미 없이 자리만 주어 자리에 있을 뿐이므로 해석하지 않고 진주어부터 해석한다.

• **It** is popular **to express** feelings through handwriting.
= **To express** feelings through handwriting is popular. 손 글씨를 통해 감정을 표현하는 것이 인기다.

■ **'It ... to부정사'의 의미상 주어**

to부정사의 동작을 실제로 하는 사람을 to부정사의 의미상 주어라고 한다. to부정사의 의미상 주어는 to부정사 바로 앞에 'for+명사의 목적격'의 형태로 쓴다. 문장에 쓰인 형용사가 nice, kind, smart, wise 등과 같이 사람의 성향, 성격을 나타내는 말일 때는 'of+목적격'을 쓴다. to부정사의 의미상 주어가 없는 경우는 특별한 사람이 아니라 일반적인 사람이기 때문이다. 또한 to부정사의 부정은 to부정사 앞에 not[never]을 써서 'not[never]+to V'로 나타내고 '…하지 않는 것은 ~하다'로 해석한다.

• Doctors say **it** is good **for** children **to wear** sunglasses.
의사들은 아이들이 선글라스를 쓰는 것이 좋다고 말한다.

• **It** was wise **of** you **to say** so. 당신이 그렇게 말한 것은 현명했습니다.

■ **it의 여러 가지 쓰임**

• Jane bought a hairpin. **It** was very cute. 〈인칭대명사〉

• **It**'s Sunday today. 〈비인칭 주어(요일)〉

• **It** is snowing. 〈비인칭 주어(날씨)〉

• **It**'s difficult to master English. 〈가주어〉

• I found **it** easy to solve the puzzle. 〈가목적어〉

핵심 Check

2. 다음 우리말과 일치하도록 빈칸에 알맞은 말을 쓰시오.

(1) 기억을 하는 것이 왜 중요할까요?

➡ Why _____ _____ _____ _____ remember?

(2) 외국어를 배우는 것은 쉽지 않다.

➡ _____ is not easy _____ _____ a foreign language.

01 다음 빈칸에 알맞은 것을 고르시오.

> A: Do you like to play *yunnori*?
> B: Yes. It is exciting _____ *yunnori*.

① play   ② plays   ③ to play
④ to playing   ⑤ of you to play

02 다음 문장에서 어법상 <u>어색한</u> 부분을 바르게 고쳐 쓰시오.

(1) I know the boy kick a ball.

_____ ➡ _____

(2) Who is the playing the piano man?

_____ ➡ _____

(3) There were lots of stars shining.

_____ ➡ _____

(4) It is exciting live in Korea.

_____ ➡ _____

(5) That is hard to make *gimchi*.

_____ ➡ _____

(6) It is difficult to not think of her.

_____ ➡ _____

03 주어진 어휘를 바르게 배열하여 우리말을 영어로 쓰시오. (필요할 경우 단어를 추가하거나 변형할 것.)

(1) 거리에서 노래를 부르고 있는 소녀들은 나의 학생들이다. (my students, the girls, on the street, sing, are)

➡ _____

(2) 다양한 프로그램을 제공하는 것은 좋은 아이디어이다. (a good idea, various programs, provide, is, to)

➡ _____

(3) 자고 있는 아기를 보아라. (sleep, look, the, baby, at)

➡ _____

01 다음 중 어법상 바르지 <u>않은</u> 것은?

① There was a man running on the playground.
② He is taking a picture in front of an old palace.
③ The river running through Seoul is the Han River.
④ The sleeping baby in the bed is really cute.
⑤ They are enjoying looking at some works of art.

02 다음 중 어법상 바른 것은?

① It is common knowledge what swimming is a good exercise.
② It's kind of you ask me some questions.
③ It is important to stay healthy.
④ It's good owns your own business.
⑤ That's necessary to say no.

03 다음 빈칸에 알맞은 말이 바르게 짝지어진 것은?

• Who is the girl _____ beside the piano?
• It is silly _____ a needless question.

① singing – asked
② singing – to ask
③ sang – asked
④ sang – to ask
⑤ sings – asking

04 다음 문장의 빈칸에 들어갈 알맞은 것은?

_____ is hard to communicate with foreigners.

① It   ② One
③ That   ④ This
⑤ What

05 밑줄 친 단어의 쓰임이 <u>다른</u> 하나는?

① The girl <u>walking</u> in the park is my sister.
② Do you know the woman <u>talking</u> to Tom?
③ The alarm clocks <u>ringing</u> noisily are Jason's.
④ The boy <u>singing</u> on the stage is my best friend.
⑤ I started <u>taking</u> a music class on weekends.

06 다음 괄호 안에서 알맞은 말을 고르시오.

(1) Who is the girl (carried / carrying) a basket?
(2) I got an e-mail (written / writing) in Chinese.
(3) The (cat sleeping / sleeping cat) is mine.
(4) It is important (to listen / listen) to others carefully.
(5) (It / That) is not easy to dance *talchum*.

07 다음 중 어법상 옳은 것은?

① The person runs fastest in our class is Angie.

② Look at the singing *pansori* men.

③ His dream is help the poor.

④ The bus taking us to the airport broke down.

⑤ The boy is washed the dog.

08 다음 중 밑줄 친 부분의 쓰임이 <u>다른</u> 하나는?

① <u>It</u> is impossible for them to do it.

② <u>It</u> was windy and rainy.

③ <u>It</u>'s important to keep traffic rules.

④ <u>It</u> is a good habit to keep a diary every day.

⑤ <u>It</u> is exciting to kick a *jegi*.

09 밑줄 친 부분 중 생략할 수 있는 것을 고르시오.

> ①Who ②is the woman ③that is ④sitting between Tom ⑤and Mike?

①   ②   ③   ④   ⑤

10 주어진 어휘를 바르게 배열하여 다음 우리말을 영작하시오.

> 외국어를 배우는 것은 중요하다.
> (language, it, a, learn, is, foreign, important, to)

➡ _____

11 다음 두 문장을 한 문장으로 바르게 연결한 것은?

> • There were many people.
> • They were waiting for the train.

① There were many people wait for the train.

② There were many people waited for the train.

③ There were many people to wait for the train.

④ There were many people were waiting for the train.

⑤ There were many people waiting for the train.

12 다음 우리말과 일치하도록 빈칸에 알맞은 것으로 묶은 것은?

> • 매일 한 문장이라도 읽는 것이 좋다.
> = _____ is good _____ even a sentence every day.

① It – to read

② It – read

③ That – to read

④ That – read

⑤ This – reading

13 다음 밑줄 친 부분이 어법상 <u>어색한</u> 것을 고르시오.

① The boy <u>played</u> soccer on the ground is my brother.

② The man <u>driving</u> the red car almost hit the person.

③ He bought a cell phone <u>made</u> in Korea.

④ Who is the boy <u>drinking</u> milk at the table?

⑤ This is the picture <u>painted</u> by Gogh.

14 다음 문장에서 어법상 <u>어색한</u> 것을 바르게 고쳐 다시 쓰시오.

(1) For me do this work would be really stupid.

➡ _____

_____

(2) That is easy to solve the puzzle.

➡ _____

_____

(3) It was amazing see such an old house there.

➡ _____

_____

(4) There was an eating ice cream girl.

➡ _____

_____

(5) A boy carried a box got on the bus.

➡ _____

_____

(6) Last week I read *Harry Potter* writing by JK Rowling.

➡ _____

_____

15 주어진 어휘를 어법에 맞게 빈칸에 쓰시오.

(1) The name of a fruit _____ with "m" is melon. (begin)

(2) It looks like a person _____ with open arms. (dance)

(3) The woman _____ at the news started to cry. (frighten)

(4) They are the photos _____ there. (take)

[16~17] 다음 우리말에 맞게 영작한 것을 고르시오.

16

나는 태권도를 배우고 있는 여자아이를 안다.

① I know the girl learn *taekwondo*.
② I know the girl learns *taekwondo*.
③ I know the girl to learn *taekwondo*.
④ I know the girl learning *taekwondo*.
⑤ I know the girl to learning *taekwondo*.

17

패스트푸드를 자주 먹는 것은 너의 건강에 좋지 않다.

① It is not good for your health eat fast food often.
② It is not good for your health eats fast food often.
③ It is not good for your health to eat fast food often.
④ That is not good for your health to eat fast food often.
⑤ That is not good for your health eating fast food often.

18 다음 중 어법상 <u>어색한</u> 것을 고르시오. (2개)

① It seemed necessary for me to attend the meeting.
② It's quite nice for her to say "Thank you."
③ It is not easy to exercise regularly.
④ The little girl singing on the stage is very cute.
⑤ I know the wearing a red cap girl.

01 다음 우리말에 맞게 주어진 어구를 바르게 배열하시오.

(1) Jack은 그의 아내에게 진주로 만든 목걸이를 주었다. (Jack, pearls, his wife, made, gave, a, necklace, of)

➡ _____

(2) 칼로 소고기 샌드위치를 자르고 있는 남자는 누구니? (the beef sandwiches, knife, the man, a, who, cutting, is, with)

➡ _____

_____

(3) 좋은 책을 발견하는 것은 멋진 일이다. (it, is, awesome, to, find, a, good book)

➡ _____

_____

(4) 캘리그래피 쓰기를 시작하는 것은 쉽다. (calligraphy, start, is, writing, easy, it, to)

➡ _____

_____

(5) 태양을 직접 보는 것은 위험합니까? (sun, it, dangerous, directly, is, look, the, to, at)

➡ _____

_____

02 다음 우리말을 (1) to부정사 주어를 써서, (2) 가주어를 써서 영작하시오.

• 제기를 차는 것은 재미있다.

➡ (1) _____

(2) _____

• 패러글라이딩을 하는 것은 위험해 보인다.

➡ (1) _____

(2) _____

03 그림을 보고, 주어진 어휘를 이용하여 빈칸에 알맞은 말을 쓰시오.

(1) (enjoy, do)

➡ Who is the man _____ B-boying?
_____ is fun _____ B-boying.

(2) (play)

➡ The men are _____ nongak. _____
is exciting _____ nongak.

04 다음 두 문장을 같은 뜻을 갖는 한 문장으로 고쳐 쓰시오.

(1) • The business woman is Sophie.
• The woman is running a big company.

➡ _____

_____

(2) • The bridge was built long time ago.
• It is a connection to the past.

➡ _____

_____

05 다음 문장을 It으로 시작하여 다시 쓰시오.

(1) To meet trouble halfway is silly.

➡ _____

(2) To get your e-mail this morning was great.

➡ _____

(3) To wear a helmet while riding a bike is safe.

➡ _____

(4) For the police to calm down the angry crowd was difficult.

➡ _____
_____

(5) That blood is thicker than water is quite true.

➡ _____

06 다음 우리말을 괄호 안에 주어진 어휘를 이용하여 영작하시오.

(1) 한복을 입고 있는 두 여자아이는 나의 친구들이다. (the, wear, *hanbok*, 8 단어)

➡ _____
_____

(2) 그 남자는 그의 집 지붕을 파랗게 칠했다. (man, roof, have, paint, 10 단어)

➡ _____
_____

(3) 과거에 대해 이야기하는 것은 재미있다. (it, the past, talk, interesting, 8 단어)

➡ _____
_____

(4) 당신이 친절한 이웃을 갖고 있는 것은 운이 좋은 것이다. (lucky, to have, neighbor, 9 단어)

➡ _____
_____

07 다음 문장에서 어법상 <u>어색한</u> 것을 바르게 고치시오.

(1) Timothy got an email sending by a stranger this morning.

_____ ➡ _____

(2) Who are the boys played soccer on the ground?

_____ ➡ _____

(3) This calligraphy shows two laughing out loud people.

_____

➡ _____

(4) Buy a ticket at the subway station is not so hard.

_____ ➡ _____ ,

_____

➡ _____

(5) This is not fun to stay in the hospital all alone.

_____ ➡ _____

(6) It is important for her eats very small amounts of food.

_____ ➡ _____

08 두 문장이 같은 뜻이 되도록 to부정사를 이용하여 문장을 완성하시오.

(1) I have difficulty in writing letters in English.

➡ It is difficult _____
_____ .

(2) Watching the horror movie was terrible for her.

➡ It was terrible _____
_____ .

Write Your Feelings

How do you express your feelings? Do you sing or dance? Do you write a poem or draw a picture? Nowadays, it is popular to express feelings through handwriting. Let's look at some works of art.

In the work of art on the right, the word includes an image of a delicious fruit, *hongsi*. It shows that autumn is a season of fruit. The work of art on the left shows a Korean word and a Chinese character.

It looks like a happy woman walking down a road with autumn leaves. Both of these works express the feeling of autumn through beautiful handwriting. This kind of art is called calligraphy.

Calligraphy is not new. Many different kinds of calligraphy works from long ago can be found all around the world. Look at the two examples from Korea and the UK below. Can you tell the difference?

The left one was created by Chusa in the period of the Joseon Dynasty.

The characters were painted with a soft brush.

express: 표현하다
poem: 시
nowadays: 요즘에는, 오늘날에는
popular: 인기 있는
handwriting: 손 글씨, 필적
include: 포함하다
autumn: 가을
season: 계절
both: 둘 다
calligraphy: 캘리그래피
below: ~의 아래에
period: 시대, 기간
dynasty: 왕조, 왕가

 확인문제

● 다음 문장이 본문의 내용과 일치하면 T, 일치하지 않으면 F를 쓰시오.

1 Nowadays, to express feelings through handwriting is popular. ☐

2 In the work of art on the right, the word excludes an image of a delicious fruit, *hongsi*. ☐

3 Both of the works express the feeling of autumn through beautiful drawing. ☐

4 Both of the works are called calligraphy. ☐

The right one, *The Canterbury Tales*, was created by Chaucer in
'The right one'과 'The Canterbury Tales'는 동격　　　과거 수동태

England in the late 1400s. It was written with a pen. Different writing
'1400년대 후반에' cf. in the early 1400s (1400년대 초반에)

tools led to different styles of calligraphy. Of course, all calligraphers

had to practice hard to make their unique styles.
to부정사의 부사적 용법(목적)

Today calligraphy is widely used around us. You can find designers'
수동태('쓰인다, 사용된다'). 부사 'widely'가 수식하는 과거분사 'used' 앞에 위치

artistic touches on movie posters, book covers, music CDs, and clothes.

Below are some examples. Look at the title on the movie poster. How
부사 'below'가 맨 앞에 오면서 '부사+동사+주어'의 어순으로 도치

do you feel? Can you imagine the monster's big mouth, sharp teeth,

and ugly, long tail? How about the title on the fantasy novel? Do you
= What about

see Harry's lightning and the wizard hats?
(남자) 마법사. witch: 마녀

Anyone can start writing calligraphy. It's not easy to write by
긍정문에서 '누구든지'　　= to write(일반적으로 '~하기를 시작하다'는 뜻일 때 동명사가 더 자주 쓰임)
가주어　　　　진주어

hand well at first, but practice makes perfect. Keep trying and make
꾸준한 연습을 강조하는 속담. 'perfect'는 원래 형용사지만 여기서는 명사처럼 쓰였음.　계속 ~하다

it part of your everyday life. Write with your feelings on birthday
= calligraphy 'make+목적어+목적격보어'의 5형식 문장으로 이루어졌음

cards, bookmarks, or gifts. Soon you will build up your own world of
만들다, 세우다

calligraphy.

어휘 (glossary)

tale: 이야기
tool: 도구, 수단
lead to: ~로 이끌다, ~로 이어지다
unique: 독특한, 특별한
widely: 널리
artistic: 예술의, 예술적인
imagine: 상상하다
monster: 괴물
sharp: 날카로운
tail: 꼬리
fantasy: 판타지, 환상, 공상
lightning: 번개
wizard: 마법사
at first: 처음에는
keep -ing: ~을 계속하다
build up: 만들다

확인문제

● 다음 문장이 본문의 내용과 일치하면 T, 일치하지 않으면 F를 쓰시오.

1　Chaucer created *The Canterbury Tales*. ▢

2　*The Canterbury Tales* was written with a brush. ▢

3　Different styles of calligraphy resulted from different writing tools. ▢

4　Today it is difficult to find calligraphy used around us. ▢

5　We see Harry's lightning and the wizard hats from the title on the fantasy novel. ▢

6　It's easy to write by hand well at first. ▢

● 우리말을 참고하여 빈칸에 알맞은 말을 쓰시오.

1 _____ Your Feelings

2 _____ do you express your _____?

3 Do you _____ or _____?

4 Do you write a poem or _____ _____ _____?

5 _____, it is popular to express feelings _____ _____.

6 Let's look at some _____ _____ _____.

7 In the work of art on the right, the word _____ _____ _____ of a delicious fruit, *hongsi*.

8 It shows that autumn is _____ _____ _____ _____.

9 The work of art on the left shows a _____ _____ and a _____ _____.

10 It _____ _____ a happy woman _____ down a road with autumn leaves.

11 Both of these works _____ _____ _____ of autumn _____ beautiful handwriting.

12 This kind of art is called _____.

13 Calligraphy is _____ _____.

14 Many different kinds of calligraphy works from long ago _____ _____ _____ all around the world.

15 Look at the two examples _____ Korea and the UK _____.

16 Can you _____ _____ _____?

17 The left one _____ _____ _____ Chusa in the period of the Joseon Dynasty.

18 The characters _____ _____ _____ a soft brush.

---

1 여러분의 느낌을 써라

2 여러분은 자신의 느낌을 어떻게 표현하는가?

3 노래를 부르거나 춤을 추는가?

4 시를 쓰거나 그림을 그리는가?

5 요즈음에는 손 글씨를 통해 감정을 표현하는 것이 인기다.

6 몇몇 작품을 살펴보자.

7 오른쪽 예술 작품에서는 단어가 맛있는 과일인 홍시의 이미지를 포함하고 있다.

8 그것은 가을이 결실의 계절임을 보여 준다.

9 왼쪽에 있는 예술 작품은 한글 단어와 한자를 보여 주고 있다.

10 그것은 마치 단풍잎이 깔린 길을 따라 걷고 있는 행복한 여인처럼 보인다.

11 이 두 작품은 아름다운 손 글씨를 통해 가을의 느낌을 표현한다.

12 이런 종류의 예술은 '캘리그래피'라고 불린다.

13 캘리그래피는 새로운 것이 아니다.

14 오래전의 다양한 종류의 많은 캘리그래피 작품들이 세계 곳곳에서 발견되고 있다.

15 아래에 있는 한국과 영국의 두 사례를 보라.

16 여러분은 그 차이를 구별할 수 있는가?

17 왼쪽 작품은 조선 왕조 시대에 추사에 의해 창작되었다.

18 그 글자들은 부드러운 붓으로 그려졌다.

19 The right one, *The Canterbury Tales*, was created by Chaucer in England _____ _____ _____ _____.

20 It _____ _____ _____ a pen.

21 _____ _____ _____ l e d t o _____ _____ o f calligraphy.

22 Of course, all calligraphers had to _____ _____ to make their _____ _____.

23 Today calligraphy _____ _____ _____ around us.

24 You can find _____ _____ _____ on movie posters, book covers, music CDs, and clothes.

25 Below _____ _____ _____.

26 Look at _____ _____ on the movie poster.

27 _____ do you feel?

28 Can you imagine the monster's big mouth, _____ _____, and _____, long tail?

29 _____ _____ the title on the fantasy novel?

30 Do you see Harry's _____ and the _____ _____?

31 _____ can start _____ calligraphy.

32 It's not easy to write _____ _____ well at first, but _____ _____ _____.

33 _____ _____ and make it _____ of your _____ life.

34 Write _____ _____ _____ on birthday cards, bookmarks, or gifts.

35 Soon you will _____ _____ your own world of calligraphy.

19 오른쪽의 '캔터베리 이야기' 는 1400년대 후반 영국에서 Chaucer에 의해 창작되었다.

20 그것은 펜으로 쓰였다.

21 각기 다른 필기구가 각기 다른 캘리그래피의 스타일을 이끌었 다.

22 물론, 모든 캘리그래피 작가들 은 자신의 독특한 스타일을 만 들어 내기 위해 열심히 연습해 야 했다.

23 캘리그래피는 요즈음 우리 주변 에서 널리 쓰이고 있다.

24 여러분은 영화 포스터, 책 표지, 음악 CD, 그리고 의류에서 디자 이너들의 예술적인 손길을 발견 할 수 있다.

25 아래에 몇 가지 예가 있다.

26 영화 포스터의 제목을 보라.

27 어떤 느낌이 드는가?

28 괴물의 커다란 입, 날카로운 이 빨, 그리고 추하고 긴 꼬리를 상 상할 수 있는가?

29 공상 소설의 제목은 어떠한가?

30 Harry의 번개와 마술사 모자가 보이는가?

31 누구든지 캘리그래피를 쓰기 시 작할 수 있다.

32 처음부터 손으로 글씨를 잘 쓰 기는 쉽지 않지만, 연습하면 완 벽해진다.

33 계속해서 노력하고 자신의 일상 의 한 부분이 되게 하라.

34 생일 카드, 책갈피, 또는 선물에 느낌을 담아 써 보라.

35 곧 자신만의 캘리그래피 세계를 만들게 될 것이다.

● 우리말을 참고하여 본문을 영작하시오.

1 여러분의 느낌을 써라
➡ _____

2 여러분은 자신의 느낌을 어떻게 표현하는가?
➡ _____

3 노래를 부르거나 춤을 추는가?
➡ _____

4 시를 쓰거나 그림을 그리는가?
➡ _____

5 요즈음에는 손 글씨를 통해 감정을 표현하는 것이 인기다.
➡ _____

6 몇몇 작품을 살펴보자.
➡ _____

7 오른쪽 예술 작품에서는 단어가 맛있는 과일인 홍시의 이미지를 포함하고 있다.
➡ _____

8 그것은 가을이 결실의 계절임을 보여 준다.
➡ _____

9 왼쪽에 있는 예술 작품은 한글 단어와 한자를 보여 주고 있다.
➡ _____

10 그것은 마치 단풍잎이 깔린 길을 따라 걷고 있는 행복한 여인처럼 보인다.
➡ _____

11 이 두 작품은 아름다운 손 글씨를 통해 가을의 느낌을 표현한다.
➡ _____

12 이런 종류의 예술은 '캘리그래피'라고 불린다.
➡ _____

13 캘리그래피는 새로운 것이 아니다.
➡ _____

14 오래전의 다양한 종류의 많은 캘리그래피 작품들이 세계 곳곳에서 발견되고 있다.
➡ _____

15 아래에 있는 한국과 영국의 두 사례를 보라.
➡ _____

16 여러분은 그 차이를 구별할 수 있는가?
➡ _____

17 왼쪽 작품은 조선 왕조 시대에 추사에 의해 창작되었다.
➡ _____

18 그 글자들은 부드러운 붓으로 그려졌다.

➡ _____

19 오른쪽의 '캔터베리 이야기'는 1400년대 후반 영국에서 Chaucer에 의해 창작되었다.

➡ _____

20 그것은 펜으로 쓰였다.

➡ _____

21 각기 다른 필기구가 각기 다른 캘리그래피의 스타일을 이끌었다.

➡ _____

22 물론, 모든 캘리그래피 작가들은 자신의 독특한 스타일을 만들어 내기 위해 열심히 연습해야 했다.

➡ _____

23 캘리그래피는 요즈음 우리 주변에서 널리 쓰이고 있다.

➡ _____

24 여러분은 영화 포스터, 책 표지, 음악 CD, 그리고 의류에서 디자이너들의 예술적인 손길을 발견할 수 있다.

➡ _____

25 아래에 몇 가지 예가 있다.

➡ _____

26 영화 포스터의 제목을 보라.

➡ _____

27 어떤 느낌이 드는가?

➡ _____

28 괴물의 커다란 입, 날카로운 이빨, 그리고 추하고 긴 꼬리를 상상할 수 있는가?

➡ _____

29 공상 소설의 제목은 어떠한가?

➡ _____

30 Harry의 번개와 마술사 모자가 보이는가?

➡ _____

31 누구든지 캘리그래피를 쓰기 시작할 수 있다.

➡ _____

32 처음부터 손으로 글씨를 잘 쓰기는 쉽지 않지만, 연습하면 완벽해진다.

➡ _____

33 계속해서 노력하고 자신의 일상의 한 부분이 되게 하라.

➡ _____

34 생일 카드, 책갈피, 또는 선물에 느낌을 담아 써 보라.

➡ _____

35 곧 자신만의 캘리그래피 세계를 만들게 될 것이다.

➡ _____

[01~03] 다음 글을 읽고 물음에 답하시오.

How do you express your feelings? Do you sing or dance? Do you write a poem or draw a picture? Nowadays, it is popular to express feelings through handwriting. Let's look at some works of art.

In the work of art on the right, the word includes a/an ⓐ of a delicious fruit, *hongsi*. It shows that autumn is a season of fruit. The work of art on the left shows a Korean word and a Chinese character. It looks like a happy woman ⓑwalking down a road with autumn leaves. Both of these works express the feeling of autumn through beautiful handwriting. This kind of art is called calligraphy.

01 위 글의 빈칸 ⓐ에 들어갈 가장 알맞은 말을 고르시오.

① scene   ② image
③ imagination   ④ figure
⑤ scenery

02 위 글의 밑줄 친 ⓑwalking과 문법적 쓰임이 다른 것을 모두 고르시오.

① Who is the boy dancing on the street?
② My hobby is drawing cartoons.
③ Who is the man talking with Sumi?
④ I'm interested in playing the piano.
⑤ The girl crying over there is Mary.

03 위 글의 내용과 일치하지 않는 것은?

① These days, to express feelings through handwriting is popular.
② The work of art on the right shows that autumn is a season of fruit.
③ We can see a Korean word and a Chinese character in the work of art on the left.
④ The work of art on the left expresses the feeling of autumn through beautiful painting.
⑤ The works of art on the right and on the left are called calligraphy.

[04~06] 다음 글을 읽고 물음에 답하시오.

Today calligraphy is widely used around us. You can find designers' artistic ⓐtouches on movie posters, book covers, music CDs, and clothes. ⓑBelow some examples are. Look at ⓒthe title on the movie poster. How do you feel? Can you imagine the monster's big mouth, sharp teeth, and ugly, long tail? How about the title on the fantasy novel? Do you see Harry's lightning and the wizard hats?

04 위 글의 밑줄 친 ⓐtouches와 같은 의미로 쓰인 것을 고르시오.

① I spent the morning putting the finishing touches to the report.
② Her story touches us all deeply.
③ The gentle touches of his hand on her shoulder made her jump.
④ He touches me on the shoulder.
⑤ He never touches alcoholic drinks.

05 위 글의 밑줄 친 ⓑ에서 어법상 **틀린** 부분을 찾아 고치시오.

_____ ➡ _____

06 위 글의 ⓒthe title on the movie poster에서 상상할 수 없는 것을 모두 고르시오.

① the monster's big mouth
② Harry's lightning
③ the monster's sharp teeth
④ the monster's ugly, long tail
⑤ the wizard hats

[07~08] 다음 글을 읽고 물음에 답하시오.

Look at the two girls learning *taekwondo*. *Taekwondo* is a traditional Korean sport, and we wear *dobok* to do it. It is exciting to learn *taekwondo*. ⓐAre you interesting? Please come and try.

07 위 글의 종류로 알맞은 것을 고르시오.

① summary   ② PR leaflet
③ review   ④ article
⑤ essay

08 위 글의 밑줄 친 ⓐ에서 어법상 **틀린** 부분을 찾아 고치시오.

_____ ➡ _____

[09~11] 다음 글을 읽고 물음에 답하시오.

Calligraphy is not new. Many different kinds of calligraphy works from long ago can be found all around the world. Look at the two examples from Korea and the UK below.

Can you tell the difference? ⓐThe left one was created by Chusa in the period of the Joseon Dynasty. The characters were painted with a soft brush.

The right one, *The Canterbury Tales*, was created by Chaucer in England in the late 1400s. It was written with a pen. ⓑ각기 다른 필기구가 각기 다른 캘리그래피의 스타일을 이끌었다. Of course, all calligraphers had to practice hard to make their unique styles.

09 다음 빈칸 (A)~(C)에 알맞은 단어를 넣어 위 글의 밑줄 친 ⓐ에 대한 소개를 완성하시오.

> It is an example of the calligraphy works from long ago. (A)_____ created it in the period of the (B)_____ _____ by painting the characters with a (C)_____ _____.

10 위 글의 밑줄 친 ⓑ의 우리말에 맞게 주어진 어휘를 이용하여 9 단어로 영작하시오.

> led to, different

➡ _____

11 위 글을 읽고 *The Canterbury Tales*에 대해 알 수 **없는** 것을 고르시오.

① 작가   ② 작가의 국적
③ 줄거리   ④ 집필된 시기
⑤ 집필할 때 사용한 필기구

[12~15] 다음 글을 읽고 물음에 답하시오.

Anyone can start writing calligraphy. ⓐ It's not easy to write by hand well at first, but practice makes perfect. Keep trying and make ⓑit part of your everyday life. Write ⓒ느낌을 담아 on birthday cards, bookmarks, or gifts. ⓓSoon you will build up your own world of calligraphy.

12 위 글의 밑줄 친 ⓐ를 바꿔 쓴 문장으로 옳지 않은 것을 모두 고르시오.

① To write by hand well at first is not easy

② That's not easy to write by hand well at first

③ It's difficult to write by hand well at first

④ Writing by hand well at first is not easy

⑤ To write by the hand well at first is not easy

서답형
13 위 글의 밑줄 친 ⓑit가 가리키는 것을 본문에서 찾아 쓰시오.

➡ _____

서답형
14 위 글의 밑줄 친 ⓒ의 우리말을 세 단어로 쓰시오.

➡ _____

서답형
15 위 글의 밑줄 친 ⓓ를 다음과 같이 바꿔 쓸 때 빈칸에 공통으로 들어갈 알맞은 단어를 쓰시오. (대·소문자 무시)

➡ = It will not be long _____ you build up your own world of calligraphy.

= _____ long you will build up your own world of calligraphy.

[16~17] 다음 한국 문화 체험 홍보문을 읽고 물음에 답하시오.

Look at the two boys playing *yunnori*. *Yunnori* is a traditional Korean (A)[board / broad] game, and we use *yuts* and *mals* (B)[to play / playing] it. It is exciting to play *yunnori*. Are you (C)[interesting / interested]? Please come and try.

서답형
16 What do we use to play *yunnori*? Answer in English in a full sentence. (5 words)

➡ _____

서답형
17 위 글의 괄호 (A)~(C)에서 문맥이나 어법상 알맞은 낱말을 골라 쓰시오.

➡ (A) _____ (B) _____ (C) _____

[18~20] 다음 글을 읽고 물음에 답하시오.

Calligraphy is not new. (①) Many different kinds of calligraphy works from long ago can be found all around the world. (②) Look at the two examples from Korea and the UK below. (③) The left one was created by Chusa in the period of the Joseon Dynasty. (④) The characters were painted with a soft brush. (⑤)

The right one, *The Canterbury Tales*, was created by Chaucer in England in the late 1400s. It was written with a pen. ⓐDifferent writing tools led to different styles of calligraphy. Of course, all calligraphers had to practice hard to make their unique styles.

중요
18 위 글의 흐름으로 보아, 주어진 문장이 들어가기에 가장 적절한 곳은?

Can you tell the difference?

①   ②   ③   ④   ⑤

서답형

19 위 글의 밑줄 친 ⓐDifferent writing tools가 가리키는 것을 본문에서 찾아 쓰시오.

➡ _____

20 위 글의 주제로 알맞은 것을 고르시오.

① Calligraphy was present in the East.
② Calligraphy was present in the West.
③ Calligraphy is not new.
④ There are various tools for writing calligraphy.
⑤ All calligraphers had to practice hard.

[21~23] 다음 글을 읽고 물음에 답하시오.

How do you express your feelings? Do you sing or dance? Do you write a poem or draw a picture? Nowadays, ⓐit is popular to express feelings through handwriting. Let's look at some works of art.

In the work of art ___(A)___ the right, the word includes an image of a delicious fruit, *hongsi*. It shows that autumn is a season of fruit. The work of art ___(A)___ the left shows a Korean word and a Chinese character. ⓑIt looks a happy woman walking down a road with autumn leaves. Both of these works express the feeling of autumn ___(B)___ beautiful handwriting. This kind of art is called calligraphy.

21 위 글의 빈칸 (A)와 (B)에 들어갈 전치사가 바르게 짝지어진 것은?

① to – through   ② in – from
③ on – from   ④ to – by
⑤ on – through

22 아래 〈보기〉에서 위 글의 밑줄 친 ⓐit과 문법적 쓰임이 같은 것의 개수를 고르시오.

┤ 보기 ├
① Did you see it?
② I make it a rule to get up early.
③ It's impossible to get there in time.
④ It's two miles from here to the beach.
⑤ It is important to choose good friends.

① 1개   ② 2개   ③ 3개   ④ 4개   ⑤ 5개

서답형

23 위 글의 밑줄 친 ⓑ에서 어법상 틀린 부분을 찾아 고치시오.

_____ ➡ _____

[24~25] 다음 글을 읽고 물음에 답하시오.

Look at the boy ⓐkicking a *jegi*. ⓑKicking a *jegi* is a traditional Korean game, and we kick it with one of our feet. It is exciting to kick a *jegi*. Are you interested? Please come and try.

24 위 글의 목적으로 알맞은 것을 고르시오.

① to promote   ② to compare
③ to survey   ④ to report
⑤ to communicate

서답형

25 다음 〈보기〉에서 위 글의 밑줄 친 ⓐkicking, ⓑKicking과 문법적 쓰임이 같은 것을 각각 골라 번호를 쓰시오.

┤ 보기 ├
① Kicking a *jegi* is interesting.
② The men kicking a *jegi* are my brothers.
③ I'm good at kicking a *jegi*.
④ We enjoyed kicking a *jegi*.
⑤ I don't like the boys kicking a *jegi* there.

➡ ⓐ와 같은 것: _____ ,
   ⓑ와 같은 것: _____

[01~03] 다음 글을 읽고 물음에 답하시오.

How do you express your feelings? Do you sing or dance? Do you write a poem or draw a picture? Nowadays, it is popular to express feelings through handwriting. Let's look at some works of art.

In the work of art on the right, the word includes an image of a delicious fruit, *hongsi*. It shows that autumn is a season of fruit. The work of art on the left shows a Korean word and a Chinese character. ⓐ그것은 마치 단풍잎이 깔린 길을 따라 걷고 있는 행복한 여인처럼 보인다. Both of these works express the feeling of autumn through beautiful handwriting. This kind of art is called calligraphy.

01 위 글에서 자신의 느낌을 표현하는 방법으로 소개된 것을 우리말로 모두 쓰시오.

➡ (1) _____ (2) _____
　 (3) _____ (4) _____
　 (5) _____

02 위 글의 밑줄 친 ⓐ의 우리말에 맞게 주어진 어휘를 알맞게 배열하시오.

> walking down / autumn leaves / like / with / a road / looks / a happy woman / it

➡ _____
　 _____

03 본문의 내용과 일치하도록 다음 빈칸 (A)와 (B)에 알맞은 단어를 쓰시오.

> At the present time, expressing feelings through (A)_____ is popular and we call this kind of art (B)_____.

[04~07] 다음 글을 읽고 물음에 답하시오.

Calligraphy is not new. Many different kinds of calligraphy works from long ago can ___ⓐ___ all around the world. Look at the two examples from Korea and the UK below. Can you tell the difference? The left one was created by Chusa in the period of the Joseon Dynasty. The characters were painted with a soft brush.

The right one, *The Canterbury Tales*, was created by Chaucer in England in the late ⓑ 1400s. It was written with a pen. Different writing tools led to different styles of calligraphy. Of course, all calligraphers had to practice hard to make their unique styles.

04 위 글의 빈칸 ⓐ에 find를 알맞은 형태로 쓰시오.

➡ _____

05 위 글을 읽고 다음 빈칸 (1)~(4)에 들어갈 알맞은 말을 〈보기〉에서 골라 쓰시오.

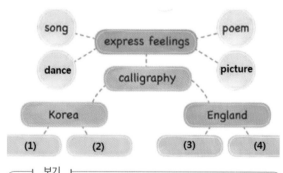

보기
• *The Canterbury Tales*　• brush
• pen　　　　　　　　• Chusa's work

➡ (1) _____ (2) _____
　 (3) _____ (4) _____

06 위 글의 밑줄 친 ⓑ1400s를 읽는 법을 영어로 쓰시오.

➡ _____

07 What did all calligraphers have to do to make their unique styles? Answer in English in a full sentence. (5 words)

➡ _____

[08~09] 다음 글을 읽고 물음에 답하시오.

Today calligraphy is widely used around us. You can find designers' artistic touches on movie posters, book covers, music CDs, and clothes. Below are ⓐsome examples. Look at the title on the movie poster. How do you feel? Can you imagine the monster's big mouth, sharp teeth, and ugly, long tail? How about the title on the fantasy novel? Do you see Harry's lightning and the wizard hats?

08 다음 빈칸에 알맞은 단어를 넣어 위 글의 밑줄 친 ⓐsome examples가 가리키는 내용을 완성하시오.

> They are some examples of movie posters, book covers, music CDs, and clothes using calligraphy, on which you can find designers' _____ _____.

09 본문의 내용과 일치하도록 다음 빈칸 (A)와 (B)에 알맞은 단어를 쓰시오.

> There are two commercial products including calligraphy titles. One is the title on the (A)_____ _____ and the other is the title on the (B)_____ _____.

[10~12] 다음 글을 읽고 물음에 답하시오.

(A)[How / What] do you express your feelings? Do you sing or dance? Do you write a poem or draw a picture? Nowadays, it is popular ⓐto express feelings through handwriting. Let's look at some works of art.

In the work of art on the right, the word (B)[excludes / includes] an image of a delicious fruit, *hongsi*. It shows that autumn is a season of fruit. The work of art on the left shows a Korean word and a Chinese character. It looks like a happy woman walking down a road with autumn leaves. Both of these works express the feeling of autumn through beautiful (C)[drawing / handwriting]. ⓑThis kind of art is called calligraphy.

10 위 글의 괄호 (A)~(C)에서 문맥이나 어법상 알맞은 낱말을 골라 쓰시오.

➡ (A) _____ (B) _____ (C) _____

11 다음 빈칸 (A)와 (B)에 알맞은 단어를 넣어 위 글의 밑줄 친 ⓐ의 예를 완성하시오.

> (1) The word including an image of a delicious fruit, *hongsi*, shows that autumn is a season of (A)_____.
> (2) The beautiful handwriting which is made up of a Korean word and a Chinese character expresses the feeling of (B)_____, and it looks like a (C)_____ woman walking down a road with autumn leaves.

12 위 글의 밑줄 친 ⓑ를 능동태로 고치시오.

➡ _____

After You Read B

These Korean characters mean "Let's laugh." This calligraphy shows two
people <u>laughing</u> out loud.
<small>앞의 명사 'two people'을 뒤에서 수식하는 현재분사의 후치 수식</small>

These Korean characters mean "tree." This calligraphy shows a tree <u>growing</u>
<small>앞의 명사 'tree'를 뒤에서 수식하는 현재분사의 후치 수식</small>
in a pot.

구문해설 · character: 글자 · mean: 의미하다 · pot: 항아리, 화분

해석

이 한글 글자는 "웃읍시다"를 의미합니다. 이 캘리그래피는 큰 소리로 웃고 있는 두 사람을 나타냅니다.

이 한글 글자는 "나무"를 의미합니다. 이 캘리그래피는 화분에서 자라는 나무를 나타냅니다.

Express Yourself C

Look at the two girls learning[doing] *taekwondo*. *Taekwondo* is a traditional
Korean sport, and we wear *dobok* to do it. It is exciting to learn *taekwondo*.
<small>to부정사의 부사적 용법(목적)　가주어　　　　　진주어</small>
Are you interested? Please come and try.

Look at the two boys playing *yunnori*. *Yunnori* is a traditional Korean board
game, and we use *yuts* and *mals* to play it. It is exciting to play *yunnori*.
<small>to부정사의 부사적 용법(목적)　가주어</small>
Are you interested? Please come and try.
<small>be interested: 관심이 있다</small>

구문해설 · traditional: 전통적인 · use: 사용하다 · wear: 입다, 신다, 착용하다

태권도를 배우고[하고] 있는 두 여자아이를 보세요. 태권도는 한국의 전통 스포츠이고, 우리는 그것을 하기 위해 도복을 입습니다. 태권도를 배우는 것은 흥미진진합니다. 관심이 있나요? 와서 한번 해 보세요.

윷놀이를 하는 두 남자아이를 보세요. 윷놀이는 한국의 전통적인 말판 놀이고, 우리는 그것을 하기 위해 윷과 말을 사용합니다. 윷놀이를 하는 것은 흥미진진합니다. 관심이 있나요? 와서 한번 해 보세요.

Link to the World

1 This is a set of Russian dolls. It <u>is called</u> matryoshka.
<small>～라고 불린다</small>

2 <u>When</u> you open it, smaller dolls <u>keep coming</u> <u>out of</u> it. It is interesting
<small>접속사 '～할 때'　　　　　계속해서 나온다　　～에서　　가주어</small>
to see a smaller doll inside each doll.
<small>진주어　　　　　　　　each+단수 명사</small>

3 <u>The first set</u> of matryoshka dolls <u>was</u> a mother doll <u>with</u> six children.
<small>　주어　　　　　　　　　　동사　　　　　～이 있는</small>

4 Today, many new styles of matryoshkas are <u>created</u> and loved by many
<small>수동태 '만들어지다'　created와 병렬 관계</small>
people.

구문해설 · Russian: 러시아의 · is called: ～라 불린다 · keep -ing: 계속 -하다
· interesting: 흥미로운 · inside: ～ 안의

1. 이것은 한 세트의 러시아 인형이다. 그것은 '마트료시카'라고 불린다.

2. 그것을 열면, 더 작은 인형들이 계속해서 나온다. 각각의 인형 안에서 더 작은 인형을 보는 것은 재미있다.

3. 최초의 '마트료시카' 인형 세트는 여섯 아이를 둔 어머니 인형이었다.

4. 오늘날에는, 많은 새로운 스타일의 '마트료시카'가 제작되어 많은 사람에게 사랑을 받고 있다.

영역별 핵심문제

Words & Expressions

01 다음 주어진 두 단어의 관계가 같도록 빈칸에 주어진 철자로 단어를 쓰시오.

include : exclude = terrible : e_____

02 다음 빈칸에 들어갈 단어로 알맞은 것은?

- You need _____ skills to draw and paint well.
- When _____ comes, the leaves will change colors.
- The tour _____ a visit to the Louvre Museum.

① handwriting – autumn – expressed
② handwriting – autumn – included
③ artistic – autumn – included
④ artistic – winter – expressed
⑤ artistic – winter – imagined

03 다음 영영풀이에 해당하는 것을 고르시오.

not the same as anything or anyone else

① artistic   ② huge   ③ similar
④ foreign   ⑤ unique

04 다음 빈칸에 들어갈 말로 알맞은 것은?

- Learning a _____ language is not easy.
- I can't recognize his _____ written in this letter.

① native – face
② foreign – handwriting
③ native – handwriting
④ foreign – dynasty
⑤ natural – face

05 다음 글의 빈칸 ⓐ와 ⓑ에 들어갈 단어로 알맞은 것은?

This is a set of Russian dolls. It is called matryoshka. When you open it, smaller dolls ⓐ_____ coming out of it. It is interesting to see a smaller doll ⓑ_____ each doll. The first set of matryoshka dolls was a mother doll with six children.

① take – inside   ② leave – behind
③ bring – between   ④ keep – inside
⑤ keep – between

06 다음 밑줄 친 부분의 의미가 바르지 <u>않은</u> 것은?

① She read the beautiful <u>poem</u> aloud. (시)
② This restaurant is very <u>popular</u> with tourists. (인기 있는)
③ The knife looks very <u>sharp</u>. (무딘)
④ The cute puppy barked and wagged its <u>tail</u>. (꼬리)
⑤ <u>Nowadays</u>, most teenagers have their own cell phones. (요즈음)

Conversation

07 대화의 밑줄 친 우리말에 맞게 주어진 단어를 알맞은 순서로 배열하시오.

G: <u>판소리를 배우고 있는 두 남자 좀 봐.</u>
B: Are you interested in pansori, Nancy?
G: Sure. I like the sound of it.

(the / men / look / learning / at / two / *pansori*)

➡ _____

08 자연스러운 대화가 되도록 알맞은 순서로 배열한 것은?

> (A) Thank you. Are you interested in dancing *talchum*?
> (B) Sure. Can you teach me?
> (C) No problem.
> (D) I enjoyed your performance. You did a good job.

① (A) – (B) – (C) – (D)
② (B) – (A) – (C) – (D)
③ (C) – (A) – (B) – (D)
④ (D) – (A) – (B) – (C)
⑤ (D) – (B) – (A) – (C)

[09~10] 다음 대화를 읽고 물음에 답하시오.

> B: _____ (A) _____
> G: Yes. Actually, I'm learning it in my calligraphy class. Look! This is my work.
> B: _____ (B) _____

09 빈칸 (A)에 알맞은 표현을 주어진 조건에 맞게 쓰시오.

> ┌─ 조건 ─┐
> • *Hangeul*을 배우는 데 관심이 있는지 묻는 표현을 쓸 것.
> • 'have'와 'interest'를 사용할 것.

➡ _____

10 위 대화의 빈칸 (B)에 들어갈 말로 알맞은 것은?

① So what?
② You know what?
③ What are you into?
④ I'm interested in musicals.
⑤ Excellent!

[11~12] 다음 대화의 빈칸에 들어갈 알맞은 표현은?

11

> A: Are you interested in going shopping?
> B: No, I'm not. _____

① I mean it's time to go shopping.
② I'm interested in riding a bike.
③ What do you want to do?
④ I'm interested in going shopping.
⑤ I feel like going shopping.

12

> *(At an art exhibition)*
> B: Good job! Someone is holding a cloud? How creative!
> G: Thank you. _____
> B: Yes, I am. Actually, I'm taking an online class for free.
> G: Oh, good for you.

① You did a good job! It's awesome.
② Are you interested in doing *taekwondo*?
③ Are you interested in taking pictures?
④ Are you interested in beatboxing?
⑤ Are you interested in cooking?

Grammar

13 다음 빈칸에 들어갈 표현이 순서대로 바르게 짝지어진 것을 고르시오.

> _____ is getting popular for students _____ themselves through selfies.

① It – to express
② It – express
③ That – to express
④ That – express
⑤ This – expressing

14 밑줄 친 부분의 쓰임이 나머지 넷과 다른 것은?

① The man driving the bus is my father.
② Did you notice her cooking food in the kitchen?
③ Look at the two boys playing *yunnori*.
④ Mary is making a call in a public phone booth.
⑤ Are you interested in watching horror movies?

15 다음 빈칸에 들어갈 말이 나머지와 다른 하나는?

① It is dangerous _____ children to walk home alone.
② It's fun _____ me to do different things.
③ It was foolish _____ him to waste his money on such trifles.
④ Wasn't it exciting _____ you to see lots of dolphins at one time?
⑤ It will be awesome _____ me to be a member of the club.

16 다음 중 밑줄 친 부분의 쓰임이 다른 하나는?

① It was not easy to go up the hill on our bicycles.
② They thought it was a good idea to make them do the work.
③ It was hard to decide which room was the largest.
④ It was behind the chair in the living room.
⑤ It was nice of you to take me to the airport.

[17~18] 다음 빈칸에 들어갈 알맞은 것은?

17

> Everyone _____ in this town knows little about him.

① live
② lives
③ lived
④ living
⑤ to live

18

> It is interesting for me _____ a smaller doll inside each doll.

① see
② sees
③ saw
④ seeing
⑤ to see

19 괄호 안에 주어진 어휘를 사용해 다음을 영작하시오.

(1) Kate는 눈으로 덮인 산을 올라갔다. (climb, cover)
➡ _____

(2) 언제 깨진 창문을 고칠 거예요? (going, fix, break)
➡ _____

(3) Mariko는 공원에서 놀고 있는 그녀의 딸을 보았다. (look, play)
➡ _____

(4) 헬멧 없이 자전거를 타는 것은 위험하다. (a bike, a helmet, dangerous, to)
➡ _____

(5) Laura가 중국어 말하기를 배운 것은 아주 현명했다. (learn, wise, how to speak, it)
➡ _____

Reading

[20~22] 다음 글을 읽고 물음에 답하시오.

How do you express your feelings? Do you sing or dance? Do you write a poem or draw a picture? Nowadays, it is popular ⓐto express feelings through handwriting. Let's look at some works of art.

In the work of art on the right, the word includes an image of a delicious fruit, *hongsi*. It shows that autumn is a season of fruit. The work of art on the left shows a Korean word and a Chinese character. It looks like a happy woman walking down a road with autumn leaves. Both of these works express the feeling of autumn through beautiful handwriting. This kind of art is called ___(A)___.

20 주어진 영영풀이를 참고하여 빈칸 (A)에 철자 c로 시작하는 단어를 쓰시오.

the art of producing beautiful handwriting using a brush or a special pen

➡ _____

21 다음 문장에서 위 글의 내용과 <u>다른</u> 부분을 찾아서 고치시오.

Both the works of art mentioned in the text express the traditional culture of autumn through beautiful handwriting.

_____ ➡ _____

22 위 글의 밑줄 친 ⓐto express와 to부정사의 용법이 같은 것을 <u>모두</u> 고르시오.

① Do you want to express feelings through handwriting?

② The best way to express feelings is using various facial expressions.

③ He danced on the stage to express feelings.

④ She was too shy to express feelings.

⑤ I decided to express feelings through handwriting.

[23~25] 다음 글을 읽고 물음에 답하시오.

Calligraphy is not new. Many different kinds of calligraphy works from long ago can be found all around the world. Look at the two examples from Korea and the UK below. Can you ⓐtell the difference? The left one was created by Chusa in the period of the Joseon Dynasty. The characters were painted with a soft brush.

The right one, *The Canterbury Tales*, was created by Chaucer in England in the late 1400s. It was written with a pen. ___(A)___ led to different styles of calligraphy. Of course, all calligraphers had to practice hard to make their unique styles.

23 위 글의 빈칸 (A)에 들어갈 알맞은 말을 고르시오.

① Difference between the subjects of the works

② Difference between the East and the West

③ Difference between the periods of creation

④ Different writing tools

⑤ Various writing styles

24 위 글의 밑줄 친 ⓐtell the difference와 바꿔 쓸 수 있는 단어를 고르시오.

① differ   ② insist   ③ distinguish

④ vary   ⑤ persuade

25 위 글의 내용과 일치하지 <u>않는</u> 것은?

① Many different kinds of calligraphy works can be found all around the world.
② The left calligraphy work was created in the late 1400s.
③ The characters of the left calligraphy work were painted with a soft brush.
④ *The Canterbury Tales* was created by Chaucer in England.
⑤ *The Canterbury Tales* was written with a pen.

[26~27] 다음 글을 읽고 물음에 답하시오.

Today calligraphy is widely used around us. (①) You can find designers' artistic touches on movie posters, book covers, music CDs, and clothes. (②) Look at the title on the movie poster. (③) How do you feel? (④) Can you imagine the monster's big mouth, sharp teeth, and ugly, long tail? (⑤) How about the title on the fantasy novel? Do you see Harry's lightning and the wizard hats?

26 위 글의 흐름으로 보아, 주어진 문장이 들어가기에 가장 적절한 곳은?

> Below are some examples.

① ② ③ ④ ⑤

27 위 글을 읽고 대답할 수 <u>없는</u> 질문은?

① Nowadays, is calligraphy widely used around us?
② Where is calligraphy used?
③ How do designers add artistic touches to calligraphy titles?
④ What can you imagine from the title on the movie poster?
⑤ What do you see from the title on the fantasy novel?

[28~29] 다음 글을 읽고 물음에 답하시오.

(A)[Anyone / Someone] can start writing calligraphy. It's not easy to write (B)[by hand / on a keyboard] well at first, but practice makes perfect. ⓐ계속해서 노력하고 자신의 일상의 한 부분이 되게 하라. Write with your feelings on birthday cards, bookmarks, or gifts. (C)[Long before / Soon] you will build up your own world of calligraphy.

28 위 글의 괄호 (A)~(C)에서 문맥상 알맞은 낱말을 골라 쓰시오.

➡ (A) _____ (B) _____ (C) _____

29 위 글의 밑줄 친 ⓐ의 우리말에 맞게 한 단어를 보충하여, 주어진 어휘를 알맞게 배열하시오.

> it / life / trying / and / of / keep / part / make / your

➡ _____

출제율 90%

01 다음 문장의 빈칸에 알맞은 말을 쓰시오.

> Hammers and saws are a carpenter's
> _____.

출제율 95%

02 다음 우리말에 맞게 빈칸에 알맞은 단어를 쓰시오.

> (A) 왼쪽 작품은 조선 왕조 시대에 추사에 의해 창작되었다.
> The left work was created by Chusa in the _____ of the Joseon Dynasty.
> (B) 공상 소설의 제목은 어떠한가?
> How about the _____ on the fantasy novel?

출제율 95%

03 다음 대화의 빈칸에 알맞은 표현은?

> B: You did a good job! It's awesome.
> G: Thanks.
> B: What is it made of? Glass?
> G: Yes, it is. Are you interested in glass art?
> B: Yes, very much. How long did it take to make it?
> G: _____

① It was not easy.
② It was 5 feet long.
③ It was 10 feet high.
④ It took one month.
⑤ It was made of glass.

출제율 95%

04 다음 영영풀이에 해당하는 단어는?

> a story about imaginary events or people

① monster   ② tool   ③ tale
④ tail   ⑤ tooth

[05~07] 다음 대화를 읽고 물음에 답하시오.

> James: What are you doing, Mina?
> Mina: I'm practicing calligraphy.
> James: You're writing with a brush. It looks fun.
> Mina: Are you interested in calligraphy?
> James: Yes, very much.
> Mina: Look at this! I just wrote it. What do you think?
> James: It looks like a person dancing with open arms.
> Mina: You got it. This Korean word means "dance."
> James: You did a good job! Can I try it?
> Mina: Why not? Take this brush.

출제율 85%

05 다음 질문에 대한 답을 대화에서 찾아 영어로 쓰시오.

> Q: What is Mina doing?
>
> ➡ _____

출제율 100%

06 위 대화의 제목으로 알맞은 것은?

① How to Write Calligraphy
② The Way to Write Calligraphy Well
③ The Meaning of Dance in Korea
④ The Importance of Practice
⑤ Fun with Calligraphy

출제율 95%

07 위 대화의 내용과 일치하지 <u>않는</u> 것은?

① They are talking about calligraphy.
② Mina is practicing calligraphy.
③ James is interested in calligraphy.
④ Mina's work is a person dancing with open arms.
⑤ James is going to try writing calligraphy.

08 다음 대화의 빈칸에 알맞은 표현은?

> A: _____
>
> B: Yes, I am. I want to eat it.

① Are you interested in *pansori*?
② Are you interested in *bibimbap*?
③ Are you interested in *taekwondo*?
④ Are you interested in *yunnori*?
⑤ Are you interested in *hanbok*?

09 다음 대화의 빈칸에 들어갈 말로 어색한 것은?

> B: Minji, _____?
>
> G: Yes. I'm good at taking care of them.
>
> B: How about plants? Are you interested in them, too?
>
> G: No, I'm not. I can't grow them well.

① are you interested in animals
② do you have an interest in animals
③ are you into animals
④ what are you interested in
⑤ do you find raising animals interesting

10 다음 두 사람의 대화가 어색한 것은?

① A: Are you interested in *yunnori*?
　 B: Yes, I am. I want to play it.
② A: Are you interested in *taekwondo*?
　 B: Yes, I am. I want to learn it.
③ A: Do you like reading books?
　 B: Yes, I do. It is boring to read books.
④ A: Are you interested in *Hangeul*, Kevin?
　 B: Yes, very much. I want to learn it.
⑤ A: Who is the woman sitting between Tom and Mike?
　 B: She's Natalie.

11 다음 ⓐ~ⓗ 중 옳은 것을 모두 고르면?

> ⓐ It is fun reads books.
> ⓑ Look at the boy enjoying *tuho*.
> ⓒ This calligraphy shows a tree to grow in a pot.
> ⓓ Isn't it exciting to see a singing contest?
> ⓔ Who was the man played the piano on the stage?
> ⓕ It's no use crying over spilt milk.
> ⓖ We live in a house built in 1906.
> ⓗ It is a lot of fun to dancing *talchum*.

① ⓐ, ⓒ, ⓕ
② ⓑ, ⓒ, ⓓ, ⓔ
③ ⓑ, ⓓ, ⓕ, ⓖ
④ ⓒ, ⓑ, ⓔ, ⓗ
⑤ ⓒ, ⓓ, ⓔ, ⓖ

12 다음 밑줄 친 부분의 쓰임이 나머지와 <u>다른</u> 것을 고르시오.

① It looks like a happy woman <u>walking</u> down a road with autumn leaves.
② Do you know the boy <u>wearing</u> a mask?
③ Jenny loves <u>going</u> hiking.
④ My brother is <u>washing</u> the dishes.
⑤ The girls <u>dancing</u> to the music are my friends.

13 다음 중 어법상 적절한 문장은?

① It is important keeps your teeth clean.
② It was boring wait for her.
③ It was impossible to estimating the flood damage this year.
④ It is a nice idea to have cold noodles in summer.
⑤ It is nice for you to help that old man.

14 다음 우리말을 주어진 어휘를 이용하여 6단어로 영작하시오.

> 건강을 유지하는 것은 중요하다. (to stay, important, healthy)

➡ _____

[15~17] 다음 글을 읽고 물음에 답하시오.

> How do you express your feelings? Do you sing or dance? Do you write a poem or draw a picture? Nowadays, it is popular to express feelings through handwriting. Let's look at some works of art.
>
>
>
> (①) In the work of art on the right, the word includes an image of a delicious fruit, *hongsi*. (②) The work of art on the left shows a Korean word and a Chinese ⓐcharacter. (③) It looks like a happy woman walking down a road with autumn leaves. (④) Both of these works express the feeling of autumn through beautiful handwriting. (⑤) This kind of art is called calligraphy.

15 위 글의 흐름으로 보아, 주어진 문장이 들어가기에 가장 적절한 곳은?

> It shows that autumn is a season of fruit.

①   ②   ③   ④   ⑤

16 위 글의 밑줄 친 ⓐcharacter와 같은 의미로 쓰인 것을 고르시오.

① He has a strong character.
② She has a face without any character.
③ Who is the major character in this book?
④ Please write in a large character.
⑤ My father is a man of fine character.

17 위 글을 읽고 대답할 수 없는 질문은?

① What is the best way to express your feelings?
② What image does the work of art on the right include?
③ What does the work of art on the left show?
④ What does the work of art on the left look like?
⑤ What is this kind of art called?

[18~20] 다음 글을 읽고 물음에 답하시오.

> Calligraphy is not new. Many different kinds of calligraphy works from long ago can be found all around the world. Look at the two examples from Korea and the UK below. Can you tell the difference? The left ____(A)____ was created by Chusa in the period of the Joseon Dynasty. The characters were painted with a soft brush.
>
>
>
> The right ____(B)____, *The Canterbury Tales*, was created by Chaucer in England in the late 1400s. It was written with a pen. Different writing tools led to different styles of calligraphy. Of course, all calligraphers had to practice hard to make their unique styles.

18 위 글의 빈칸 (A)와 (B)에 공통으로 들어갈 알맞은 대명사를 쓰시오.

➡ _____

19 다음 영영풀이에 해당하는 단어를 본문에서 찾아 쓰시오.

> a series of rulers of a country who all belong to the same family

➡ _____

20 위 글의 왼쪽 그림에 대해 알 수 없는 것을 고르시오.

① 작가 ② 제작된 국가
③ 제작된 시기 ④ 사용한 필기구
⑤ 시를 인용한 이유

[21~23] 다음 글을 읽고 물음에 답하시오.

　Today calligraphy is widely used around us. You can find designers' (A)[artistic / awkward] touches on movie posters, book covers, music CDs, and clothes. Below are some examples. Look at the title on the movie poster. How do you feel? Can you imagine the monster's big mouth, sharp teeth, and ugly, long (B)[tail / tale]? How about ⓐthe title on the fantasy novel? Do you see Harry's (C)[lightning / lightening] and the wizard hats?

21 위 글의 제목으로 알맞은 것을 고르시오.

① How to Find Designers' Artistic Touches
② What Can You Find on the Movie Poster?
③ Examples of Calligraphy Used around Us
④ Let's Find Calligraphy Used on the Movie Poster
⑤ Let's Find Calligraphy Used on the Fantasy Novel

22 위 글의 괄호 (A)~(C)에서 문맥상 알맞은 낱말을 골라 쓰시오.

➡ (A) _____ (B) _____ (C) _____

23 위 글을 읽고 밑줄 친 ⓐthe title on the fantasy novel에서 볼 수 있는 것 두 가지를 우리말로 쓰시오.

➡ (1) _____ (2) _____

[24~25] 다음 글을 읽고 물음에 답하시오.

　Anyone can start writing calligraphy. ⓐ It's easy to write by hand well at first, but _____(A)_____. Keep trying and make it part of your everyday life. Write with your feelings on birthday cards, bookmarks, or gifts. Soon you will build up your own world of calligraphy.

24 위 글의 빈칸 (A)에 들어갈 알맞은 말을 고르시오.

① look before you leap
② practice makes perfect
③ two heads are better than one
④ make hay while the sun shines
⑤ haste makes waste

25 위 글의 밑줄 친 ⓐ에서 흐름상 어색한 부분을 찾아 고치시오.

_____ ➡ _____

01 다음 대화의 빈칸에 들어갈 표현을 주어진 〈조건〉에 맞게 완성하시오.

> B: Good job! Someone is holding a cloud? How creative!
> G: Thank you. _____
> B: Yes, I am. Actually, I'm taking an online class for free.
> G: Oh, good for you.

┤ 조건 ├
- 관심이 있는지 묻는 표현을 쓸 것.
- 'take pictures'를 활용할 것.
- 'interested'를 사용할 것.

➡ _____

02 다음 대화의 밑줄 친 우리말에 맞게 주어진 단어를 이용하여 쓰시오.

> B: You did a good job! It's awesome.
> G: Thanks.
> B: What is it made of? Glass?
> G: Yes, it is. Are you interested in glass art?
> B: Yes, very much. 그거 만드는 데 시간이 얼마나 걸렸니?
> G: It took one month.

(long / take / make / it)

➡ _____

03 다음 대화를 읽고 아래의 요약문을 완성하시오.

> James: What are you doing, Mina?
> Mina: I'm practicing calligraphy.
> James: You're writing with a brush. It looks fun.
> Mina: Are you interested in calligraphy?

> James: Yes, very much.
> Mina: Look at this! I just wrote it. What do you think?
> James: It looks like a person dancing with open arms.
> Mina: You got it. This Korean word means "dance."
> James: You did a good job! Can I try it?
> Mina: Why not? Take this brush.

⬇

> Mina and James are talking about Mina's _____ work. Mina is _____ calligraphy with a _____. She writes a Korean word meaning "_____." James thinks she did a _____ job. He is going to try _____ calligraphy.

04 다음 문장을 주어진 말로 시작하여 다시 쓰시오.

(1) Dick must be sent to hospital because of his illness.
➡ It is necessary _____
_____.

(2) Jane thinks she should eat lots of vegetables.
➡ Jane thinks it is necessary _____
_____.

05 다음 두 문장을 관계대명사를 사용하지 않고 하나의 문장으로 고쳐 쓰시오.

> - She bought a smartphone.
> - The smartphone was made in Korea.

➡ _____

[06~08] 다음 글을 읽고 물음에 답하시오.

How do you express your feelings? Do you sing or dance? Do you write a poem or draw a picture? Nowadays, ⓐ손 글씨를 통해 감정을 표현하는 것이 인기다. Let's look at some works of art.

In the work of art on the right, the word includes an image of a delicious fruit, *hongsi*. It shows that autumn is a season of fruit. ⓑ The work of art on the left shows a Korean word and a Chinese character. It looks like a happy woman walking down a road with autumn leaves. Both of these works express the feeling of autumn through beautiful handwriting. This kind of art is called calligraphy.

06 위 글의 밑줄 친 ⓐ의 우리말에 맞게 주어진 어휘를 이용하여 8단어로 영작하시오.

it, through

➡ _____

07 다음 빈칸 (A)와 (B)에 알맞은 단어를 넣어 위 글의 밑줄 친 ⓑ에 대한 소개를 완성하시오.

It is the calligraphy expressing the (A)_____ of autumn, and it shows a (B)_____ _____ and a (C)_____ _____. It looks like a happy woman walking down a road with autumn leaves.

08 본문의 내용과 일치하도록 다음 빈칸 (A)와 (B)에 알맞은 단어를 쓰시오.

Calligraphy is the (A)_____ through which we can express (B)_____.

[09~11] 다음 글을 읽고 물음에 답하시오.

Calligraphy is not (A)[new / old]. Many different kinds of calligraphy works from long ago can be found all around the world. Look at the two examples from Korea and the UK below. Can you tell the difference? ⓐThe left one was created by Chusa in the period of the Joseon Dynasty. The characters were painted with a soft brush.

The right one, *The Canterbury Tales*, was created by Chaucer in England in the late 1400s. It was written with a pen. Different writing tools led to different styles of calligraphy. Of course, all calligraphers had to practice (B)[hard / hardly] to make their (C)[common / unique] styles.

09 위 글의 괄호 (A)~(C)에서 문맥이나 어법상 알맞은 낱말을 골라 쓰시오.

➡ (A) _____ (B) _____ (C) _____

10 위 글의 밑줄 친 ⓐ를 능동태로 고치시오.

➡ _____

11 다음 빈칸 (A)와 (B)에 알맞은 단어를 넣어 위 글의 *The Canterbury Tales*에 대한 소개를 완성하시오.

(A)_____ created it in England in the late 1400s. He wrote it with (B)_____ _____.

창의사고력 서술형 문제

01 주어진 십대의 취미 중 하나를 선택하여, 관심이 있는지 묻고 그에 대한 긍정의 답과 부정의 답을 〈보기〉의 문장과 같이 쓰시오. (부정의 답에는 관심 있는 취미를 쓰시오.)

〈Teens Hobbies〉

go shopping / watch horror movies / take selfies / listen to music / play soccer / ride a bike / collect figures / read detective stories

〈보기〉

A: Are you interested in watching horror movies?

B: Yes, I am. I watch horror movies very often. / No, I'm not. I'm interested in reading detective stories.

02 주어진 어휘와 가주어를 이용하여 3 문장 이상을 쓰시오.

learn English	play *yunnori*	keep promises
study history	swim in this river	see his art collection

(1) _____

(2) _____

(3) _____

(4) _____

(5) _____

(6) _____

03 다음 내용을 바탕으로 한국 문화 체험을 홍보하는 글을 쓰시오.

- 전통적인 한국의 문화 활동: kicking a *jegi*, a traditional Korean game
- 하는 방법: kick a *jegi* with one of our feet
- 기타: It is exciting to kick a *jegi*

Look at the boy (A)_____ a *jegi*. Kicking a *jegi* is a (B)_____, and we kick it with (C)_____. It is (D)_____ to kick a *jegi*. Are you interested? Please come and try.

단원별 모의고사

01 다음 단어에 대한 영어 설명이 <u>어색한</u> 것은?

① wildly: by a lot of people or in a lot of places
② imagine: to think about something and form a picture or idea of it
③ sharp: pointed
④ include: to make someone or something part of a group
⑤ tool: a piece of equipment, usually one you hold in your hand, that is designed to do a particular type of work

02 우리말에 맞게 문장의 빈칸에 알맞은 단어를 쓰시오.

> 각기 다른 필기구가 각기 다른 캘리그래피의 스타일을 이끌었다.
> ➡ Different writing tools _____ different styles of calligraphy.

03 다음 영영풀이에 해당하는 단어를 고르시오.

> beautiful writing, often created with a special pen or brush

① handwriting   ② character
③ calligraphy   ④ painting
⑤ selfie

04 대화의 빈칸 (A)와 (B)에 들어갈 말을 쓰시오.

> B: Minji, are you (A)_____ in animals?
> G: Yes, I am. I'm good at (B)_____ care of them.
> B: How about plants? Are you interested in them, too?
> G: No, I'm not. I can't grow them well.

05 그림을 보고 빈칸에 들어갈 알맞은 단어를 쓰시오.

> The work of art above shows a Korean word and a Chinese _____. It looks like a happy woman walking down a road with autumn leaves.

① painting   ② culture
③ handwriting   ④ character
⑤ tale

06 대화의 빈칸에 들어갈 말로 알맞은 것은?

> B: Look! Two girls are learning *Hangeul*.
> G: Are you interested in *Hangeul*, Kevin?
> B: _____ I want to join them and learn it.

① Good for you.
② No, I'm not.
③ Minji is interested in *Hangeul*.
④ Of course not.
⑤ Yes, very much

07 다음 대화의 빈칸 ⓐ와 ⓑ에 들어갈 알맞은 말을 쓰시오.

> B: _____ⓐ_____! It's awesome.
> G: Thanks.
> B: What is it made of? Glass?
> G: Yes, it is. _____?
> B: Yes, very much. How long did it take to make it?
> G: It took one month.

조건
ⓐ • 상대방을 칭찬하는 표현을 쓸 것.
  • 'do', 'job'을 활용하여 5단어로 쓸 것.
ⓑ • glass art에 관심이 있는지 묻는 표현을 쓸 것.
  • 'be'동사 의문문으로 쓸 것.

➡ ⓐ _____

  ⓑ _____

[08~09] 다음 대화를 읽고 물음에 답하시오.

James: What are you doing, Mina?
Mina: I'm practicing calligraphy. (①)
James: You're writing with a brush. It looks fun. (②)
Mina: Are you interested in calligraphy?
James: Yes, very much.
Mina: Look at this! I just wrote it. (③)
James: It looks like a person dancing with open arms. (④)
Mina: You got it. This Korean word means "dance." (⑤)
James: You did a good job! Can I try it?
Mina: _____(A)_____ Take this brush.

08 주어진 문장이 들어갈 위치로 알맞은 것은?

What do you think?

① ② ③ ④ ⑤

09 위 대화의 흐름상 빈칸 (A)에 들어갈 말로 알맞은 것은?

① Are you interested in calligraphy?
② I'm afraid not.
③ How kind you are!
④ Why not?
⑤ Well done!

10 대화의 빈칸에 들어갈 표현으로 알맞은 것은?

A: You're writing something. What's this?
B: It's my art homework. Do you like it?
A: Sure. _____

① I think you did a good job!
② Anyone can start painting.
③ You have to practice more.
④ I don't like it.
⑤ I want to learn it.

11 다음 대화의 빈칸에 적절한 말은?

B: Julie, are you interested in *hanbok*?
G: Not really.
B: Then, _____
G: Well, I'm interested in *taekwondo*. It is a traditional Korean sport. It's awesome.

① are you interested in *bibimbap*?
② what are you going to do?
③ I think you did a good job!
④ are you interested in cooking?
⑤ what are you interested in?

12 대화의 밑줄 친 우리말에 맞게 주어진 단어를 활용하여 영어로 쓰시오.

Mina: Look at this! I just wrote it. What do you think?
James: 두 팔을 벌리고 춤을 추는 사람처럼 보여. (look like / dance / with open arms)
Mina: You got it. This Korean word means "dance."
James: You did a good job!

➡ _____

13 빈칸에 괄호 안에 주어진 동사를 알맞게 쓰시오.

> The boy _____ on the grass is my son.
> (sit)

14 가주어를 사용하여 주어진 문장과 같은 의미가 되도록 쓰시오.

(1) Knives and forks are easy to use.

➡ _____

(2) To read books is important.

➡ _____

15 다음 문장에서 어법상 어색한 것을 바르게 고치시오.

(1) There is a sign said "No smoking."

_____ ➡ _____

(2) That's fun to watch basketball games.

_____ ➡ _____

16 다음 중 어법상 어색한 것을 고르시오.

① It is exciting to learn *taekwondo*.
② It is not wise for you to put all your eggs in one basket.
③ It is important to save energy.
④ Look at the man cooking *bibimbap*.
⑤ There was a fence painted green.

[17~19] 다음 글을 읽고 물음에 답하시오.

How do you express your feelings? Do you sing or dance? Do you write a poem or draw a picture? Nowadays, it is popular to express feelings through handwriting. Let's look at some ⓐworks of art.

In ⓑthe work of art on the right, the word includes an image of a delicious fruit, *hongsi*. It shows that autumn is a season of fruit. The work of art on the left shows a Korean word and a Chinese character. It looks like a happy woman walking down a road with autumn leaves. Both of these works express the feeling of autumn through beautiful handwriting. This kind of art is called calligraphy.

17 위 글의 주제로 알맞은 것을 고르시오.

① There are many ways to express your feelings.
② The word can include an image of a delicious fruit.
③ It is possible to express feelings through handwriting.
④ A Korean word and a Chinese character can be used together in calligraphy.
⑤ There are many kinds of calligraphy.

18 위 글의 밑줄 친 ⓐworks와 같은 의미로 쓰인 것을 고르시오.

① She works for an engineering company.
② This machine works by electricity.
③ The engineering works are closed today.
④ This pill works on me.
⑤ Kate bought the complete works of Shakespeare.

19 다음 빈칸 (A)와 (B)에 알맞은 단어를 넣어 위 글의 밑줄 친 ⓑ에 대한 소개를 완성하시오.

> It is the calligraphy including an (A)_____ of a delicious fruit, *hongsi*, which shows that (B)_____ is a season of fruit.

[20~22] 다음 글을 읽고 물음에 답하시오.

ⓐThe right one, *The Canterbury Tales,* was created by Chaucer in England in the late 1400s. ⓑIt was written with a pen. Different writing tools ⓒled to different styles of calligraphy. Of course, all calligraphers had to practice hard ⓓto make their unique styles.

20 위 글의 밑줄 친 ⓐ와 ⓑ를 능동태로 고치시오.

➡ ⓐ _____

_____

ⓑ _____

21 위 글의 밑줄 친 ⓒled to와 바꿔 쓸 수 없는 말을 모두 고르시오.

① resulted from   ② caused
③ came about   ④ resulted in
⑤ brought about

22 아래 〈보기〉에서 위 글의 밑줄 친 ⓓto make와 문법적 쓰임이 같은 것의 개수를 고르시오.

┌─ 보기 ├─
① They thought it difficult to make their unique styles.
② They were happy to make their unique styles.
③ They studied many other styles to make their unique styles.
④ They explained the plan to make their unique styles to me.
⑤ They were creative enough to make their unique styles.
└──────────

① 1개   ② 2개   ③ 3개   ④ 4개   ⑤ 5개

[23~24] 다음 글을 읽고 물음에 답하시오.

ⓐ캘리그래피는 요즈음 우리 주변에서 널리 쓰이고 있다. You can find designers' artistic touches on movie posters, book covers, music CDs, and clothes. Below are some examples. Look at the title on the movie poster. How do you feel? Can you imagine the monster's big mouth, sharp teeth, and ugly, long tail? How about the title on the fantasy novel? Do you see Harry's lightning and the wizard hats?

23 위 글의 밑줄 친 ⓐ의 우리말에 맞게 주어진 어휘를 이용하여 7 단어로 영작하시오.

┌──────────────────────┐
│   Today, is, around   │
└──────────────────────┘

➡ _____

24 위 글의 내용과 일치하지 않는 것은?

① It's possible to find designers' artistic touches on movie posters.
② We use calligraphy in movie posters, book covers, music CDs, and clothes.
③ We can imagine the monster's big mouth, sharp teeth, and ugly, long tail from the title on the movie poster.
④ We see Harry's lightning and the wizard hats from the title on the fantasy novel.
⑤ The title on the fantasy novel is a good example of drawing used around us.

Lesson 8

Design for All

🎙 의사소통 기능

- 불평하기
  I'm not happy about the desk.
- 의도 표현하기
  I'm thinking of putting some pads on it.

🎙 언어 형식

- so ~ that ... can't
  The shoes were **so** uncomfortable **that** she **couldn't** walk well.
- 사역동사
  What **made** her **do** all this?

Words & Expressions

Key Words

- **add** [æd] 동 더하다, 추가하다
- **almost** [ɔ́:lmoust] 부 거의
- **another** [ənʌ́ðər] 형 또 하나의, 또 다른
- **bath** [bæθ] 명 목욕
- **bathtub** [bǽθtʌb] 명 욕조
- **below** [bilóu] 전 (위치가 …보다) 아래에
- **blind** [blaind] 형 눈이 먼
- **bookshelf** [búkʃelf] 명 책꽂이
- **Braille** [breil] 명 점자
- **cold answer** 냉담한 대답
- **company** [kʌ́mpəni] 명 회사
- **cotton** [kátn] 명 솜
- **cross** [krɔːs] 동 건너다
- **crowded** [kráudid] 형 붐비는
- **cushion** [kúʃən] 명 쿠션, 방석
- **decide** [disáid] 동 결심하다
- **decorate** [dékərèit] 동 장식하다
- **difficulty** [dífikʌ̀lti] 명 어려움
- **dirty** [də́ːrti] 형 더러운
- **easily** [íːzili] 부 쉽게
- **either** [íːðər] 부 (부정문에서) …도 또한[역시]
- **finally** [fáinəli] 부 마침내
- **flat** [flæt] 형 평평한
- **fountain** [fáuntən] 명 분수, 원천
- **handle** [hǽndl] 명 손잡이
- **hang** [hæŋ] 동 매달다, 걸다
- **hearing** [híriŋ] 명 청력
- **however** [hauévər] 부 그러나, 하지만
- **journey** [dʒə́ːrni] 명 여행, 여정

- **jump rope** 줄넘기를 하다
- **locker** [lákər] 명 사물함
- **low(–lower–lowest)** [lou] 형 낮은
- **moment** [móumənt] 명 순간
- **pad** [pæd] 명 패드, 깔개
- **point of view** 관점
- **product** [prádʌkt] 명 상품, 제품
- **reach** [riːtʃ] 동 …에 닿다
- **seat** [siːt] 명 자리, 좌석
- **sign** [sain] 명 표지판
- **solution** [səlúːʃən] 명 해결책
- **station** [stéiʃən] 명 역, 정류장
- **step** [step] 명 계단
- **step box** 디딤대
- **stick** [stik] 명 지팡이, 막대기
- **swing** [swiŋ] 명 그네
- **switch** [switʃ] 명 스위치
- **thick** [θik] 형 두꺼운
- **tight** [tait] 형 꽉 조이는, 딱 붙는
- **together** [təgéðər] 부 함께
- **traffic** [trǽfik] 명 교통
- **traffic light** 신호등
- **uncomfortable** [ənkʌ́mfərtəbəl] 형 불편한
- **universal** [jùːnəvə́ːrsəl] 형 보편적인
- **view** [vjuː] 명 견해, 관점
- **way** [wei] 명 방법
- **wheelchair** [hwíːltʃər] 명 휠체어
- **wiper** [wáipər] 명 닦개, 와이퍼

Key Expressions

- **be planning to+동사원형** …할 계획이다
- **be thinking of** …할 것을 고려[생각] 중이다
- **by oneself** 혼자서
- **get hurt** 다치다
- **get in** …에 들어가다(= **enter**)
- **get on** …을 타다
- **go through** …을 겪다
- **How about –ing?** …하는 게 어때?
- **in danger** 위험에 처한
- **lots of (= a lot of)** 많은

- **more and more** 점점 더 많은
- **put A on B** A를 B에 놓다[두다]
- **put on** …을 입다
- **so+형용사/부사+that+주어+can't …**
  너무 ~해서 …할 수 없다
- **such a(n)+형용사+명사+that+주어+can …**
  아주 ~해서 …할 수 있다
- **tired of** …에 지친, …에 싫증 난
- **turn on** …을 켜다
- **watch out** 조심하다

Word Power

※ 형용사 뒤에 -ly를 붙여 부사로 만들기

- [ ] **easy**(쉬운) – **easily**(쉽게)
- [ ] **final**(마지막의) – **finally**(마침내)
- [ ] **comfortable**(편안한) – **comfortably**(편안하게)

- [ ] **difficult**(어려운) – **difficultly**(어렵게)
- [ ] **safe**(안전한) – **safely**(안전하게)
- [ ] **thick**(두꺼운) – **thickly**(두껍게)

※ 서로 반대되는 뜻을 가진 어휘

- [ ] **difficulty** (어려움) ↔ **ease** (쉬움)
- [ ] **dirty** (더러운) ↔ **clean** (깨끗한)
- [ ] **comfortable** (편안한) ↔ **uncomfortable** (불편한)

- [ ] **thick** (두꺼운) ↔ **thin** (마른, 야윈)
- [ ] **low** (낮은) ↔ **high** (높은)
- [ ] **tight** (꽉 조이는) ↔ **loose** (느슨한)

English Dictionary

- [ ] **below** …의 아래에
  → in a lower place or position 더 낮은 장소나 위치에

- [ ] **blind** 눈이 먼
  → unable to see 볼 수 없는

- [ ] **company** 회사
  → a business organization that makes money by producing or selling goods or services
  물건이나 서비스를 생산하거나 팔아서 돈을 버는 사업 조직

- [ ] **cross** 건너다
  → to go across from one side of something to the other
  어떤 것의 한쪽 편에서 반대편으로 가로질러 가다

- [ ] **crowded** 붐비는
  → having a lot of people or too many people
  많은 사람들 또는 너무 많은 사람들이 있는

- [ ] **decorate** 장식하다
  → to add something to an object or place, especially in order to make it more attractive
  특히 더 매력적으로 만들기 위해 물건이나 장소에 어떤 것을 더하다

- [ ] **flat** 평평한
  → not having a part that is higher or lower than another
  다른 부분보다 더 높거나 더 낮은 부분을 가지지 않은

- [ ] **handle** 손잡이
  → a part that is designed especially to be held by the hand 특히 손에 쥐어지게 설계된 부분

- [ ] **journey** 여행, 여정
  → an act of traveling from one place to another
  한 장소에서 또 다른 장소로 여행하는 행위

- [ ] **locker** 사물함
  → a cupboard, often tall and made of metal, in which you can keep your possessions, and leave them for a period of time 소유물을 보관할 수 있고 일정 기간 동안 남겨둘 수 있는 금속으로 만들어진 종종 큰 벽장

- [ ] **low** 낮은
  → small in height or smaller than the usual height
  높이가 작은 또는 일반적인 높이보다 더 작은

- [ ] **product** 제품
  → something that is made or grown for selling
  팔기 위해 만들어지거나 재배되는 것

- [ ] **solution** 해결책
  → the answer to a problem
  문제에 대한 해답

- [ ] **station** 역, 정류장
  → a building or place where buses or trains stop so that people can get on or off
  사람들이 타고 내릴 수 있도록 버스나 기차가 멈춰서는 건물이나 장소

- [ ] **stick** 지팡이
  → a long, thin wooden pole that especially old or injured people use to walk
  노인들이나 부상당한 사람들이 걷기 위해 사용하는 길고 가는 나무로 된 막대

- [ ] **switch** 스위치
  → a button or key that controls the light or machine
  전구나 기계를 통제하는 버튼이나 키

- [ ] **uncomfortable** 불편한
  → not feeling comfortable and pleasant
  편안하거나 유쾌하게 느끼지 않는

- [ ] **universal** 보편적인
  → related to everyone in the world
  세상의 모든 사람과 관련된

- [ ] **view** 관점, 견해
  → a personal opinion or belief about a situation or subject
  어떤 상황이나 주제에 관한 개인적인 의견이나 믿음

01 다음 빈칸에 들어갈 말로 알맞은 것은?

> She couldn't see or hear well. She couldn't walk well without a stick. With all these _____, the woman had to climb stairs in subway stations and get on crowded buses.

① difference ② products ③ steps
④ difficulties ⑤ journey

서답형

02 다음 문장의 빈칸에 주어진 영영풀이에 해당하는 말을 쓰시오.

> • One example of her _____ design ideas is low-floor buses.
> <영영풀이> related to everyone in the world

➡ _____

서답형

03 다음 우리말에 맞게 두 단어로 쓰시오.

> 그녀는 혼자서 전등을 켤 수 없어요.
> ➡ She can't turn on the light _____.

➡ _____

중요

04 다음 중 밑줄 친 단어의 우리말 뜻이 잘못된 것은?

① Sometimes she got hurt or found herself in danger. (위험에 처한)
② She became tired of the same cold answer. (싫증 난)
③ She put on her grandmother's clothes, uncomfortable shoes, and thick glasses. (불편한)
④ During her journey, Patricia felt the difficulties old people go through. (겪다)
⑤ Every moment was very difficult for her. (다른)

[05~06] 다음 영영풀이에 해당하는 단어를 고르시오.

05

> a long, thin wooden pole that especially old or injured people use to walk

① stroller ② stick
③ wheelchair ④ seat
⑤ handle

중요

06

> in a lower place or position

① on ② below
③ beyond ④ above
⑤ between

서답형

07 다음 빈칸에 공통으로 들어갈 단어를 쓰시오.

> • Which _____ do I press to turn it off?
> • I can't work next weekend. Will you _____ with me?

➡ _____

서답형

08 다음 우리말에 맞게 빈칸에 주어진 철자로 시작하는 단어를 쓰시오.

> 그녀와 나는 내일 분수에서 만날 것이다.
> • She and I will meet at the f_____ tomorrow.

01 빈칸에 들어갈 단어를 주어진 철자로 시작하여 쓰시오.

> In 1979, a woman started a j_____ to cities in the U.S. and Canada. Every moment was very difficult for her, but she visited more than 115 cities and ended her trip in 1982.

02 우리말에 맞게 주어진 단어를 이용하여 문장의 빈칸을 채우시오. (어형 변화 필수)

(1) 그 여인은 지하철역에서 계단을 올라가거나 붐비는 버스에 올라타야 했다.

➡ The woman had to climb stairs in subway stations and get on _____ buses. (crowd)

(2) 그녀는 똑같은 냉담한 대답에 지쳤다.

➡ She became _____ _____ the same cold answer. (tire)

(3) 그녀는 자신의 할머니 옷을 입고, 불편한 신발을 신고, 두꺼운 안경을 썼다.

➡ She put on her grandmother's clothes, _____ shoes, and thick glasses. (comfortable)

03 다음 빈칸에 영영풀이에 해당하는 단어를 주어진 철자로 시작하여 쓰시오.

> • Products like big f_____ light switches are helping people live better lives.
> <영영풀이> not having a part that is higher or lower than another

04 우리말과 같은 뜻이 되도록 빈칸에 알맞은 단어를 쓰시오.

(1) 나는 그의 견해에 동의하지 않는다.

➡ I don't agree with his _____.

(2) 이 재킷은 내겐 너무 꽉 조인다.

➡ This jacket is too _____ for me.

(3) 그녀의 유니버설 디자인 아이디어의 한 가지 예는 저상 버스이다. 그것은 계단이 없고 낮은 바닥을 가지고 있어서 휠체어를 탄 사람조차 아무 도움 없이 이용할 수 있다.

➡ One _____ of her universal design ideas is low-floor buses. They have no steps and have such a low floor that even a person in a _____ can use them _____ any help.

(4) 1970년대 동안, 그녀는 큰 디자인 회사에서 일했다.

➡ _____ the 1970's, she worked for a big design _____.

05 영영풀이에 해당하는 단어를 <보기>에서 찾아 첫 번째 칸에 쓰고, 두 번째 칸에는 우리말 뜻을 쓰시오.

> ┤ 보기 ├
> view / cross / product / low

(1) _____: something that is made or grown for selling: _____

(2) _____: small in height or smaller than the usual height: _____

(3) _____: a personal opinion or belief about a situation or subject: _____

(4) _____: to go across from one side of something to the other: _____

Conversation

1 불평하기

I'm not happy about the desk. 나는 책상이 마음에 들지 않아.

- "I'm not happy about …"은 '나는 …이 마음에 들지 않는다'라는 의미로, 만족스럽지 못한 것에 대해 불평하는 표현이다.

  e.g. A: I'm not happy about this restaurant.
  B: Is there anything wrong?

불평하는 표현

- It's not fair.
- I don't like ….
- I'm not satisfied with ….
- I'm not content with ….
- I want to complain about ….
- … is not satisfactory to me.
- … is not good enough for me.

핵심 Check

1. 다음 대화의 빈칸에 들어갈 말로 알맞지 <u>않은</u> 것은?

   A: _____

   B: What's the problem?

   A: The power button doesn't work.

   ① I want to complain about this computer.
   ② I'd like to complain about this computer.
   ③ I'm not happy with this computer.
   ④ I'm not satisfied with this computer.
   ⑤ This computer is good enough for me.

② 의도 표현하기

I'm thinking of putting some pads on it. 나는 그 위에 몇 장의 패드를 놓을까 생각 중이야.

■ "I'm thinking of …"는 '나는 …할까 생각 중이다'라는 뜻으로, 의도나 계획을 나타낼 때 쓰는 표현이다. 'of'는 전치사이므로 뒤에 명사나 동명사(-ing)가 와야 한다.

> *e.g.* A: I'm thinking of inviting Ms. Kim to the party.
> B: That's a good idea.

"I'm thinking of …"는 "I'm considering -ing …" 또는 "I intend to ~."와 바꿔 쓸 수 있다. 의지를 조금 더 강하게 표현할 때는 "I will ~"로 나타낼 수 있으며, 전치사 of 대신 about을 사용하여 "I'm thinking about ~"으로도 표현한다.

의도 표현하기

- I will ….
- I'm going to ….
- I'm planning to ….
- I'm considering -ing ….
- I intend to ….

- I'm thinking of buying a car. 나는 차를 살까 생각 중이다.
  = I'm considering buying a car.
  = I intend to buy a car.

핵심 Check

2. 다음 문장과 바꿔 쓸 수 있는 것은?

I'm thinking of putting some pads on it.

① I will putting some pads on it.
② I intend putting some pads on it.
③ I'm intend to put some pads on it.
④ I'm considering putting some pads on it.
⑤ I'm considering to putting some pads on it.

3. 다음 우리말에 맞게 대화의 빈칸에 알맞은 말을 쓰시오.

A: Are you _____ of buying a used car? (너는 중고차를 살 생각이니?)

B: No, I'm _____ to buy a new one. (아니. 난 새 차를 살 계획이야.)

🔖 **Get Ready 2**

(1) B: ❶I'm not happy about this fountain. It's too high for some kids.

    G: Well, ❷I'm planning to put lower fountains together with it.

    B: That's a good idea.

(2) G: ❸I don't like the high steps here. People in wheelchairs can't get in.

    B: Right. ❹I'm thinking of building a new way with no steps.

(3) G: I'm not happy about this swing. People in wheelchairs can't get on it easily.

    B: Right. I'm planning to hang a bigger and safer seat for them.

    G: Good idea.

(1) B: 나는 이 음수대가 마음에 들지 않아. 몇몇 아이들에게는 너무 높아.
G: 음, 나는 그것과 함께 더 낮은 음수대들을 놓으려고 계획 중이야.
B: 좋은 생각이야.
(2) G: 나는 여기 높은 계단이 마음에 들지 않아. 휠체어를 탄 사람들은 들어설 수가 없잖아.
B: 맞아. 나는 계단 없는 새 길을 짓는 것을 생각 중이야.
(3) G: 나는 이 그네가 마음에 들지 않아. 휠체어를 탄 사람들은 그것을 쉽게 탈 수 없어.
B: 맞아. 나는 그들을 위해 더 크고 더 안전한 자리를 매달려고 계획 중이야.
G: 좋은 생각이야.

❶ '나는 …이 마음에 들지 않는다.'라는 의미로, 만족스럽지 못한 것에 대해 불평하는 표현이다.
❷ 'be planning to+동사원형' 형태로 '나는 …할까 생각 중이다'라는 뜻으로, 의도나 계획을 나타낼 때 쓰는 표현이다.
❸ 'I don't like …'는 만족스럽지 못한 것에 대해 불평하는 표현이다.
❹ "I'm thinking of …"는 '나는 …할까 생각 중이다'라는 뜻으로, 의도나 계획을 나타낼 때 쓰는 표현이다. 'of'는 전치사이므로 뒤에 명사나 동명사(동사-ing)가 와야 한다.

Check(√) True or False

(1) B doesn't like this fountain because it is too high for some kids.   T ☐ F ☐

(2) B isn't satisfied with the steps, so he is planning to build a new way with low steps.   T ☐ F ☐

(3) B intends to hang a bigger and safer seat for those in wheelchairs.   T ☐ F ☐

🔖 **Start Off Listen & Talk A**

(1) G: I'm not happy about the button.

    B: Why? ❶What's wrong with it?

    G: It's too high. Children or people in wheelchairs can't reach it. I'm thinking of putting ❷another switch for them.

(2) G: I'm not happy about the sign. There are some people ❸who can't see.

    B: Right. Do you have any ideas?

    G: Well, I'm thinking of adding Braille on the sign.

    B: That's a good idea.

(1) G: 나는 그 버튼이 마음에 들지 않아.
B: 왜? 뭐가 잘못됐니?
G: 그것은 너무 높아. 아이들이나 휠체어를 탄 사람들은 거기까지 닿을 수가 없어. 나는 그들을 위해 또 다른 스위치를 달까 생각 중이야.
(2) G: 나는 표지판이 마음에 들지 않아. 볼 수 없는 사람들도 좀 있잖아.
B: 맞아. 너는 어떤 아이디어라도 있니?
G: 음, 나는 표지판 위에 점자를 추가할까 생각 중이야.
B: 그거 좋은 생각이다.

❶ What's the matter with it?과 같은 표현이다.
❷ another+단수명사
❸ 관계대명사절로 선행사 people을 꾸며주는 역할을 한다.

Check(√) True or False

(4) G isn't satisfied with the button, so she's planning to fix it.   T ☐ F ☐

(5) G is thinking of adding Braille on the sign for blind people.   T ☐ F ☐

Start Off Listen & draw

B: I'm not happy about the lights.
G: ❶What's wrong with them?
B: The traffic lights look the same to some people ❷who are blind to colors.
G: Oh, I see. How about putting an image on each light?
B: A walking man on the green light and a standing man on the red light? Good idea!

❶ 무엇이 문제인지 물어보는 표현이다.
❷ 관계대명사절로 선행사 people을 수식하고, 'be blind to ...'는 '…을 못보다'라는 뜻이다.

Speak Up Look and talk

A: I'm not happy about the desk. It's too low.
B: ❶Right. I'm thinking of putting some pads on it.
A: ❷Good idea.

❶ 상대방의 말에 동의하는 말로 You're right.이라고 해도 좋다.
❷ 상대방의 말에 동의하는 표현이다.

Speak Up Mission

A: I'm not happy about the bookshelf. It's too small.
B: ❶I think so, too. Do you have any ideas?
A: I'm thinking of putting another bookshelf on it.
B: That's a good idea.

❶ 상대방의 말에 동의하는 표현이다.

Step Up Real-life Scene

Dad: What are you doing here?
Son: I'm thinking of ways ❶to help Miso.
Dad: What's wrong?
Son: She can't turn on the light ❷by herself. This switch is too high for her.
Dad: That's right. I'm not happy about it, ❸ either. Do you have any good ideas about that?
Son: I'm thinking of putting a step box here below the switch.

Dad: Good idea. And I'll change the switch to a bigger ❹one.
Son: Great. Grandma will like it, too. She can turn on the light more easily.

❶ ways를 수식하는 형용사적 용법이다.
❷ by oneself: 혼자서
❸ either: 부정문에서 '~도 역시'의 뜻이다.
❹ one은 부정대명사로 'switch'를 가리킨다.

Express Yourself A

(1) G: I'm not happy about my brother's chair. It's too low and too hard.
　　B: Right. I'm thinking of buying ❶this one. What do you think?
　　G: Looks great. I think he can use it ❷for so long, even after he grows taller.
(2) B: I'm not happy about the door handles in my house. They are not easy ❸to use for my grandma.
　　G: How about this one? She will pull it and open the door easily.
　　B: That's good.
(3) G: I'm thinking of buying this spoon. It will help my grandma eat soup easily.
　　B: Right. ❹She doesn't have to hold it with her fingers.

❶ this one = this chair
❷ for so long: 아주 오랫동안
❸ 형용사 easy를 꾸며주는 부정사의 부사 용법이다.
❹ doesn't have to+동사원형: …할 필요가 없다

Learning Diary Check Yourself

G: I'm not happy about this light switch.
B: Why? What's wrong?
G: It's too small. Grandma can't use it easily.
B: ❶Do you have any ideas?
G: I'm thinking of changing it with ❷a bigger one. That'll help her turn on the light easily.
B: Good idea.

❶ 무슨 아이디어가 있느냐고 묻는 표현이다.
❷ a bigger one = a bigger switch

● 다음 우리말과 일치하도록 빈칸에 알맞은 말을 쓰시오.

Get Ready 2

(1) B: I'm _____ _____ _____ this _____. It's _____ _____ for some kids.
 G: Well, I'_____ _____ _____ _____ lower fountains together with it.
 B: That's a _____ _____.

(2) G: I _____ _____ the high steps here. People _____ _____ can't _____ _____.
 B: Right. I'm _____ _____ _____ a new way _____ no _____.

(3) G: I'm not _____ about this swing. People in wheelchairs can't _____ _____ it _____.
 B: Right. I'm _____ _____ _____ a bigger and safer seat for them.
 G: Good idea.

Start Off Listen & Talk A

(1) G: I'm _____ _____ _____ the button.
 B: Why? What's _____ with it?
 G: It's too high. Children or people in wheelchairs can't _____ it. _____ _____ _____ putting _____ switch for them.

(2) G: I'm not _____ _____ the sign. There are some people _____ can't see.
 B: Right. Do you have _____ ideas?
 G: Well, I'm _____ of _____ Braille on the sign.
 B: That's a _____ _____.

Start Off Listen & draw

B: _____ _____ _____ _____ _____ the lights.
G: _____ _____ _____ _____ them?
B: The traffic lights look _____ _____ to some people _____ are _____ _____ _____.
G: Oh, I see. _____ _____ _____ an image on each light?
B: A _____ man on the green light and a _____ man on the red light? Good idea!

Speak Up Look and talk

B: _____ _____ _____ _____ _____ the desk. It's _____ _____.
G: Right. I'm _____ _____ _____ some pads on it.
B: Good idea.

Speak Up Mission

A: I'm _____ _____ the _____. It's too small.
B: I think so, too. Do you have _____ _____?
A: I'm _____ _____ _____ another bookshelf on it.
B: That's a good idea.

Speak Up Real-life Scene

Dad: What are you _____ here?
Son: I'm _____ of _____ to help Miso.
Dad: What's _____?
Son: She can't _____ _____ the light _____ _____. This switch is _____ _____ for her.
Dad: That's right. I'm not _____ _____ it, _____. Do you have any good ideas _____ _____?
Son: I'm _____ of putting a _____ _____ here _____ the switch.
Dad: Good idea. And I'll _____ the switch to a _____ _____.
Son: Great. Grandma will like it, too. She can _____ _____ the light more _____.

Express Yourself A

(1) G: _____ _____ _____ _____ _____ my brother's chair. It's _____ _____ and _____ _____.
   B: Right. _____ _____ _____ _____ _____ this one. _____ do you _____?
   G: _____ _____. I think he can use it for _____ _____, even after he _____ _____.

(2) B: I'm _____ _____ _____ the door _____ in my house. They are not _____ _____ _____ for my grandma.
   G: _____ _____ this one? She will pull it and open the door easily.
   B: That's good.

(3) G: _____ _____ _____ buying this spoon. It will help my grandma eat soup easily.
   B: Right. She _____ _____ _____ hold it with her fingers.

Learning Diary Check Yourself

G: I'm _____ _____ about this _____ _____.
B: Why? What's _____?
G: It's _____ _____. Grandma can't use it easily.
B: Do you have _____ _____?
G: _____ _____ _____ _____ it _____ a bigger one. That'll help her _____ _____ the light easily.
B: Good idea.

해석

A: 나는 책꽂이가 마음에 들지 않아. 그것은 너무 작아.
B: 나도 그렇게 생각해. 어떤 아이디어라도 있니?
A: 나는 그 위에 또 다른 책꽂이를 놓을까 생각 중이야.
B: 그거 좋은 생각이다.

아빠: 너는 여기서 무엇을 하고 있니?
아들: 저는 미소를 도울 방법을 생각하고 있어요.
아빠: 뭐가 잘못됐니?
아들: 그녀는 혼자서 전등을 켤 수 없어요. 이 스위치는 그녀에게 너무 높아요.
아빠: 그렇구나. 나도 그것이 마음에 들지 않는구나. 그것에 대한 어떤 아이디어라도 있니?
아들: 저는 여기 스위치 아래에 디딤대를 놓을까 생각하고 있어요.
아빠: 좋은 생각이구나. 그럼 나는 스위치를 더 큰 것으로 바꾸마.
아들: 좋아요. 할머니께서도 그것을 좋아하실 거예요. 할머니께서는 전등을 더 쉽게 켜실 수 있어요.

(1) G: 나는 내 남동생의 의자가 마음에 안 들어. 그것은 너무 낮고 딱딱해.
   B: 맞아. 나는 이것을 살까 생각 중이야. 너는 어때?
   G: 좋아 보이네. 나는 그가 키가 더 자란 후에도 그것을 오랫동안 사용할 수 있을 거라고 생각해.
(2) B: 나는 우리 집의 문손잡이가 마음에 안 들어. 그것들은 우리 할머니께서 사용하시기에 쉽지 않아.
   G: 이것은 어때? 그녀는 그것을 당겨서 문을 쉽게 여실 거야.
   B: 그것 좋네.
(3) G: 나는 이 숟가락을 살까 생각 중이야. 그것은 우리 할머니께서 국을 쉽게 드실 수 있도록 도와줄 거야.
   B: 맞아. 그녀는 그것을 손가락으로 잡으실 필요가 없어.

G: 나는 이 조명 스위치가 마음에 들지 않아.
B: 왜? 뭐가 잘못됐니?
G: 그것은 너무 작아. 할머니께서 그것을 쉽게 사용하실 수가 없어.
B: 어떤 아이디어라도 있니?
G: 나는 그것을 좀 더 큰 것으로 바꿀까 생각 중이야. 그것은 할머니께서 조명을 쉽게 켜실 수 있도록 도와줄 거야.
B: 좋은 생각이다.

01 다음 대화의 빈칸에 들어갈 말로 알맞은 것은?

> B: _____ It's too high for some kids.
>
> G: Well, I'm planning to put lower fountains together with it.
>
> B: That's a good idea.

① I want this fountain.

② I'm satisfied with this fountain.

③ I'm not interested in this fountain.

④ I like this fountain.

⑤ I'm not happy about this fountain.

02 다음 대화의 빈칸에 들어갈 말로 적절한 것은?

> G: I don't like the high steps here. People in wheelchairs can't get in.
>
> B: Right. _____ building a new way with no steps.

① I intend to   ② I'm thinking of

③ I'm planning to   ④ I'm going to

⑤ I will

03 다음 대화의 우리말에 맞게 주어진 단어를 이용하여 영어로 쓰시오.

> B: 나는 셔츠가 마음에 들지 않아. (happy / the shirt)
>
> G: What's wrong with it?
>
> B: It's too tight for me.

➡ _____

04 다음 대화를 알맞은 순서대로 배열하시오.

> (A) That's a good idea.
>
> (B) I'm thinking of putting another bookshelf on it.
>
> (C) I'm not happy about the bookshelf. It's too small.
>
> (D) I think so, too. Do you have any ideas?

➡ _____

[01~02] 다음 대화를 읽고 물음에 답하시오.

> G: _____(A)_____ this swing. People in wheelchairs can't get on it easily.
>
> B: Right. (B)I'm planning to hang a bigger and safer seat for them.
>
> G: Good idea.

01 위 대화의 빈칸 (A)에 들어갈 말로 어색한 것은?

① I'm not happy about
② I'm not satisfied with
③ I'm not content with
④ I don't like
⑤ I don't complain about

02 위 대화의 밑줄 친 (B)의 의도로 알맞은 것은?

① 금지하기   ② 계획 표현하기
③ 부탁하기   ④ 허용 여부 묻기
⑤ 불평하기

서답형

03 다음 대화의 빈칸에 관심을 묻는 말을 주어진 조건에 따라 완성하시오.

> G: I'm not happy about the button.
> B: Why? _____
> G: It's too high. Children or people in wheelchairs can't reach it. I'm thinking of putting another switch for them.

┤ 조건 ├

• 상대방이 문제를 제기할 때, '무슨 일이야?'라고 묻는 표현
• 'wrong'과 'with'를 사용할 것

➡ _____

[04~05] 다음 대화를 읽고 물음에 답하시오.

> B: I'm not ⓐhappy about the lights.
>
> G: What's ⓑwrong with them?
>
> B: The traffic lights look ⓒdifferent to some people who are ⓓblind to colors.
>
> G: Oh, I see. (A)How about putting an ⓔimage on each light?
>
> B: A walking man on the green light and a standing man on the red light? Good idea!

04 위 대화의 밑줄 친 ⓐ~ⓔ 중 어휘의 쓰임이 어색한 것은?

① ⓐ   ② ⓑ   ③ ⓒ   ④ ⓓ   ⑤ ⓔ

05 위 대화의 밑줄 (A)와 같은 의미가 아닌 것은?

① What about putting
② Why don't we put
③ Shall we put
④ Why are you putting
⑤ What do you say to putting

[06~07] 다음 대화를 읽고 물음에 답하시오.

> G: _____(A)_____ It will help my grandma eat soup easily.
>
> B: Right. (B)그녀는 그것을 손가락으로 잡으실 필요가 없어.

06 위 대화의 빈칸 (A)에 들어갈 말로 어색한 것은?

① I'm thinking of buying this spoon.
② I'm considering buying this spoon.
③ I intend to buy this spoon.
④ I'm planning to buy this spoon.
⑤ I want to complain about buying this spoon.

07 위 대화의 밑줄 친 (B)의 우리말에 맞게 주어진 단어를 활용하여 영어로 쓰시오.

> (have to / hold / her fingers)

➡ _____

[08~09] 다음 대화를 읽고 물음에 답하시오.

G: I'm not happy about this light switch.
B: Why? What's wrong?
G: (A)_____ Grandma can't use it easily.
B: Do you have any ideas?
G: I'm thinking of changing it with a bigger one. (B)That'll help her turning on the light easily.
B: Good idea.

08 위 대화의 빈칸 (A)에 들어갈 말로 적절한 것은?

① This switch is too bright.
② This switch is too big.
③ This switch is too high for her.
④ This switch is too small.
⑤ This switch is too low.

서답형

09 위 대화의 밑줄 친 (B)에서 어법상 틀린 부분을 찾아 바르게 고쳐 완전한 문장으로 쓰시오.

➡ _____

중요

10 다음 중 짝지어진 대화가 어색한 것을 고르시오.

① A: I'm happy with the lights.
  B: Why? What's wrong?
② A: What's wrong?
  B: I lost my ticket.

③ A: I'm not happy about the desk. It's too low.
  B: Right.
④ A: I'm thinking of putting another bookshelf on it.
  B: That's a good idea.
⑤ A: I want to complain about this spaghetti.
  B: Me, too. It tastes bad.

중요

11 대화의 밑줄 친 부분의 의도로 알맞은 것은?

> A: I'm not happy about the bookshelf. It's too small.
> B: I think so, too.

① 부탁하기   ② 제안하기   ③ 불평하기
④ 선호 묻기   ⑤ 관심 표현하기

[12~13] 다음 대화를 읽고 물음에 답하시오.

B: (A)I'm not happy about the shirt.
G: What's wrong with it?
B: _____

12 위 대화의 빈칸에 들어갈 말은?

① I'm interested in this shirt.
② I'm thinking of buying this shirt.
③ It's too tight for me.
④ This shirt is so comfortable.
⑤ I want to buy some shirts.

서답형

13 위 대화의 밑줄 친 (A)와 같은 의미가 되도록 동사 'want'와 'complain'을 사용하여 문장을 쓰시오.

➡ _____

01 다음 제시된 물건의 문제점과 해결책을 보고, 주어진 단어를 이용하여 대화의 빈칸을 완성하시오.

• problem – old
• solution – decorate its door

A: (1)_____(happy) the locker. It's too old.
B: I think so, too. Do you have any ideas?
A: (2)_____(think of) its door.
B: That's a good idea.

02 대화의 흐름상 빈칸에 들어갈 표현을 주어진 〈조건〉에 맞게 쓰시오.

A: _____
B: Why? What's wrong?
A: They are too bright.

┤ 조건 ├
• 전등에 대해 불만을 나타내는 표현을 쓸 것.
• 동사 'like'를 이용할 것.

➡ _____

[03~05] 다음 대화를 읽고 물음에 답하시오.

Dad: What are you doing here?
Son: I'm thinking of ways to help Miso.
Dad: What's wrong?

Son: (a)그녀는 혼자서 전등을 켤 수 없어요. This switch is too high for her.
Dad: That's right. _____(A)_____ Do you have any good ideas about that?
Son: I'm thinking of putting a step box here below the switch.
Dad: Good idea. And I'll change the switch to a bigger one.
Son: Great. Grandma will like it, too. She can turn on the light more easily.

03 위 대화의 빈칸 (A)에 들어갈 표현을 주어진 〈조건〉에 맞게 영어로 쓰시오.

┤ 조건 ├
• 아들이 말한 불평에 동의하는 표현을 쓸 것.
• 'happy, about'을 사용할 것.

➡ _____

04 위 대화의 밑줄 친 (a)의 우리말을 주어진 〈조건〉에 맞게 영어로 쓰시오.

┤ 조건 ├
• 재귀대명사를 사용할 것.
• 조동사 can을 활용할 것.
• 8 단어의 문장으로 쓸 것.

➡ _____

05 위 대화를 읽고 다음 물음에 영어로 답하시오.

Q: What will Dad do for Miso and Grandma?

➡ _____

Grammar

교과서

① so+형용사/부사+that+주어+can't ...

> • The shoes were **so** uncomfortable **that** she **couldn't** walk well.
> 신발이 너무 불편해서 그녀는 잘 걸을 수 없었다.

■ so+형용사[부사]+that+주어+can't ...'
  - 의미: 너무 ~해서 …할 수 없다(결과)
  - 형태: so+형용사/부사+that+주어+can't ...

■ 'so+형용사[부사]+that+주어+동사' 구문은 '너무 ~해서 …하다'라는 뜻으로 so 다음에는 형용사나 부사가 나오고 that 다음에는 주어와 동사가 있는 절이 온다. so 다음에 나오는 말이 '원인', that 다음에 나오는 절이 그에 따른 '결과'를 나타낸다.

■ 'so+형용사[부사]+that+주어+can't ...' 구문은 'too+형용사[부사]+to ...' 구문으로 바꿔 쓸 수 있으며, 'so+형용사[부사]+that+주어+can ...' 구문은 '형용사[부사]+enough+to ...' 구문으로 바꿔 쓸 수 있다.

  - It's **so** cold **that** I **can't** go outside. 너무 추워서 나는 밖에 나갈 수 없다.
    = It's **too** cold **to** go outside.
  - My sister was **so** smart **that** she **could** solve the problem.
    = My sister was smart **enough to** solve the problem. 내 여동생은 너무 똑똑해서 그 문제를 풀 수 있었다.

■ 'so ... that' 구문에서 that 앞에 형용사나 부사 대신 명사가 오면 so 대신 such를 쓴다.

  - The buses have **such** a low floor **that** even a person in a wheelchair can use them without any help. 그 버스들은 낮은 바닥을 가지고 있어서 휠체어를 탄 사람조차도 아무 도움 없이 이용할 수 있다.

■ 'so that+주어+동사'는 목적을 나타내어 '~하기 위해서' 혹은 '~하도록'이라는 의미로 쓰인다. 'so ~ that ...'과 혼동하지 않도록 유의한다.

  - Amy swims every day **so that** she can stay healthy. Amy는 건강을 유지하기 위해 매일 수영한다.

핵심 Check

1. 다음 괄호 안에서 알맞은 말을 고르시오.
   (1) She was (so / very) tired that she couldn't exercise.
   (2) The dress was so beautiful (that / what) Ann wanted to buy it.
   (3) The box was (too / very) heavy to carry.

② 사역동사

- What **made** her **do** all this? 무엇이 그녀로 하여금 이 모든 것을 하게 만들었을까?
- I **had** him **wash** my car. 나는 그에게 내 차를 닦게 시켰다.

■ **사역동사**

- 의미: ~하게 하다, ~시키다
- 종류: make, have, let 등
- 형태: 5형식 문장에서 '주어+동사+목적어+동사원형'

(5형식 문장: '주어+동사+목적어+목적격보어'의 어순으로 이루어진 문장을 말한다.)

■ 사역동사는 '사역동사+목적어+목적격보어'의 형태로 '~하게 하다(하라고 시키다)'의 뜻을 가지며 사역 동사에는 make, have, let 등이 있다.

- He can **make** us **laugh** all day long. 그는 하루 종일 우리를 웃게 할 수도 있어.
- **Let** your body **relax**. 몸의 긴장을 풀어라.

■ 목적격보어로 동사원형이 오면 능동의 의미로 '~(목적어)가 …(목적격보어)을 하게 하다'의 뜻을 가지며 과거분사가 오면 수동의 의미로 '~(목적어)가 …(목적격보어)을 당하게[되게] 하다'의 뜻을 갖는다.

- I **had** him **write** the letter. 〈능동〉 나는 그에게 그 편지를 쓰게 하였다. (그가 편지를 쓰는 것으로 능동)
- I want to **have** my car **repaired**. 〈수동〉 제 차를 수리하려고 합니다. (차가 수리되는 것으로 수동)

■ **'help'와 'get'의 쓰임**

– help는 목적격보어로 동사원형이나 to부정사가 나오며 뜻의 차이는 없다.

- Of course, this **helps** other people **get** on the bus more comfortably, too.
  = Of course, this **helps** other people **to get** on the bus more comfortably, too.
  물론, 이것은 다른 사람들도 버스를 더 편안하게 탈 수 있도록 도와준다.

– get이 '~하게 하다'라는 사역동사의 뜻으로 쓰일 때 목적격보어로 to부정사를 쓴다.

- Mom **got** me **to clean** the room. 〈능동〉 엄마는 내게 방청소를 시키셨다.
- I **got** my car **repaired**. 〈수동〉 나는 내 차가 수리되도록 했다.

핵심 Check

2. 다음 괄호 안에서 알맞은 말을 고르시오.

(1) Mom had my sister (clean / to clean) her room.

(2) My brother helped me (to do / doing) my science project.

(3) The doctor got him (quit / to quit) smoking.

Grammar 시험대비 기본평가

01 다음 문장에서 어법상 <u>어색한</u> 부분을 바르게 고쳐 쓰시오.

(1) Dad made me to wash the car.

_____ ➡ _____

(2) I had him swimming across the river.

_____ ➡ _____

(3) Linda was very sick that she could not go out.

_____ ➡ _____

(4) Eugine was so busy to take a rest.

_____ ➡ _____

02 주어진 단어를 어법에 맞게 빈칸에 쓰시오.

(1) Ms. Kim had the boy _____ a line. (draw)

(2) Mom had the trash _____ away. (throw)

(3) Jessy got her dad _____ her off at her school. (drop)

(4) Courage helped him _____ the game. (win)

03 다음 우리말을 영어로 바르게 옮긴 것은?

> • 창문이 너무 더러워서 밖을 볼 수가 없어.

① The window is very dirty that I can't see through it.

② The window is so dirty that I can't see through it.

③ The window is dirty so that I can't see through it.

④ The window is dirty enough that I can't see through it.

⑤ The window is too dirty that I can't see through it.

04 주어진 단어를 바르게 배열하여 다음 우리말을 영어로 쓰시오. 필요하다면 단어를 변형하시오.

> • 그는 아무도 자신을 찾을 수 없도록 숨었다.
> (he / him / himself / one / find / so / hid / can / no / that)

➡ _____

01 다음 빈칸에 알맞은 말이 순서대로 바르게 짝지어진 것은?

• Mr. Kim let the students _____ the classroom.
• This soup is _____ hot that I can't eat it.

① to leave – too
② leaving – very
③ leaving – so
④ leave – very
⑤ leave – so

02 다음 빈칸에 들어갈 말로 적절한 것을 모두 고르시오.

He helped me _____ the chair.

① makes   ② making
③ made   ④ make
⑤ to make

03 다음 빈칸에 알맞은 말이 바르게 짝지어진 것을 고르시오.

The seat is _____ high _____ I can't sit on it.

① so – that   ② that – so
③ very – that   ④ too – that
⑤ too – to

서답형

04 주어진 단어를 이용하여 다음 우리말을 영어로 쓰시오. (9 단어)

당신이 너무 빨리 말해서 이해할 수가 없어요.
(I, speak, fast, get)

➡ _____

05 다음 중 어법상 바르지 않은 것은?

① The teacher let her students listen to the music.
② She got her two boys to divide a cake exactly in half.
③ She will have her son to close the window.
④ He says television helped him to learn English.
⑤ Mom made me go to bed.

서답형

06 괄호 안에서 알맞은 것을 고르시오.

(1) Kate had her son (do / to do) the dishes.
(2) I finished my homework, so Mom let me (watch / watching) TV.
(3) Abigail got her chair (to paint / painted).
(4) Did you (make / help) your kid to take a bath?
(5) Mike got up so late (that / which) he was late for school.
(6) Bill was (so / very) tired that he couldn't take a walk.
(7) The ice cream was (too / very) sweet for me to eat.
(8) He is (too smart / smart enough) to understand this book.

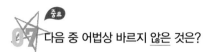

07 다음 중 어법상 바르지 <u>않은</u> 것은?

> Annabell ①had ②some water ③boil ④ to prepare ⑤for dinner.

① ② ③ ④ ⑤

서답형

08 다음 문장에서 어법상 <u>틀린</u> 부분을 찾아 바르게 고쳐 쓰시오.

> He was tall so that he could hardly find any pants that fitted him.

_____ ➡ _____

[09~10] 다음 우리말을 영어로 바르게 옮긴 것을 <u>모두</u> 고르시오.

09

> 그녀는 내가 숙제를 끝낼 수 있도록 도와주었다.

① She helped me finishes my homework.
② She helped me finished my homework.
③ She helped me finish my homework.
④ She helped me to finish my homework.
⑤ She helped me finishing my homework.

10

> 나는 부주의하게도 그 사람을 신용했다.

① I was very careless that I trusted the man.
② I was careless so that I trusted the man.
③ I was so careless that I trusted the man.
④ I was too careless to trust the man.
⑤ I was careless enough to trust the man.

11 다음 문장의 빈칸에 알맞지 <u>않은</u> 말은?

> Merriam _____ him go jogging every morning.

① wanted   ② helped
③ let   ④ had
⑤ made

12 다음 중 어법상 올바른 문장을 <u>모두</u> 고르시오.

① Emily had her daughters to take care of her dogs.
② I helped my brother to do his homework.
③ This rock is heavy so that I can't lift it.
④ The room was so dark that I turned on the light.
⑤ It was so a nice concert that the $15 for the ticket seemed cheap.

13 다음 중 (A)~(C)에서 어법상 옳은 것끼리 바르게 짝지은 것은?

> • Eddy made Sharon (A)(take / taking) some pictures of him.
> • He got Alexander (B)(teach / to teach) his daughter everything.
> • Andrew had his car (C)(drive / driven) by his son.

(A)	(B)	(C)
① taking	teach	driven
② taking	to teach	drive
③ taking	teach	drive
④ take	to teach	drive
⑤ take	to teach	driven

서답형

14 다음 괄호 안에 주어진 단어를 이용하여 우리말을 영어로 옮기시오.

(1) 창문이 너무 무거워서 나는 그것을 열 수가 없어. (the window, open, heavy, so)

➡ _____

_____

(2) 나의 형의 의자는 너무 낮아서 그가 편안하게 앉을 수 없다. (my brother, sit, low, comfortably, too, on)

➡ _____

_____

(3) 이 벽들은 충분히 두꺼워서 외부의 소리를 차단해 주고 있다. (these walls, shut out, thick, outside, to)

➡ _____

_____

(4) 숙제를 끝마쳐서 엄마는 내가 TV를 보도록 했다. (Mom, TV, watch, finish, let, so)

➡ _____

_____

(5) 체육 선생님은 그 남자아이가 그 공을 가져오게 했다. (the P.E. teacher, the boy, bring, have)

➡ _____

_____

서답형

15 다음 문장에서 어법상 <u>어색한</u> 부분을 바르게 고치시오.

(1) I got the man repairing my car.

_____ ➡ _____

(2) The school makes all the students to wear uniforms.

_____ ➡ _____

(3) The girl was too strong to solve the difficulties.

_____ ➡ _____

중요

16 다음 두 문장을 한 문장으로 바르게 연결한 것은?

• The dress was very expensive.
• So I didn't buy it.

① The dress was very expensive that I didn't buy it.

② The dress was expensive so that I didn't buy it.

③ The dress was so expensive that I didn't buy it.

④ The dress was expensive enough that I didn't buy it.

⑤ The dress was too expensive that I didn't buy it.

17 다음 중 밑줄 친 단어의 쓰임이 〈보기〉 같은 것은?

┌── 보기 ├──
Susan <u>makes</u> her daughter clean her room.

① Melanie will <u>make</u> a wise mother.

② He went into the kitchen and <u>made</u> me a sandwich.

③ Everyone wonders if money can <u>make</u> us happy.

④ Our doubts about the weather <u>made</u> us cancel the picnic.

⑤ A cool slice of melon <u>makes</u> an excellent dessert in hot weather.

서답형

18 다음 문장을 주어진 어휘를 이용하여 바꿔 쓰시오.

The box is too heavy for me to move.

(1) so

➡ The box is _____.

(2) because

➡ I can't move the box _____

_____.

01 다음 문장에서 어법상 <u>어색한</u> 부분을 바르게 고쳐 다시 쓰시오.

(1) They made the students to wear school uniforms.

➡ _____

_____

(2) She doesn't let her kids watching TV late at night.

➡ _____

_____

(3) I had my puppy gets me the ball.

➡ _____

_____

(4) My sister asked me to have her computer repair.

➡ _____

(5) I helped my cousin baked some cookies.

➡ _____

_____

(6) He got his sister help him with his homework.

➡ _____

_____

02 다음 두 문장을 〈보기〉와 같이 사역동사를 이용하여 한 문장으로 완성하시오.

┌─ 보기 ├─
- Nick was busy.
- So, he asked his brother to wash his car.
→ Nick had his brother wash his car.

- Patricia had a broken computer.
- So, she asked Benjamin to repair it.

➡ _____

03 다음 문장을 to부정사를 이용하여 바꿔 쓰시오.

(1) My brother is so young that he can't understand the words.

➡ _____

_____

(2) Sam was so smart that he could understand what the scientist said.

➡ _____

_____

(3) This coffee is so hot that I can't drink it.

➡ _____

_____

(4) The bookshelf is so low that my little brother can reach it.

➡ _____

_____

04 〈보기〉에서 의미상 적절한 단어를 골라 빈칸에 알맞은 형태로 쓰시오.

┌─ 보기 ├─
repair   carry   do   wait

(1) She had me _____ the box for her.

(2) My dad had his car _____ by the man.

(3) His girl friend got him _____ for her on the street.

(4) I helped my brother _____ his homework.

05 다음 두 문장을 〈보기〉와 같이 한 문장으로 쓰시오.

┌─ 보기 ─┐
The food was very hot. I couldn't eat it.
→ The food was so hot that I couldn't eat it.
└────────┘

(1) • The storm was really strong.
  • We couldn't go out.
  ➡ _____

(2) • I was very tired.
  • I didn't go there.
  ➡ _____

(3) • I can't hear the music.
  • It's because the bus is very noisy.
  ➡ _____

(4) • The fog was very thick.
  • So, driving became really dangerous.
  ➡ _____
  _____

06 그림을 보고 괄호 안에 주어진 어구들을 바르게 배열하여 문장을 완성하시오.

(the button, it, people, reach, is, that, in wheelchairs, high, can't, so)

➡ _____
_____

07 다음 문장을 〈보기〉와 같이 주어진 동사를 이용하여 바꿔 쓰시오.

┌─ 보기 ─┐
Mr. Kim got Jack to open the window. (have)
→ Mr. Kim had Jack open the window.
└────────┘

(1) Eve let him use her pen. (allow)
  ➡ _____

(2) She forced Dan to follow her advice. (make)
  ➡ _____

08 빈칸을 알맞게 채워 다음 문장과 같은 의미의 문장을 쓰시오.

┌────────────────┐
The button is very high, so the boy can't push the button.
└────────────────┘

= The boy can't push the button _____
_____.

= The button is _____
_____.

= The button is _____
_____.

09 다음 그림을 참고하여 단어 take의 알맞은 형태를 빈칸에 채우시오.

➡ The man let the girl _____ a rest under the tree.

Reading

Patricia Moore – Mother of Universal Design

In 1979, a woman started a journey to cities in the U.S. and Canada. She looked over 80. She couldn't see or hear well. She couldn't walk well without a stick.

With all these difficulties, the woman had to climb stairs in subway stations and get on crowded buses. She had to open heavy doors and use can openers with her weak hands. Sometimes she got hurt or found herself in danger. Every moment was very difficult for her, but she visited more than 115 cities and ended her trip in 1982.

Who was the woman and what made her do all this? She was Patricia Moore, a 26-year-old designer. During the 1970's, she worked for a big design company. She often asked at meetings, "How about designing for old or weak people?" The other designers always answered, "We don't design for those people."

She became tired of the same cold answer. Finally, she decided to become one of "those people" and travel around many cities to understand their difficulties better. For this, she put on her grandmother's clothes, uncomfortable shoes, and thick glasses. The shoes were so uncomfortable that she couldn't walk well without a stick. The glasses were so thick that she couldn't see well with them. She also put lots of cotton in her ears to make her hearing bad.

universal: 보편적인
journey: 여행, 여정
station: 역, 정류장
get on: ~을 타다
crowded: 붐비는, 복잡한
company: 회사
tired of: ~에 지친, 실증 난
uncomfortable: 불편한(↔ **comfortable** 편한)

- 다음 문장이 본문의 내용과 일치하면 T, 일치하지 않으면 F를 쓰시오.

1 In 1979, a woman who looked over 80 started a journey to cities in the U.S. and Canada. ☐

2 Every moment was very difficult, so she gave up her trip. ☐

3 Patricia's glasses were so thick that she couldn't see well without them. ☐

4 Patricia put lots of cotton in her ears to make her hearing bad. ☐

During her journey, Patricia felt the difficulties old people go
<small>old 앞에 관계대명사 which[that]가 생략</small>

through. From this experience, she designed products anybody could
<small>anybody 앞에 관계대명사 which[that]가 생략</small>

use safely and easily. This was the beginning of "universal design,"

or "design for all."
<small>즉, 다시 말해서: 동격 어구를 연결</small>

One example of her universal design ideas is low-floor buses.
<small>주어   동사, are(×)</small>

They have no steps and have such a low floor that even a person
<small>such ~ that 주어 can ...: 아주 ~해서 …할 수 있다 such+a[an]+형용사+명사</small>

in a wheelchair can use them without any help. Of course, this

helps other people get on the bus more comfortably, too.
<small>준사역동사 help의 목적격보어: 동사원형 또는 to부정사 (5형식 문장)</small>

Today more and more designers are following Patricia's way.
<small>점점 더 많은   현재진행형(be동사+동사-ing)</small>

Products like big flat light switches, doors with easy handles, and
<small>주어   ~ 같은(전치사)</small>

phones with touch buttons are helping people live better lives.
<small>준사역동사 help의 목적격보어: 동사원형 또는 to부정사 (5형식 문장)   동족목적어</small>

Look around you, feel the difficulties of people who are older or
<small>동사원형 'Look. feel. try'가 and로 이어진 명령문.   old의 비교급</small>

weaker, and try to find solutions from their point of view. You could
<small>weak의 비교급</small>

be the next Patricia Moore and make the world a better place for
<small>5형식 문장</small>

everybody.

---

go through: ~을 겪다
product: 상품, 제품
low: 낮은
flat: 평평한
switch: 스위치
handle: 손잡이
view: 견해, 관점

확인문제

● 다음 문장이 본문의 내용과 일치하면 T, 일치하지 않으면 F를 쓰시오.

1 During her journey, Patricia felt the difficulties old people go through. ☐

2 One example of Patricia's universal design ideas is low-floor buses. ☐

3 Low-floor buses have no steps and have such a low floor that even a person in a wheelchair can use them with some help. ☐

4 Low-floor buses are uncomfortable for people who are healthy. ☐

5 Today, there are few designers who are following Patricia's way. ☐

6 Products such as big flat light switches, doors with easy handles, and phones with touch buttons are helping people live better lives. ☐

● 우리말을 참고하여 빈칸에 알맞은 말을 쓰시오.

1 Patricia Moore – Mother of _____ _____

2 In 1979, a woman _____ _____ _____ to cities in the U.S. and Canada.

3 She _____ _____ _____.

4 She _____ _____ _____ _____ well.

5 She couldn't walk well _____ _____ _____.

6 _____ _____ _____ _____, the woman had to climb stairs in subway stations and get on crowded buses.

7 She had to open heavy doors and use can openers _____ _____ _____ _____.

8 Sometimes she got hurt or _____ _____ _____ _____.

9 Every moment was _____ _____ _____ _____, but she visited _____ _____ 115 cities and ended her trip in 1982.

10 Who was the woman and _____ _____ _____ _____ all this?

11 She was Patricia Moore, _____ _____ _____.

12 _____ _____ _____, she worked for a big design company.

13 She often asked at meetings, "_____ _____ _____ for old or weak people?"

14 The other designers always answered, "We don't design _____ _____ _____."

15 She _____ _____ _____ the same cold answer.

16 _____, she decided to become one of "those people" and travel around many cities _____ _____ _____ _____ better.

---

1 Patricia Moore – 유니버설 디자인의 어머니

2 1979년에, 한 여성이 미국과 캐나다의 도시로 여행을 시작했다.

3 그녀는 80세가 넘어 보였다.

4 그녀는 잘 보거나 잘 들을 수 없었다.

5 그녀는 지팡이가 없이는 잘 걸을 수 없었다.

6 이 모든 어려움을 가진 채, 그 여성은 지하철역에서 계단을 올라가거나 붐비는 버스에 올라타야 했다.

7 그녀는 무거운 문을 열거나 그녀의 약한 손으로 깡통 따개를 사용해야 했다.

8 때때로 그녀는 다치거나 위험에 처하기도 했다.

9 모든 순간이 그녀에게 매우 어려웠으나, 그녀는 115개 이상의 도시를 방문하였으며 1982년에 여행을 끝마쳤다.

10 그 여성은 누구였고 무엇이 그녀로 하여금 이 모든 것을 하게 만들었을까?

11 그녀는 26살의 디자이너인 Patricia Moore였다.

12 1970년대 동안, 그녀는 큰 디자인 회사에서 일했다.

13 그녀는 종종 회의에서 물었다. "나이 들거나 약한 사람들을 위해 디자인하는 게 어떨까요?"

14 다른 디자이너들은 항상 대답했다. "우리는 그런 사람들을 위해 디자인하지 않습니다."

15 그녀는 똑같은 냉담한 대답에 지쳤다.

16 마침내, 그녀는 '그런 사람들' 중의 하나가 되어 그들의 어려움을 더 잘 이해하기 위해 많은 도시를 여행하기로 결심했다.

17 _____ _____, she put on her grandmother's clothes, _____ shoes, and _____ _____.

18 The shoes were _____ uncomfortable _____ she _____ walk well _____ _____ _____.

19 The glasses were _____ thick _____ she _____ see well _____ _____.

20 She also put lots of cotton in her ears _____ _____ _____ _____ _____.

21 _____ her journey, Patricia felt the difficulties old people _____ _____.

22 _____ this experience, she designed products anybody could use _____ and _____.

23 This was the beginning of "_____ _____," or "_____ _____."

24 _____ _____ of her universal design ideas is low-floor _____.

25 They have _____ _____ and have _____ _____ _____ _____ that even a person _____ _____ _____ can use them _____ _____ _____.

26 Of course, this helps other people get on the bus _____ _____, too.

27 Today more and more designers are _____ _____ _____.

28 Products _____ big flat light switches, doors with easy handles, and phones with touch buttons are helping people _____ _____ _____.

29 Look around you, feel the difficulties of people who are older or weaker, and try to find solutions _____ _____ _____ _____.

30 You could be the _____ Patricia Moore and make the world _____ _____ _____ _____ _____.

17 이를 위해, 그녀는 자신의 할머니 옷을 입고, 불편한 신발을 신고, 두꺼운 안경을 썼다.

18 신발은 너무 불편해서 그녀는 지팡이가 없이는 잘 걸을 수 없었다.

19 안경은 너무 두꺼워서 그녀는 안경을 쓰고는 잘 볼 수 없었다.

20 그녀는 또한 그녀의 청력을 나쁘게 하려고 귀에 많은 솜을 넣었다.

21 여행 동안, Patricia는 나이 든 사람들이 겪는 어려움을 느꼈다.

22 이 경험으로부터, 그녀는 누구나 안전하고 쉽게 사용할 수 있는 제품들을 고안했다.

23 이것이 '유니버설 디자인' 또는 '모두를 위한 디자인'의 시작이었다.

24 그녀의 유니버설 디자인 아이디어의 한 가지 예는 저상 버스이다.

25 그것은 계단이 없고 낮은 바닥을 가지고 있어서 휠체어를 탄 사람조차 아무 도움 없이 이용할 수 있다.

26 물론, 이것은 다른 사람들도 버스를 더 편안하게 탈 수 있도록 도와준다.

27 오늘날 점점 더 많은 디자이너가 Patricia의 방식을 따르고 있다.

28 크고 평평한 조명 스위치, 편한 손잡이를 가진 문, 터치 버튼을 가진 전화기와 같은 제품들은 사람들이 더 나은 삶을 살도록 도와주고 있다.

29 여러분의 주위를 둘러보고, 더 나이 들거나 더 약한 사람들의 어려움을 느껴 보고, 그들의 관점에서 해결책을 찾으려고 노력해 봐라.

30 여러분은 다음의 Patricia Moore가 되어 세상을 모두에게 더 나은 곳으로 만들 수 있을 것이다.

● 우리말을 참고하여 본문을 영작하시오.

1 Patricia Moore – 유니버설 디자인의 어머니

➡ _____

2 1979년에, 한 여성이 미국과 캐나다의 도시로 여행을 시작했다.

➡ _____

3 그녀는 80세가 넘어 보였다.

➡ _____

4 그녀는 잘 보거나 잘 들을 수 없었다.

➡ _____

5 그녀는 지팡이 없이는 잘 걸을 수 없었다.

➡ _____

6 이 모든 어려움을 가진 채, 그 여성은 지하철역에서 계단을 올라가거나 붐비는 버스에 올라타야 했다.

➡ _____

7 그녀는 무거운 문을 열거나 그녀의 약한 손으로 깡통 따개를 사용해야 했다.

➡ _____

8 때때로 그녀는 다치거나 위험에 처하기도 했다.

➡ _____

9 모든 순간이 그녀에게 매우 어려웠으나, 그녀는 115개 이상의 도시를 방문하였으며 1982년에 여행을 끝마쳤다.

➡ _____

10 그 여성은 누구였고 무엇이 그녀로 하여금 이 모든 것을 하게 만들었을까?

➡ _____

11 그녀는 26살의 디자이너인 Patricia Moore였다.

➡ _____

12 1970년대 동안, 그녀는 큰 디자인 회사에서 일했다.

➡ _____

13 그녀는 종종 회의에서 물었다. "나이 들거나 약한 사람들을 위해 디자인하는 게 어떨까요?"

➡ _____

14 다른 디자이너들은 항상 대답했다. "우리는 그런 사람들을 위해 디자인하지 않습니다."

➡ _____

15 그녀는 똑같은 냉담한 대답에 지쳤다.

➡ _____

16 마침내, 그녀는 '그런 사람들' 중의 하나가 되어 그들의 어려움을 더 잘 이해하기 위해 많은 도시를 여행하기로 결심했다.

➡ _____

_____

17 이를 위해, 그녀는 자신의 할머니 옷을 입고, 불편한 신발을 신고, 두꺼운 안경을 썼다.

➡ _____

18 신발은 너무 불편해서 그녀는 지팡이 없이는 잘 걸을 수 없었다.

➡ _____

19 안경은 너무 두꺼워서 그녀는 안경을 쓰고는 잘 볼 수 없었다.

➡ _____

20 그녀는 또한 그녀의 청력을 나쁘게 하려고 귀에 많은 솜을 넣었다.

➡ _____

21 여행 동안, Patricia는 나이 든 사람들이 겪는 어려움을 느꼈다.

➡ _____

22 이 경험으로부터, 그녀는 누구나 안전하고 쉽게 사용할 수 있는 제품들을 고안했다.

➡ _____

23 이것이 '유니버설 디자인' 또는 '모두를 위한 디자인'의 시작이었다.

➡ _____

24 그녀의 유니버설 디자인 아이디어의 한 가지 예는 저상 버스이다.

➡ _____

25 그것은 계단이 없고 낮은 바닥을 가지고 있어서 휠체어를 탄 사람조차 아무 도움 없이 이용할 수 있다.

➡ _____

_____

26 물론, 이것은 다른 사람들도 버스를 더 편안하게 탈 수 있도록 도와준다.

➡ _____

27 오늘날 점점 더 많은 디자이너가 Patricia의 방식을 따르고 있다.

➡ _____

28 크고 평평한 조명 스위치, 편한 손잡이를 가진 문, 터치 버튼을 가진 전화기와 같은 제품들은 사람들이 더 나은 삶을 살도록 도와주고 있다.

➡ _____

_____

29 여러분의 주위를 둘러보고, 더 나이 들거나 더 약한 사람들의 어려움을 느껴 보고, 그들의 관점에서 해결책을 찾으려고 노력해 봐라.

➡ _____

_____

30 여러분은 다음의 Patricia Moore가 되어 세상을 모두에게 더 나은 곳으로 만들 수 있을 것이다.

➡ _____

[01~04] 다음 글을 읽고 물음에 답하시오.

Who was the woman and what made her do all this? She was Patricia Moore, a (A)[26-year-old / 26-years-old] designer. During the 1970's, she worked for a big design company. She often asked at meetings, "How about designing for ①old or weak people?" (B)[Another / The other] designers always answered, "②We don't design for ③those people."

She became tired of ⓐthe same cold answer. Finally, she decided to become one of "④those people" and travel around many cities to understand ⑤their difficulties better. For this, she put on her grandmother's clothes, uncomfortable shoes, and thick glasses. The shoes were so uncomfortable that she couldn't walk well without a stick. The glasses were so thick that she couldn't see well with (C)[it / them]. She also put lots of cotton in her ears to make her hearing bad.

서답형

01 위 글의 괄호 (A)~(C)에서 문맥이나 어법상 알맞은 낱말을 골라 쓰시오.

➡ (A) _____ (B) _____ (C) _____

중요

02 위 글의 밑줄 친 ①~⑤ 중에서 가리키는 대상이 나머지 넷과 다른 것은?

①   ②   ③   ④   ⑤

서답형

03 위 글의 밑줄 친 ⓐthe same cold answer가 가리키는 것을 본문에서 찾아 쓰시오.

➡ _____

중요

04 위 글의 제목으로 알맞은 것을 고르시오.

① Patricia's Real Age
② Designers Refused Patricia's Proposal
③ Patricia Tried to Understand the Old in Person
④ Patricia Looked Old for Her Age
⑤ The Difficulties the Old Experience

[05~07] 다음 글을 읽고 물음에 답하시오.

In 1979, a woman started a journey to cities in the U.S. and Canada. She looked over 80. She couldn't see or hear well. She couldn't walk well without a stick.

With all these _____ⓐ_____, the woman had to climb stairs in subway stations and get on crowded buses. She had to open heavy doors and use can openers with her weak hands. ⓑSometimes she got hurt or found herself in danger. Every moment was very difficult for her, but she visited more than 115 cities and ended her trip in 1982.

서답형

05 본문의 한 단어를 변형하여 위 글의 빈칸 ⓐ에 들어갈 알맞은 단어를 쓰시오.

➡ _____

06 위 글의 밑줄 친 ⓑSometimes와 바꿔 쓸 수 없는 말을 고르시오.

① Once in a while   ② Rarely
③ Now and then   ④ At times
⑤ From time to time

서답형

07 본문의 내용과 일치하도록 다음 빈칸 (A)와 (B)에 알맞은 단어를 쓰시오.

> She started a (A)_____ to cities in the U.S. and Canada in 1979, and after visiting over (B)_____ _____, she ended it in 1982.

➡ (A) _____ (B) _____

[08~10] 다음 글을 읽고 물음에 답하시오.

During her journey, Patricia felt the difficulties old people go through. From this experience, she designed products anybody could use (A)[safe and easy / safely and easily]. This was the beginning of "universal design," or "design for all."

One example of her universal design ideas is low-floor buses. They have no steps and have (B)[so / such] a low floor that even a person in a wheelchair can use ⓐthem without any help. Of course, this helps other people ___(a)___ on the bus more (C)[comfortable / comfortably], too.

08 위 글의 빈칸 (a)에 들어갈 알맞은 말을 <u>모두</u> 고르시오.

① to get
② got
③ having got
④ get
⑤ getting

서답형

09 위 글의 괄호 (A)~(C)에서 어법상 알맞은 낱말을 골라 쓰시오.

➡ (A) _____ (B) _____
(C) _____

10 위 글의 밑줄 친 ⓐthem이 가리키는 것을 본문에서 찾아 쓰시오.

➡ _____

[11~13] 다음 글을 읽고 물음에 답하시오.

Today more and more designers are following Patricia's way. Products ⓐlike big flat light switches, doors with easy handles, and phones with touch buttons are helping people live better lives. Look around you, feel the difficulties of people ___(A)___ are older or weaker, and try to find solutions from their ⓑpoint of view. You could be ⓒ the next Patricia Moore and make the world a better place for everybody.

11 위 글의 빈칸 (A)에 들어갈 알맞은 말을 <u>모두</u> 고르시오.

① what
② who
③ whom
④ which
⑤ that

서답형

12 위 글의 밑줄 친 ⓐlike, ⓑpoint of view와 바꿔 쓸 수 있는 단어들을 각각 쓰시오.

➡ ⓐ _____ ⓑ _____

서답형

13 위 글의 밑줄 친 ⓒthe next Patricia Moore가 되기 위해 해야 할 일을 우리말로 쓰시오.

➡ _____
_____
_____

[14~16] 전시 중인 제품에 대한 다음 글을 읽고 물음에 답하시오.

> ⓐThe washing machine door in my house is so high that my little brother can't put clothes easily into it. ___(A)___, this machine has a side door. It'll help my brother put clothes in more easily.

14 위 글의 빈칸 (A)에 들어갈 알맞은 말을 고르시오.

① Therefore ② For example
③ In addition ④ However
⑤ In other words

서답형

15 위 글의 밑줄 친 ⓐ를 다음과 같이 바꿔 쓸 때 빈칸에 들어갈 알맞은 말을 쓰시오.

➡ The washing machine door in my house is _____ high _____ my little brother _____ put clothes easily into it.

서답형

16 현재 집에 있는 세탁기의 단점과 전시 중인 제품에서 개선된 점을 우리말로 쓰시오.

➡ 현재 집에 있는 세탁기의 단점: _____

_____

전시 중인 제품에서 개선된 점: : _____

_____

[17~19] 다음 글을 읽고 물음에 답하시오.

> In 1979, a woman started a journey to cities ___ⓐ___ the U.S. and Canada. She looked over 80. She couldn't see or hear well. She couldn't walk well without a stick.
>
> With all these difficulties, the woman had to climb stairs ___ⓑ___ subway stations and get on crowded buses. She had to open heavy doors and use can openers with her weak

hands. Sometimes she got hurt or found herself ___ⓒ___ danger. Every moment was very difficult ___ⓓ___ her, but she visited (a)more than 115 cities and ended her trip ___ⓔ___ 1982.

서답형

17 위 글의 빈칸 ⓐ~ⓔ에 들어갈 전치사가 나머지와 다른 것을 고르시오.

➡ _____

서답형

18 위 글의 밑줄 친 (a)more than과 바꿔 쓸 수 있는 단어를 본문에서 찾아 쓰시오.

➡ _____

19 위 글의 내용과 일치하지 않는 것은?

① A woman started a trip to cities in the U.S. and Canada in 1979.
② It was difficult for her to see or hear well.
③ Her eyesight and hearing were not good.
④ From time to time, she got hurt.
⑤ With so many difficulties, she gave up her journey.

[20~22] 다음 글을 읽고 물음에 답하시오.

> During her journey, Patricia felt the difficulties old people ⓐgo through. ___(A)___ this experience, ⓑ그녀는 누구나 안전하고 쉽게 사용할 수 있는 제품들을 고안했다. This was the beginning of "universal design," or "design for all."
>
> One example of her universal design ideas is low-floor buses. They have no steps and have such a low floor that even a person ___(B)___ a wheelchair can use them without any help. Of course, this helps other people get on the bus more comfortably, too.

20 위 글의 빈칸 (A)와 (B)에 들어갈 전치사가 바르게 짝지어진 것은?

① For – by ② From – in
③ With – in ④ For – to
⑤ From – by

서답형

21 위 글의 밑줄 친 ⓐgo through와 바꿔 쓸 수 있는 한 단어를 본문에서 찾아 쓰시오.

➡ _____

서답형

22 위 글의 밑줄 친 ⓑ의 우리말에 맞게 주어진 어휘를 이용하여 9 단어로 영작하시오.

products, anybody, safely, easily

➡ _____

_____

[23~25] 다음 글을 읽고 물음에 답하시오.

She became tired of the same cold answer. (①) For this, she put on her grandmother's clothes, uncomfortable shoes, and thick glasses. (②) ⓐThe shoes were so uncomfortable that she couldn't walk well without a stick. (③) The glasses were so thick that she couldn't see well with ⓑthem. (④) She also put lots of cotton in her ears to make her hearing bad. (⑤)

중요

23 위 글의 흐름으로 보아, 주어진 문장이 들어가기에 가장 적절한 곳은?

Finally, she decided to become one of "those people" and travel around many cities to understand their difficulties better.

① ② ③ ④ ⑤

24 위 글의 밑줄 친 ⓐ와 같은 의미의 문장을 모두 고르시오.

① The shoes were such uncomfortable that she couldn't walk well without a stick.
② The shoes were too uncomfortable for her to walk well without a stick.
③ The shoes were very uncomfortable, so she couldn't walk well without a stick.
④ The shoes were uncomfortable enough for her to walk well without a stick.
⑤ The shoes were uncomfortable in order that she couldn't walk well without a stick.

서답형

25 위 글의 밑줄 친 ⓑthem이 가리키는 것을 본문에서 찾아 쓰시오.

➡ _____

[26~28] 전시 중인 제품에 대한 다음 글을 읽고 물음에 답하시오.

The desk in my house is so high that my little sister can't use it ___ⓐ___. However, this desk has special legs. ⓑIt'll help my sister read books more comfortably.

서답형

26 위 글의 빈칸 ⓐ에 with ease와 같은 뜻의 한 단어를 쓰시오.

➡ _____

서답형

27 다음 빈칸에 알맞은 단어를 넣어 밑줄 친 ⓑIt에 대한 설명을 완성하시오.

this desk with _____ _____

28 Why is it difficult for the little sister to use her desk in her house? Fill in the blanks with the suitable words.

➡ It's because it is _____ for her _____ with ease.

[01~03] 다음 글을 읽고 물음에 답하시오.

In ⓐ1979, a woman started a journey to cities in the U.S. and Canada. She (A)[looked / looked like] over 80. She couldn't see or hear well. ⓑShe couldn't walk well with a stick.

ⓒWithout all these difficulties, the woman had to climb stairs in subway stations and get on (B)[crowding / crowded] buses. She had to open heavy doors and use can openers with her weak hands. Sometimes she got hurt or found (C)[her / herself] in danger. Every moment was very difficult for her, but she visited more than ⓓ115 cities and ended her trip in ⓔ1982.

중요

01 위 글의 괄호 (A)~(C)에서 어법상 알맞은 낱말을 골라 쓰시오.

➡ (A) _____ (B) _____ (C) _____

02 위 글의 밑줄 친 ⓐ1979, ⓓ115, ⓔ1982를 영어로 읽는 법을 쓰시오.

➡ ⓐ _____ ⓓ _____

   ⓔ _____

03 위 글의 밑줄 친 ⓑ와 ⓒ에서 흐름상 어색한 부분을 찾아 고치시오.

➡ ⓑ _____ ⓒ _____

[04~06] 다음 글을 읽고 물음에 답하시오.

Who was the woman and what made her do all this? She was Patricia Moore, a 26-year-old designer. During the 1970's, she worked for a big design company. She often asked at meetings, "How about designing for old or weak people?" The other designers always answered, "We don't design for those people."

She became tired of the same cold answer. Finally, she decided ⓐto become one of "those people" and travel around many cities to understand their difficulties better. For this, she put on her grandmother's clothes, uncomfortable shoes, and thick glasses. The shoes were so uncomfortable that she couldn't walk well without a stick. ⓑThe glasses were so thick that she couldn't see well with them. She also put lots of cotton in her ears to make her hearing bad.

04 위 글에서 Patricia가 밑줄 친 ⓐ의 결심을 실천하기 위해 했던 일을 우리말로 쓰시오.

➡ (1) _____

   _____

   (2) _____

   _____

중요

05 위 글의 밑줄 친 ⓑ를 다음과 같이 바꿔 쓸 때 빈칸에 들어갈 알맞은 말을 쓰시오.

➡ The glasses were _____ thick _____ her _____ see well with them.

06 본문의 내용과 일치하도록 다음 빈칸 (A)와 (B)에 알맞은 단어를 쓰시오.

Patricia tried to understand the difficulties of (A)_____ _____ _____ people better by becoming one of "(B)_____ _____" and traveling around many cities.

[07~08] 다음 글을 읽고 물음에 답하시오.

During her journey, Patricia felt the difficulties old people go through. ⓐFrom this experience, she designed products anybody could use them safely and easily. This was the beginning of "universal design," or "design for all."

One example of her universal design ideas is low-floor buses. They have no steps and have such a low floor that even a person in a wheelchair can use them without any help. Of course, this helps other people get on the bus more ⓑcomfort, too.

07 위 글의 밑줄 친 ⓐ에서 어법상 **틀린** 부분을 찾아 고치시오.

_____ ➡ _____

08 위 글의 밑줄 친 ⓑ를 알맞은 형으로 바꿔 쓰시오.

➡ _____

[09~11] 다음 글을 읽고 물음에 답하시오.

Today more and more designers are following Patricia's way. Products like big flat light switches, doors with easy handles, and ⓐphones with touch buttons are helping people living better lives. Look around you, feel the difficulties of people who are older or weaker, and try to find solutions ⓑfrom their point of view. You could be the next Patricia Moore and make the world a better place for everybody.

09 위 글에서 Patricia의 방식을 따라 디자이너들이 만든 제품의 예를 우리말로 쓰시오. (세 가지)

➡ (1) _____ (2) _____
　　(2) _____

10 위 글의 밑줄 친 ⓐ에서 어법상 **틀린** 부분을 찾아 고치시오.

_____ ➡ _____

11 위 글의 밑줄 친 ⓑ를 다음과 같이 바꿔 쓸 때 빈칸에 들어갈 알맞은 말을 쓰시오.

➡ from the point of view of _____ or _____ people

[12~13] 다음 글을 읽고 물음에 답하시오.

ⓐThe hole cover was so dangerous that I couldn't ride my bike on it. So I want to change the cover like this. The new cover will help people ride a bike ___(A)___.

12 위 글의 빈칸 (A)에 in safety와 바꿔 쓸 수 있는 한 단어를 쓰시오.

➡ _____

13 위 글의 밑줄 친 ⓐ를 다음과 같이 바꿔 쓸 때 빈칸에 들어갈 알맞은 말을 쓰시오.

➡ The hole cover was _____ dangerous, _____ I couldn't ride my bike on it.

Express Yourself C1

The washing machine door in my house is so high that my little brother can't
<u>so+형용사/부사+that+주어+can't … = too ~ to … = very ~. so+주어+can't …</u>

put clothes easily into it. However, this machine has a side door. It'll help my
<u>put을 수식하는 부사</u>

brother put clothes in more easily.
<u>= to put</u>　　　<u>easily의 비교급</u>

> 우리 집에 있는 세탁기 문은 너무 높아서 나의 남동생은 그 안에 옷을 쉽게 넣을 수 없다. 그러나, 이 기계는 옆문을 가지고 있다. 그것은 내 남동생이 옷을 더 쉽게 넣을 수 있도록 도와줄 것이다.

구문해설　• washing machine: 세탁기　• however: 그러나　• side door: 옆문　• clothes: 옷

Project Step 3

The hole cover was so dangerous that I couldn't ride my bike on it. So I want
<u>so+형용사+that+주어+can't … = too ~ to … = the hole cover</u>

to change the cover like this. The new cover will help people ride a bike
<u>전치사</u>　　　　　　　　　　　　<u>준사역동사</u>　<u>목적격보어(= to ride)</u>

safely.

> 맨홀 덮개가 너무 위험해서 나는 그 위에서 자전거를 탈 수 없었다. 그래서 나는 덮개를 이렇게 바꾸고 싶다. 새로운 덮개는 사람들이 자전거를 안전하게 타도록 도와줄 것이다.

구문해설　• hole cover: 맨홀 덮개

Link to the World

• Kim Mandeok was born to a poor family in Jeju. She worked hard and
　　　　　　　<u>…에서 태어났다</u>

became rich.

• In 1794, lots of people in Jeju were dying of hunger because of bad weather.
　　　　　　　　　　　　　　<u>…로 죽어가고 있었다</u>　　　<u>'~ 때문에' 뒤에 명사가 나온다.</u>

• She spent almost all she had and saved a lot of people.
　　　　　　　　　　<u>목적격 관계대명사절로 선행사 'all'을 수식</u>

• King Jeongjo let her take a trip to Mountain Geumgang.
　　　　　　<u>let+목적어+동사원형: …가 ~하도록 허락하다</u>

> • 김만덕은 제주의 가난한 가정에서 태어났다. 그녀는 열심히 일해서 부자가 되었다.
>
> • 1794년에 제주의 많은 사람이 나쁜 날씨로 인해 굶주림으로 죽어가고 있었다.
>
> • 그녀는 자신이 가진 거의 모든 것을 써서 많은 사람을 구했다.
>
> • 정조 임금은 그녀가 금강산으로 여행을 하도록 허락했다.

구문해설　• lots of: 많은　• hunger: 굶주림　• because of+명사(구): … 때문에　• save: 구하다
　　　　　• take a trip: 여행하다

01 다음 주어진 두 단어의 관계가 같도록 빈칸에 주어진 철자로 단어를 쓰시오.

> comfortable : uncomfortable
> = loose : _____

02 다음 빈칸에 들어갈 말이 바르게 짝지어진 것은?

> Look around you, feel the _____ of people who are older or weaker, and try to find _____ from their point of _____.

① difficulties – solutions – place
② difficulties – help – place
③ difficulties – solutions – view
④ experience – help – design
⑤ experience – solutions – view

03 다음 영영풀이에 해당하는 것을 고르시오.

> having a lot of people or too many people

① station ② huge
③ vacant ④ crowded
⑤ company

04 다음 빈칸에 들어갈 말이 바르게 짝지어진 것은?

> • I have _____ finished my homework.
> • The dog helps the _____ man.
> • Be careful when you _____ the street.

① almost – old – across
② almost – blind – cross
③ almost – old – reach
④ most – blind – cross
⑤ most – old – across

05 다음 그림을 보고, 빈칸에 알맞은 단어를 쓰시오.

➡ Ted _____ _____ with his dog every day.

06 다음 밑줄 친 부분의 의미가 바르지 않은 것은?

① She designed products anybody could use safely and easily. (생산적인)
② One example of her universal design ideas is low-floor buses. (예, 사례)
③ This helps other people get on the bus more comfortably. (편안하게)
④ This room has a low ceiling. (낮은)
⑤ Laughter is a universal language. (보편적인)

07 대화의 밑줄 친 우리말에 맞게 주어진 단어를 알맞은 순서로 배열하시오.

> G: I'm not happy about the sign. 볼 수 없는 사람들도 좀 있잖아.
> B: Right.

(are / can't / people / who / there / some / see)

➡ _____

08 자연스러운 대화가 되도록 알맞은 순서로 배열한 것은?

> (A) They are too bright.
> (B) Why? What's wrong?
> (C) I'm not happy about the lights.
> (D) I see. Let's switch to other lights.

① (A) – (B) – (C) – (D)
② (B) – (A) – (C) – (D)
③ (C) – (A) – (B) – (D)
④ (C) – (B) – (A) – (D)
⑤ (D) – (B) – (A) – (C)

09 주어진 문장이 들어갈 위치로 알맞은 것은?

> G: I'm not happy about my brother's chair. (①) It's too low and too hard.
> B: Right. (②) I'm thinking of buying this one. (③)
> G: Looks great. (④) I think he can use it for so long, even after he grows taller. (⑤)

> What do you think?

①   ②   ③   ④   ⑤

[10~12] 다음 대화를 읽고 물음에 답하시오.

> Dad: What are you doing here?
> Son: _____(A)_____ ways to help Miso.
> Dad: What's wrong?
> Son: She can't turn on the light ⓐby herself. This switch is ⓑtoo high for her.
> Dad: That's right. I'm not happy about it, ⓒtoo. Do you have any good ideas about that?
> Son: _____(B)_____ putting a step box here below the switch.
> Dad: Good idea. And I'll change the switch to a ⓓbigger one.

> Son: Great. Grandma will like it, too. She can turn on the light ⓔmore easily.

10 위 대화의 빈칸 (A)와 (B)에 공통으로 들어갈 말로 알맞은 것은?

① I know
② I'm going to
③ I'm not satisfied with
④ I'm interested in
⑤ I'm thinking of

11 위 대화의 밑줄 친 ⓐ~ⓔ 중, 어법상 어색한 것은?

① ⓐ   ② ⓑ   ③ ⓒ   ④ ⓓ   ⑤ ⓔ

12 위 대화를 읽고 답할 수 없는 질문은?

① Can Miso turn on the light by herself?
② What will Dad do for Miso and Grandma?
③ What will the boy do to help Miso?
④ What's wrong with the step box?
⑤ Who came up with the idea of a bigger switch?

Grammar

13 다음 중 어법상 바르지 않은 것은?

① The river is too deep for you to swim in.
② He is rich enough to buy the car.
③ The food was so salty that I couldn't eat it.
④ It was such a fine day that we took a walk to the park.
⑤ I was very thirsty that I drank a bottle of water.

14 주어진 어휘를 이용하여 다음 우리말을 영어로 옮길 때 두 번째와 다섯 번째로 오는 단어를 쓰시오.

> 그것은 나의 할머니께서 문을 더 편안하게 여실 수 있도록 도와줄 것이다.
> (It'll, my grandma, comfortably)

➡ _____

15 다음 문장을 so와 that을 이용하여 바꾸어 쓰시오.

(1) This question is too difficult for me to solve.

➡ _____

(2) The big panel was light enough to float on the water.

➡ _____

(3) He held her by the sleeve very tightly, so she couldn't ran away.

➡ _____
_____

(4) I can't hear the music because the bus is very noisy.

➡ _____

(5) He took a taxi not to be late.

➡ _____

[16~17] 다음 빈칸에 알맞은 것을 고르시오.

16
> Mike's room is a mess. I'll have it _____.

① clean   ② cleans
③ cleaned   ④ cleaning
⑤ to clean

17
> My grandma is _____ sick that she can't go out.

① too   ② enough
③ so   ④ such
⑤ very

18 다음 그림을 보고 괄호 안에 주어진 어휘를 이용하여 빈칸에 알맞은 말을 쓰시오.

> My friend got hurt. I should have him _____ to the hospital. (take)

19 다음 빈칸에 알맞은 말이 순서대로 짝지어진 것은?

> • The princess got her maid _____ her hair smoothly.
> • Olivia helped me _____ a birthday cake.

① brushing – make
② to brush – making
③ to brush – to make
④ brush – made
⑤ brush – make

20 다음 중 어법상 올바른 것은?

① He is enough tall to touch the ceiling.

② Nobody could catch up with her so that she ran fast.

③ Ron asked me to have his computer repair.

④ The teacher let the students play outside.

⑤ I'll have him copied all the files for the meeting.

21 다음 중 어법상 올바른 문장의 개수는?

ⓐ Ella had her pictures taken.

ⓑ The teacher let Joseph play the guitar singing a song.

ⓒ Sarah always lets me to use her laptop computer.

ⓓ It'll help my grandma eating food more comfortably.

ⓔ My dad got the robot to do a lot of house work.

ⓕ He had his bicycle repaired yesterday.

ⓖ Charlotte did her best to have the project finish on time.

① 1개　② 2개　③ 3개　④ 4개　⑤ 5개

Reading

[22~24] 다음 글을 읽고 물음에 답하시오.

(A)[During / For] her journey, ⓐPatricia felt the difficulties old people go through. (①) From this experience, she designed products (B)[anybody / somebody] could use safely and easily. (②)

One example of her universal design ideas (C)[is / are] low-floor buses. (③) They have no steps and have such a low floor that even a person in a wheelchair can use them without any help. (④) Of course, this helps other people get on the bus more comfortably, too. (⑤)

22 위 글의 괄호 (A)~(C)에서 문맥이나 어법상 알맞은 낱말을 골라 쓰시오.

➡ (A) _____ (B) _____ (C) _____

23 위 글의 밑줄 친 문장 ⓐ에 생략된 말을 넣어 문장을 다시 쓰시오.

➡ _____

_____

24 위 글의 흐름으로 보아, 주어진 문장이 들어가기에 가장 적절한 곳은?

This was the beginning of "universal design," or "design for all."

①　　②　　③　　④　　⑤

[25~26] 다음 글을 읽고 물음에 답하시오.

In 1979, a woman started a journey to cities in the U.S. and Canada. She looked over 80. She couldn't see or hear well. She couldn't walk well without a stick.

With ⓐall these difficulties, the woman had to climb stairs in subway stations and get on crowded buses. ⓑShe had to open heavy doors and used can openers with her weak hands. Sometimes she got hurt or found herself in danger. Every moment was very difficult for her, but she visited more than 115 cities and ended her trip in 1982.

25 위 글의 밑줄 친 ⓐall these difficulties가 가리키는 내용을 우리말로 쓰시오.

➡ (1) _____

　　(2) _____

26 위 글의 밑줄 친 ⓑ에서 어법상 틀린 부분을 찾아 고치시오.

_____ ➡ _____

[27~29] 다음 글을 읽고 물음에 답하시오.

　She became ⓐtired of the same cold answer. Finally, she decided to become one of "those people" and travel around many cities to understand their difficulties better. For this, she put on her grandmother's clothes, uncomfortable shoes, and thick glasses. The shoes were so uncomfortable that she couldn't walk well without a stick. The glasses were so thick that she couldn't see well with them. She also put lots of cotton in her ears to ⓑmake her hearing bad.

27 위 글의 밑줄 친 ⓐtired of와 바꿔 쓸 수 있는 말을 모두 고르시오.

① sick of　　　　② tired with
③ worn out　　　④ bored with
⑤ tired from

28 위 글의 밑줄 친 ⓑ와 문장의 형식이 같은 것을 모두 고르시오.

① make me a dress
② make him play the piano
③ make him very happy
④ make toward home
⑤ make a fortune

29 다음 중 Patricia에 대한 설명으로 옳지 않은 것은?

① 많은 도시를 여행하기로 결심했다.
② 자신의 할머니 옷을 입었다.
③ 자신의 할머니의 불편한 신발을 신었다.
④ 자신의 할머니의 두꺼운 안경을 썼다.
⑤ 청력이 나쁜 사람이었다.

[30~31] 다음 글을 읽고 물음에 답하시오.

　Today more and more designers are following Patricia's way. Products like big flat light switches, doors with easy handles, and phones with touch buttons are helping people live better lives. Look around you, feel the difficulties of people who are older or weaker, and try ⓐto find solutions from their point of view. You could be the next Patricia Moore and make the world a better place for everybody.

30 아래 〈보기〉에서 위 글의 밑줄 친 ⓐto find와 문법적 쓰임이 다른 것의 개수를 고르시오.

┌─ 보기 ┤
① It's not easy to find solutions to this.
② He decided to find solutions to this.
③ I was so happy to find solutions to this.
④ She wants to find solutions to this.
⑤ Show me the way to find solutions to this.
└─────

① 1개　② 2개　③ 3개　④ 4개　⑤ 5개

31 위 글의 제목으로 알맞은 것을 고르시오.

① How to Follow Patricia's Way
② Produce Big Flat Light Switches
③ Popular Phones with Touch Buttons
④ Find Solutions from Others' Viewpoint
⑤ The Invention of Eco-friendly Products

01 출제율 90%

다음 문장의 빈칸에 적당한 말을 쓰시오.

> She couldn't walk well without a
> _____.

02 출제율 95%

우리말에 맞게 빈칸에 알맞은 단어를 쓰시오.

> (A) 과거에 사람들은 지구가 평평하다고 믿었다.
> ➡ In the past, people believed the Earth
> was _____.
> (B) 문을 열고 싶다면 문손잡이를 돌리세요.
> ➡ Turn the door _____ if you want to
> open the door.

03 출제율 95%

다음 대화의 빈칸에 알맞은 표현은?

> G: I'm not happy about the button.
> B: Why? What's wrong with it?
> G: _____ Children or people in
> wheelchairs can't reach it. I'm thinking
> of putting another switch for them.

① It's too small.　② It's too tight.
③ It's too high.　④ It takes long time.
⑤ It's too bright.

04 출제율 85%

다음 영영풀이에 해당하는 단어는?

> a cupboard, often tall and made of metal,
> in which you can keep your possessions,
> and leave them for a period of time

① backpack　② tool
③ pad　④ swing
⑤ locker

[05~07] 다음 대화를 읽고 물음에 답하시오.

> Dad: What are you doing here?
> Son: I'm thinking of ways to help Miso.
> Dad: What's wrong? (①)
> Son: She can't turn on the light by herself. This
> switch is too high for her.
> Dad: That's right. (②) Do you have any good
> ideas about that?
> Son: (③) I'm thinking of putting a step box
> here below the switch.
> Dad: (④) Good idea. And I'll change the
> switch to a bigger one.
> Son: Great. (⑤) Grandma will like it, too. She
> can turn on the light more easily.

05 출제율 95%

위 대화의 ①~⑤ 중, 주어진 문장이 들어갈 위치로 알맞은 것은?

> I'm not happy about it, either.

①　②　③　④　⑤

06 출제율 95%

위 대화의 제목으로 알맞은 것은?

① Importance of Helping Others
② Difficulty of Doing the Housework
③ How to Install the Switch
④ Good Ideas for Family
⑤ Being Good to Grandma

07 출제율 100%

위 대화의 내용과 일치하지 않는 것은?

① The switch is too high for Miso.
② The boy will put a step box below the
switch.
③ Both the boy and his dad aren't happy
with the switch.
④ The boy's grandma can't turn on the
switch by herself.
⑤ The boy's grandma will like the new switch.

[08~09] 다음 대화를 읽고 물음에 답하시오.

G: _____(A)_____

B: Why? What's wrong?

G: It's too small. Grandma can't use it easily.

B: Do you have any ideas?

G: _____(B)_____ That'll help her turn on the light easily.

B: Good idea.

08 위 대화의 빈칸 (A)에 알맞은 표현은?

① I'm not happy about the locker.

② I'm not happy about the TV.

③ I'm not happy about this light switch.

④ I'm not happy about the board.

⑤ I'm not happy about the mirror.

09 위 대화의 빈칸 (B)에 알맞은 표현은?

① I'm thinking of putting a cushion on it.

② I'm thinking of hanging a wiper on it.

③ I'm thinking of putting a step box below it.

④ I'm thinking of hanging a bigger and safer seat.

⑤ I'm thinking of changing it with a bigger one.

10 다음 대화의 빈칸에 문제의 해결책을 주어진 〈조건〉에 맞게 쓰시오.

G: I'm not happy about the sign. There are some people who can't see.

B: Right. Do you have any ideas?

G: Well, _____

B: That's a good idea.

┤ 조건 ├

• '나는 …할까 생각 중이다'라는 뜻으로, 의도나 계획을 나타내는 표현을 쓸 것.

• 'be / think of / add / Braille / the sign' 을 이용할 것.

➡ _____

11 다음 우리말을 주어진 표현을 이용하여 영작하시오.

그녀는 매우 친절해서 나에게 역으로 가는 길을 말해 주었다. (so ~ that)

➡ _____
_____

12 다음 글에서 어법상 틀린 부분을 모두 찾아 바르게 고쳐 쓰시오.

The hole cover was very dangerous that I couldn't ride my bike on it. So I want to change the cover like this. The new cover will help people riding a bike safely.

➡ _____, _____

[13~14] 어법상 올바른 문장을 모두 고르시오.

13 ① It'll help my grandma take a bath more comfortably.

② Ms. Han made her son to go to bed immediately.

③ It gave him so a shock that he couldn't say a word.

④ I am such tired that I can't walk any more.

⑤ The car is so expensive that I can't buy it.

14 ⓐ출제율 95%

① I'm so tired to go there.

② The man is rich enough that he can buy the big house.

③ This problem is too difficult to solve.

④ King Jeongjo let her take a trip to Mountain Geumgang.

⑤ Mom made me cleaning my room.

[15~16] 다음 글을 읽고 물음에 답하시오.

Who was the woman and what made her _____ⓐ_____ all this? She was Patricia Moore, a 26-year-old designer. During the 1970's, she worked for a big design company. She often asked at meetings, "How about designing for old or weak people?" The other designers always answered, "We don't design for those people."

She became tired of the same cold answer. Finally, she decided ⓑto become one of "those people" and travel around many cities ⓒto understand their difficulties better. For this, she put on her grandmother's clothes, uncomfortable shoes, and thick glasses. The shoes were so uncomfortable that she couldn't walk well without a stick. The glasses were so thick that she couldn't see well with them. She also put lots of cotton in her ears to make her hearing bad.

15 ⓐ출제율 90%

위 글의 빈칸 ⓐ에 들어갈 알맞은 말을 고르시오.

① to do   ② do   ③ done

④ doing   ⑤ to have done

16 ⓐ출제율 95%

다음 〈보기〉에서 위 글의 밑줄 친 ⓑto become, ⓒto understand와 to부정사의 용법이 같은 것을 각각 고르시오.

┌─ 보기 ─┐

① It was not easy to understand their difficulties.

② She was very happy to become one of "those people."

③ I tried to understand their difficulties.

④ He wanted to understand their difficulties.

⑤ Tom went to New York to become one of "those people."

➡ ⓑ와 용법이 같은 것: _____

ⓒ와 용법이 같은 것: _____

[17~19] 다음 글을 읽고 물음에 답하시오.

During her journey, Patricia felt the difficulties old people go through. From this experience, she designed products anybody could use safely and easily. This was the beginning of "universal design," or "design for all."

One example of her universal design ideas is low-floor buses. ⓐ그것들은 계단이 없고 낮은 바닥을 가지고 있어서 that even a person in a wheelchair can use them without any help. Of course, this helps other people get on the bus more comfortably, too.

17 ⓐ출제율 90%

위 글의 밑줄 친 ⓐ의 우리말에 맞게 주어진 어휘를 알맞게 배열하시오.

such / steps / have / floor / and / no / a / have / low / they

18 ⓐ출제율 100%

위 글의 주제로 알맞은 것을 고르시오.

① the difficulties old people go through

② how to design safely and easily

③ the beginning of "universal design"

④ the strong points of low floor buses

⑤ people who can help other people

19 본문의 내용과 일치하도록 다음 빈칸 (A)와 (B)에 알맞은 단어를 쓰시오.

> Patricia created "(A)_____ _____"
> from the experience she went through
> in person, and it could be "(B)_____
> _____ _____" as you can see in the
> case of low floor buses.

[20~22] 다음 글을 읽고 물음에 답하시오.

In 1979, a woman started a ⓐjourney to cities in the U.S. and Canada. (①) She looked over 80. (②) She couldn't see or hear well. She couldn't walk well without a stick.

(③) She had to open heavy doors and use can openers with her weak hands. (④) Sometimes she got hurt or found herself in danger. (⑤) Every moment was very difficult for her, but she visited more than 115 cities and ended her trip in 1982.

20 위 글의 흐름으로 보아, 주어진 문장이 들어가기에 가장 적절한 곳은?

> With all these difficulties, the woman had to climb stairs in subway stations and get on crowded buses.

①　　②　　③　　④　　⑤

21 위 글의 밑줄 친 ⓐjourney와 바꿔 쓸 수 있는 단어를 쓰시오.

➡ _____

22 본문의 내용과 일치하도록 다음 빈칸 (A)와 (B)에 알맞은 단어를 쓰시오.

> Though there were many (A)_____,
> the woman visited more than (B)_____
> _____ in the U.S. and Canada and
> ended her trip in 1982.

[23~24] 다음 글을 읽고 물음에 답하시오.

Today more and more designers are following Patricia's way. Products like big ____ⓐ____ light switches, doors with easy ____ⓑ____, and phones with ____ⓒ____ buttons are helping people live better lives. Look around you, feel the difficulties of people who are older or weaker, and try to find solutions from their point of view. You could be the next Patricia Moore and make the world a better place for everybody.

23 다음 그림을 참조하여 위 글의 빈칸 ⓐ~ⓒ에 들어갈 알맞은 말을 쓰시오.

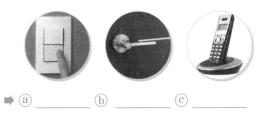

➡ ⓐ _____　　ⓑ _____　　ⓒ _____

24 다음 문장에서 위 글의 내용과 다른 부분을 찾아서 고치시오.

> To be the next Patricia Moore and make the world a better place for everybody, you should feel the difficulties of people who are older or weaker, and try to find solutions from your viewpoint.

_____ ➡ _____

01 대화의 우리말 해석에 맞게 주어진 어구를 알맞은 순서로 배열하시오.

> B: I'm not happy about the lights.
> G: What's wrong with them?
> B: 색맹인 사람들에게는 신호등이 똑같아 보일 거야.
> G: Oh, I see. How about putting an image on each light?
> B: A walking man on the green light and a standing man on the red light? Good idea!

> (the traffic / the same / who / to / lights / look / blind to / some people / colors / are)

➡ _____

_____

02 주어진 그림과 글을 보고 대화의 빈칸을 완성하시오.

My brother's chair is so low that he can't sit on it comfortably. However, this chair has special pads. They'll help my brother read books more comfortably.

> G: _____ my brother's chair. It's _____ and too hard.
> B: Right. _____ buying this one. What do you think?
> G: Looks great. I think he can read books more _____.

03 다음 대화를 읽고 아래의 요약문을 완성하시오.

> Dad: What are you doing here?
> Son: I'm thinking of ways to help Miso.
> Dad: What's wrong?
> Son: She can't turn on the light by herself. This switch is too high for her.
> Dad: That's right. I'm not happy about it, either. Do you have any good ideas about that?
> Son: I'm thinking of putting a step box here below the switch.
> Dad: Good idea. And I'll change the switch to a bigger one.
> Son: Great. Grandma will like it, too. She can turn on the light more easily.

> Miso can't turn on the light _____ because the switch is too _____ for her. So, her brother decides to put _____ _____ the switch to help her. Dad also will _____ the switch to a _____ one for Miso and Grandma so that they can turn it on _____.

04 다음 문장을 make를 이용하여 비슷한 의미의 문장으로 바꿔 쓰시오.

(1) Mom told me to throw away the trash.

➡ _____

(2) The teacher ordered the students to do homework.

➡ _____

(3) Anna asked her daughter to come home early at night.

➡ _____

중요

05 다음 문장을 to부정사를 이용하여 다시 쓰시오.

(1) Betty was so busy that she couldn't come to the party.

➡ _____

(2) This food is so delicious that I can eat it all.

➡ _____

(3) This problem is so easy that anyone can solve it.

➡ _____

06 다음 두 문장을 to부정사를 이용하여 하나의 문장으로 쓰시오.

(1) • This ice cream is very cold.
　　• I can't eat it.

➡ _____

(2) • It rained really hard.
　　• We couldn't play soccer.

➡ _____

[07~09] 다음 글을 읽고 물음에 답하시오.

　Who was the woman and ⓐwhat made her do all this? She was Patricia Moore, a 26-year-old designer. During the 1970's, she worked for a big design company. She often asked at meetings, "ⓑHow about designing for ⓒold or weak people?" The other designers always answered, "We don't design for those people."

07 위 글의 밑줄 친 ⓐ를 다음과 같이 바꿔 쓸 때 빈칸에 들어갈 알맞은 말을 쓰시오.

➡ _____ did she do all this?

중요

08 위 글의 밑줄 친 ⓑ를 다음과 같이 바꿔 쓸 때 빈칸에 들어갈 알맞은 말을 쓰시오.

➡ (1) _____ about designing

(2) _____ don't we design

(3) _____ we design

09 위 글의 밑줄 친 ⓒ와 같은 뜻이 되도록 다음 빈칸에 알맞은 단어를 쓰시오.

➡ _____ old or _____ weak

[10~12] 다음 글을 읽고 물음에 답하시오.

　During her journey, Patricia felt the difficulties old people go through. From ⓐthis experience, she designed products anybody could use safely and easily. This was the beginning of "ⓑuniversal design," or "design for all."

　One example of her universal design ideas is low-floor buses. ⓒThey have no steps and have such a low floor that even a person in a wheelchair can use them without any help. Of course, this helps other people get on the bus more comfortably, too.

10 위 글의 밑줄 친 ⓐthis experience가 가리키는 내용을 우리말로 쓰시오.

➡ _____

_____

중요

11 위 글에서 ⓑuniversal design의 예를 찾아 영어로 쓰시오.

➡ _____

12 위 글의 밑줄 친 ⓒ를 다음과 같이 바꿔 쓸 때 빈칸에 들어갈 알맞은 말을 쓰시오.

➡ They have no steps and their floor is _____ low

01 각 물건의 문제점과 그에 대한 해결책을 제시하는 대화를 〈보기〉와 같이 쓰시오.

〈물건의 문제점〉

locker – too old / bookshelf – too small

〈해결책〉

decorate its door / put another bookshelf on it

〈보기〉

A: I'm not happy about the bookshelf. It's too small.

B: I think so, too. Do you have any ideas?

A: I'm thinking of putting another bookshelf on it.

B: That's a good idea.

02 〈보기〉에 주어진 표현과 사역동사나 so와 that을 이용하여 4 문장 이상 쓰시오.

보기

clean his room	fix her computer	go to the K-pop concert

cried very loudly / covered my ears   spoke very fast / could not understand him

(1) _____

(2) _____

(3) _____

(4) _____

03 다음 내용을 바탕으로, 불편한 점을 개선하여 디자인한 작품의 안내문을 쓰시오.

• 불편한 점: The desk is too high for my little sister to use easily.

• 개선한 점: This desk has special legs.

The desk in my house is (A)_____ high (B)_____ my little sister (C)_____ use it easily. However, this desk has (D)_____. It'll help my sister read books more comfortably.

단원별 모의고사

01 다음 단어에 대한 영어 설명이 <u>어색한</u> 것은?

① company: a business organization that makes money by producing or selling goods or services

② pad: a button or key that controls the light or machine

③ handle: a part that is designed especially to be held by the hand

④ solution: the answer to a problem

⑤ uncomfortable: not feeling comfortable and pleasant

02 우리말에 맞게 문장의 빈칸에 세 단어를 쓰시오.

> 여러분의 주위를 둘러보고, 더 나이 들거나 더 약한 사람들의 어려움을 느껴 보고, 그들의 관점에서 해결책을 찾으려고 노력해 봐라.
> ➡ Look around you, feel the difficulties of people who are older or weaker, and try to find solutions from their _____.

03 다음 영영풀이에 해당하는 단어를 고르시오.

> a building or place where buses or trains stop so that people can get on or off

① company   ② bathtub
③ cushion   ④ station
⑤ seat

04 그림을 보고 대화의 빈칸 (A)와 (B)에 들어갈 말을 쓰시오.

> G: I'm (A)_____ of buying this spoon. It will help my grandma eat soup easily.
> B: Right. She (B)_____ it with her fingers.

05 다음 대화의 빈칸에 들어갈 말로 <u>어색한</u> 것은?

> A: _____
> B: Why? What's wrong?
> A: There are not enough chairs here. I'm thinking of telling the guide to give us more chairs.

① I'm not happy about this place.

② I'm not satisfied with this place.

③ This place is not satisfactory to me.

④ I'm not content with this place.

⑤ I don't want to complain about this place.

06 대화의 빈칸에 들어갈 말로 알맞은 것은?

> G: I'm not happy about the button.
> B: Why? What's wrong with it?
> G: It's too high. Children or people in wheelchairs can't _____ it. I'm thinking of putting another switch for them.

① reach   ② take   ③ bring
④ distinguish   ⑤ add

07 다음 대화의 빈칸에 들어갈 말로 알맞은 것은?

> B: I'm not happy about the desk. It's too low.
>
> G: Right. _____
>
> B: Good idea.

┤ 조건 ├
- 계획이나 의도를 말하는 표현을 쓸 것.
- B가 한 불만에 대한 해결책으로 'put some pads'를 사용할 것.
- 'intend to'를 사용할 것.

➡ _____

[08~09] 다음 대화를 읽고 물음에 답하시오.

Dad: What are you doing here?

Son: I'm thinking of ways to help Miso.

Dad: What's wrong?

Son: She can't turn on the light by herself. This switch is too high for her.

Dad: That's right. 나도 그것이 마음에 들지 않는구나. Do you have any good ideas about that?

Son: _____(A)_____

Dad: Good idea. And I'll change the switch to a bigger one.

Son: Great. Grandma will like it, too. She can turn on the light more easily.

08 위 대화의 흐름상 빈칸 (A)에 들어갈 말로 알맞은 것은?

① I'm thinking of buying this spoon.

② I'm not happy about my brother's chair.

③ I'm thinking of hanging a wiper on it.

④ I'm thinking of putting a step box here below the switch.

⑤ I'm thinking of putting another bookshelf on it.

09 밑줄 친 우리말에 맞게 'happy'를 사용하여 영어로 쓰시오.

➡ _____

10 대화의 빈칸에 들어갈 말로 가장 알맞은 것은?

> G: I don't like the high steps here. _____
>
> B: Right. I'm thinking of building a new way with no steps.

① The music is too loud.

② It's too low and too hard.

③ People in wheelchairs can't get in.

④ There are some people who are blind to colors.

⑤ There are some people who can't see.

11 다음 대화의 빈칸에 적절한 말은?

> G: I'm not happy about the sign. _____
>
> B: Right. Do you have any ideas?
>
> G: Well, I'm thinking of adding Braille on the sign.
>
> B: That's a good idea.

① People in wheelchairs can't get on it easily.

② There are some people who are blind to colors.

③ There are some people who can't see.

④ It's too low and too hard.

⑤ There are not enough signs here.

12 대화의 밑줄 친 우리말에 맞게 주어진 단어를 활용하여 영어로 쓰시오.

> G: I'm not happy about this light switch.
> B: Why? What's wrong?
> G: It's too small. Grandma can't use it easily.
> B: Do you have any ideas?
> G: 나는 그것을 더 큰 것으로 바꿀까 생각 중이야. That'll help her turn on the light easily.
> B: Good idea.

> (think of / change / with / one)

➡ _____

13 다음 두 문장을 'so ~ that' 구문을 사용하여 한 문장으로 연결하여 쓰시오.

(1) • The noise was very loud.
    • So, I couldn't sleep.

    ➡ _____

(2) • I can't get on the bus.
    • Because the steps are so high.

    ➡ _____

14 다음 중 어법상 올바르지 않은 것은?

① The teacher had his students to follow the rules.
② Minsu helped his friend walk to the school nurse.
③ Mr. Yi let the girl get some rest under the tree.
④ This chair was so uncomfortable that nobody could sit on it for a long time.
⑤ The bus handle is so high that I can't hold it.

15 다음 문장에서 어법상 어색한 부분을 바르게 고치시오.

(1) The bathtub in my house is too high for my grandma to get in it easily.

    _____ ➡ _____

(2) The man had me to carry his luggage.

    _____ ➡ _____

[16~17] 다음 글을 읽고 물음에 답하시오.

Today more and more designers are following ⓐPatricia's way. Products like big flat light switches, doors with easy handles, and phones with touch buttons are helping people live better lives. Look around you, feel the difficulties of people who are older or weaker, and try to find solutions ⓑfrom their point of view. You could be the next Patricia Moore and make the world a better place for everybody.

16 다음 빈칸 (A)와 (B)에 알맞은 단어를 넣어 ⓐPatricia's way에 대한 설명을 완성하시오.

> It's the way to help people live (A)_____ _____ by feeling the difficulties of people who are older or weaker, and trying to find (B)_____ from their viewpoint.

17 위 글의 밑줄 친 ⓑ를 다음과 같이 바꿔 쓸 때 빈칸에 들어갈 알맞은 말을 쓰시오.

➡ by putting yourself in _____ shoes

[18~19] 다음 글을 읽고 물음에 답하시오.

During her journey, Patricia felt the difficulties old people go through. From this experience, she designed products anybody could use safely and easily. This was the beginning of "universal design," or "design for all."

One example of her universal design ideas is low-floor buses. They have no steps and have such a low floor that even a person in a wheelchair can use them without any help. Of course, ⓐthis helps other people get on the bus more comfortably, too.

18 위 글의 밑줄 친 ⓐthis가 가리키는 것을 본문에서 찾아 쓰시오.

➡ _____

_____

19 위 글의 내용과 일치하지 <u>않는</u> 것은?

① Patricia는 여행 동안 나이 든 사람들이 겪는 어려움을 느꼈다.

② 이 경험으로부터, 그녀는 누구나 안전하고 쉽게 사용할 수 있는 제품들을 고안했다.

③ Patricia가 자신의 여행 경험으로부터 제품들을 고안한 것이 '유니버설 디자인'의 시작이었다.

④ 유니버설 디자인 아이디어의 한 가지 예는 저상 버스이다.

⑤ 휠체어를 타지 않은 사람들은 저상 버스를 탈 때 불편함을 느낀다.

[20~21] 다음 글을 읽고 물음에 답하시오.

She became tired of the same cold answer. ⓐFinally, she decided to become one of "those people" and travel around many cities to understand their difficulties better. For this, she put on her grandmother's clothes,

uncomfortable shoes, and thick glasses. ⓑThe shoes were so uncomfortable that she couldn't walk well with a stick. ⓒThe glasses were so thick that she couldn't see well without them. She also put lots of cotton in her ears to make her hearing bad.

20 위 글의 밑줄 친 ⓐFinally와 바꿔 쓸 수 <u>없는</u> 말을 <u>모두</u> 고르시오.

① In the end   ② Actually

③ Especially   ④ At last

⑤ In the long run

21 위 글의 밑줄 친 ⓑ와 ⓒ에서 흐름상 어색한 부분을 찾아 고치시오.

➡ ⓑ _____ ⓒ _____

[22~23] 다음 글을 읽고 물음에 답하시오.

With all these difficulties, the woman had to climb stairs in subway stations and get ⟨ⓐ⟩ crowded buses. She had to open heavy doors and use can openers with her weak hands. ⓑSometimes she got hurt or found her in danger. Every moment was very difficult ⟨ⓒ⟩ her, but she visited more than 115 cities and ended her trip in 1982.

22 위 글의 빈칸 ⓐ와 ⓒ에 알맞은 전치사로 짝지어진 것은?

① on – for   ② in – with

③ on – from   ④ to – for

⑤ in – from

23 위 글의 밑줄 친 ⓑ에서 어법상 어색한 것을 고쳐 쓰시오.

_____ ➡ _____

Lesson

Special

Teens' Magazine

Words & Expressions

교과서

Key Words

- **activity** [əktívəti] 명 활동
- **bread** [bred] 명 빵
- **break time** 쉬는 시간
- **bright** [brait] 형 밝은, 똑똑한
- **brrr** 감 부르르, 부들부들
- **can** [kæn] 명 캔, 깡통
- **change** [tʃeindʒ] 동 갈아입다, 바꾸다
- **choose** [tʃuːz] 동 고르다
- **circle** [sə́rkl] 명 동그라미, 원
- **close** 부 [klous] 가까이 동 [klouz] 닫다
- **clothes** [klouz] 명 옷
- **cute** [kjuːt] 형 귀여운
- **delicious** [dilíʃəs] 형 맛있는
- **dessert** [dizə́ːrt] 명 후식, 디저트
- **enjoy** [indʒɔ́i] 동 즐기다
- **exactly** [igzǽktli] 부 정확하게
- **favorite** [féivərit] 형 가장 좋아하는
- **finish** [fíniʃ] 동 끝나다, 끝내다
- **friendly** [fréndli] 형 친근한, 다정한
- **grade** [greid] 명 성적
- **handwriting** [hǽndràitiŋ] 명 손 글씨
- **hopeful** [hóupful] 형 희망적인
- **like** [laik] 전 ~처럼, ~와 같이
- **mirror** [mírər] 명 거울

- **most** [moust] 형 대부분의
- **never** [névər] 부 결코 ~ 하지 않다
- **ocean** [óuʃən] 명 바다, 대양
- **outside** [áutsàid] 부 밖에
- **P.E. class** 체육 수업
- **place** [place] 명 장소 동 놓다, 두다
- **recycle bin** 재활용 수거함
- **save** [seiv] 동 절약하다
- **second** [sékənd] 명 초, 짧은 시간, 두 번째
- **slow** [slou] 형 느린
- **shape** [ʃeip] 명 모양, 도형
- **sky** [skai] 명 하늘
- **special** [spéʃəl] 형 특별한
- **sweet** [swiːt] 명 단것, 단 음식
- **though** [ðou] 접 비록 ~일지라도
- **trash can** 쓰레기 통
- **umbrella** [ʌmbrélə] 명 우산
- **visit** [vízit] 동 방문하다
- **wave** [weiv] 동 파도치다, 손을 흔들다
- **wet** [wet] 형 젖은
- **wheel** [hwiːl] 명 바퀴
- **winner** [wínər] 명 승자
- **youth** [juːθ] 명 젊음, 청춘

Key Expressions

- **add A to B** A를 B에 더하다
- **a lot of** 많은
- **be full of** ~로 가득 차다
- **break down into** ~로 부서지다
- **cover A up with B** B로 A를 덮다
- **cut A into B** A를 B로 자르다
- **don't need to** ~할 필요가 없다
- **in such a way that ~** ~하게 되는 방식으로
- **in the middle of** ~의 한가운데에

- **make a presentation** 발표하다
- **wait a second** 잠깐만
- **such as** ~와 같은
- **take a break** 휴식을 취하다
- **take a test** 시험을 치다
- **take A to B** A를 B로 데려가다
- **up and down** 위아래로
- **up to** ~까지
- **walk back** 물러서다

Word Power

※ 서로 반대되는 뜻을 가진 어휘

- □ **fun** (재미있는) ↔ **boring** (지루한)
- □ **handsome** (잘생긴) ↔ **ugly** (못생긴)
- □ **push** (누르다) ↔ **pull** (당기다)
- □ **hungry** (배고픈) ↔ **full** (배부른)
- □ **close** (닫다) ↔ **open** (열다)

- □ **wet** (젖은) ↔ **dry** (마른)
- □ **slow** (느린) ↔ **fast** (빠른)
- □ **outside** (밖에) ↔ **inside** (안에)
- □ **same** (같은) ↔ **different** (다른)
- □ **close** (가까이) ↔ **far** (멀리)

※ 서로 비슷한 뜻을 가진 어휘

- □ **a lot of : lots of** (많은)
- □ **delicious : tasty** (맛있는)
- □ **sleepy : drowsy** (졸린)
- □ **finish : end** (끝내다)
- □ **choose : pick** (고르다)
- □ **exactly : accurately** (정확하게)

- □ **handsome : good-looking** (잘생긴)
- □ **though : although** (비록 ~일지라도)
- □ **be full of : be filled with** (~으로 가득 차다)
- □ **such as : like** (~와 같은)
- □ **shape : figure** (도형)
- □ **bright : clever** (똑똑한)

English Dictionary

□ **bread** 빵
→ a food made from flour, water, and usually yeast, mixed together and baked
밀가루, 물 및 보통 효모로 만들어지고 함께 섞어서 구워진 음식

□ **choose** 고르다
→ to decide what you want from two or more things or possibilities
둘 또는 그 이상의 것이나 가능성으로부터 원하는 것을 결정하다

□ **circle** 원
→ a continuous curved line, the points of which are always the same distance away from a fixed central point
고정된 중심점으로부터 항상 동일한 거리인 점들의 연속된 곡선

□ **friendly** 친절한
→ behaving in a pleasant, kind way towards someone
누군가를 향해 유쾌하고 친절하게 행동하는

□ **grade** 성적
→ a number or letter that shows how good someone's work or performance is
누군가의 일이나 수행이 얼마나 좋은지 보여주는 숫자나 글자

□ **save** 절약하다
→ to keep something, especially money, for use in the future
미래에 사용하기 위해 어떤 것, 특히 돈을 간직하다

□ **wave** 손을 흔들다
→ to raise your hand and move it from side to side as a way of greeting someone
누군가에게 인사하는 방식으로써 손을 들어올려 옆으로 흔들다

□ **wheel** 바퀴
→ a circular object connected at the centre to a bar, used for making vehicles or parts of machines move
중심에서 막대기에 연결되어 차량 또는 기계 부품을 이동시키기 위해 사용되는 원형 물체

□ **youth** 젊음
→ the period of your life when you are young, or the state of being young
당신이 젊을 때의 인생 시기, 혹은 젊은 상태

Reading

교과서

Teens' Magazine

Works of Art in Shapes

Like a Circle

I love you like a circle because a circle never ends.
전치사(~처럼, ~와 같이)

Snowman

It's cold outside.
밖에(는)

I don't want to go out and play.

But Mom says I have to.

It's starting to snow and I'm going to be cold.

I don't like playing outside on days like these.
=like to play

But wait a second, I have the most wonderful idea!

I'll cover myself up with snow and I'll hide here! brrr... brrr...

Looking Back with Your Handwriting

Life is art. Live yours in COLOR.
=your life

IT ISN'T OVER UNTIL IT'S OVER.
be over: 끝나다

I am a slow walker, but I never walk back.
빈도부사로, be동사 뒤에, 일반동사 앞에 위치

I love the little things you do.
'you' 앞에 목적격 관계대명사 'that'이 생략

Follow your dream.

My Bike

Two wheels take me / To any place / To school / Back home / To the
take ~ to ...: ~을 ...로 데려가다
mountain / To the river / I love my bike / I enjoy riding it every day
'enjoy'는 동명사를 목적어로 취하는 동사

Giving Tree

Out there – wet

In here – dry

Pretty big umbrella
형용사 앞에서: (부사) '꽤, 상당히'
Between me and the sky

 확인문제

- 다음 문장이 본문의 내용과 일치하면 T, 일치하지 않으면 F를 쓰시오.

1 The bike takes the writer to any place. ☐

2 The giving tree is like an umbrella between the writer and the sky. ☐

circle: 동그라미, 원
second: 초, 짧은 시간, 두 번째
wait a second: 잠깐만
cover ~ up with ...: ~의 위까지
...로 덮다
brrr: 부르르, 부들부들
slow: 느린 ↔ fast 빠른
never: 결코 ...하지 않다
walk back: 물러서다
wheel: 바퀴
wet: 젖은, 축축한
dry 마른
sky: 하늘

Selfies of This Year

Though we lost the game, we had a lot of fun.
양보의 뜻을 지닌 접속사(비록 …이지만)

Look at the robots we made. Aren't they cute?
'we made' 앞에는 목적격 관계대명사 that[which]이 생략

We made a big cake for Mr. Han. It made him happy.
5형식. him은 목적어이고 happy는 목적격 보어로 형용사

Have you ever seen a handsome Peter Pan like me?
'경험'을 묻는 현재완료의 의문문   전치사(…와 같이)

What Do You Think of Your School Life?

The most uncomfortable moment
→ comfortable

1. When I take tests

2. When I am really hungry and have nothing to eat
to부정사의 형용사적 용법

3. When I change clothes before and after P.E. class
cloth: 옷감 clothes: 옷

4. others: When I am sleepy in class

When the teacher doesn't finish classes after the bell rings

The most lovely time

1. Lunch time

2. Class with my favorite teacher

3. The last class on Friday

4. others: When I am sleeping during break time

When I see myself in the mirror
재귀대명사(주어와 목적어가 동일인)

The most awesome news

1. I got better grades than before

2. School finishes earlier today
early의 비교급

3. I don't go to school because it rains or snows a lot

4. others: We eat delicious sweets for dessert

My best friend and I are in the same class

cute: 귀여운

break time: 쉬는 시간

grade: 등급, 성적

choose: 고르다

sweet: 단것

📎 **확인문제**

● 다음 문장이 본문의 내용과 일치하면 T, 일치하지 <u>않으면</u> F를 쓰시오.

1 Thanks to the cake that Mr. Han made, we felt happy. ☐

2 To students, taking tests is the most uncomfortable. ☐

3 The students don't like the last class on Friday. ☐

The most difficult work to do
형용사적 용법의 to부정사

1. Washing trash cans

2. Studying

3. Making a presentation in front of friends
~ 앞에(서)

4. others: Being on time every day
동명사

        Group work

Places We Love in Our Village

Daehan Traditional Market - 10 Likes

  If you want to eat something delicious, visit Daehan Market. You can buy "*yeopjeon*" and use it to make your lunch box full. You can choose many kinds of food and add them to your lunch box.
목적을 나타내는 to부정사의 부사적 용법

Saebom Youth Center - 12 Likes

  This is Saebom Youth Center in the middle of our town. We like this place because we can learn many things, such as dance and music. We can also play board games and take a break here.
~와 같은

Mr. Kim's Bakery - 12 Likes

  This is a small bakery near the school. We like to go there after school because we're always hungry! It is good to enjoy delicious bread with friends.
가주어   진주어

Let's Have Fun with Puzzles!

Shape Puzzles

  If you cut the shape A into two same pieces, you can then make all the other shapes(B, C, D, E, F, G) from those two pieces.

Ten Balls in Five Lines

  Place 10 balls in 5 lines in such a way that each line has exactly 4 balls on it.
a way를 수식하는 관계대명사절

make a presentation 발표하다

youth: 젊음, 청춘

such as: …와 같은

take a break: 휴식을 취하다

cut ~ into …: ~을 …로 자르다

place: 놓다, 두다; 장소, 곳

in such a way that …: …하게 되는 방식으로

exactly: 정확하게

📎 **확인문제**

● 다음 문장이 본문의 내용과 일치하면 T, 일치하지 않으면 F를 쓰시오.

1   To students, the most difficult work to do is doing their homework. ☐

2   At Saebom Youth Center, students can learn many things. ☐

You Are Eating Plastic Spoons!

1. A lot of plastic spoons are thrown away every year.
   'be동사+과거분사' 형태의 수동태이다. thrown은 throw의 과거분사
2. Most plastic breaks down into smaller pieces in the ocean.
   대부분의
3. Very small pieces of plastic go into fish.

4. If you eat the fish, you eat the plastic, too. Up to 11,000 pieces
   up to: ~까지
   each year!

Let's Make a Dream School!

We had a universal design contest for our school last month. Here
are the winners' works.

1. When your hands come close, water comes out. When you pull
   your hands away, the water stops. You don't need to turn or touch
   any parts. We can save lots of water with this. – by O Juyeon(1-3)

2. This is our school park between two buildings. Anybody can go up
   anybody가 긍정문에 쓰여 '어떤 누구라도'의 의미
   and down easily here. Also we can sit and get some rest here. – by
   Gim Jimin(3-5)

3. These are special desks and chairs for the classroom. For group
   activities, you can get them together and make a wonderful group
   table for three, four, or five students. – by Choi Yumi(2-1)

LET'S LAUGH

Funny Earth Day Jokes Ha! Ha! Ha!

Why are recycle bins hopeful?

- Because they're full of cans.
  be full of: ~으로 가득 차다
How can you tell the ocean is friendly?
  'the ocean' 앞에 접속사 that이 생략된 문장. that절은 tell의 목적어
- It waves.

Why did the sun go to school?

- To get brighter.
  get+형용사: ~해지다

break down into: …로 부서지다

winner: 승자

close: 가까이

don't need to: …할 필요가 없다

up and down: 위아래로

recycle bin: 재활용 수거함

can: 캔, 깡통

friendly: 친근한, 다정한

wave: 파도치다, 손을 흔들다

bright: 밝은, 똑똑한

 확인문제

● 다음 문장이 본문의 내용과 일치하면 T, 일치하지 <u>않으면</u> F를 쓰시오.

1   Many plastic spoons are thrown away every year. ☐

2   The fish eat the plastic up to 11,000 pieces each year. ☐

3   The sun goes to school to get brighter. ☐

● 우리말을 참고하여 빈칸에 알맞은 말을 쓰시오.

1 _____ Magazine

2 Works of Art _____ _____

3 _____ a Circle

4 I love you _____ a circle _____ a circle never ends.

5 _____

6 It's cold _____ .

7 I don't want to _____ _____ and _____ .

8 But Mom says I _____ _____ .

9 It's starting _____ _____ and I'm going to _____ _____ .

10 I don't like playing outside _____ _____ _____ .

11 But wait _____ _____ , I have _____ _____ _____ idea!

12 I'll _____ _____ _____ with snow and I'll _____ _____ !

13 _____ _____ with Your Handwriting

14 Life is _____ .

15 Live _____ in COLOR.

16 IT ISN'T OVER _____ IT'S _____ .

17 I am a _____ _____ , but I never walk back.

18 I love the _____ _____ you do.

19 _____ your dream.

20 _____ _____

21 Two wheels _____ me / _____ _____ _____ / To school / Back _____ / To the mountain / To the river / I love my bike / I _____ _____ it every day

22 _____ Tree

23 Out _____ – wet

24 In _____ – dry

25 Pretty big _____

1	십대들의 잡지
2	모양으로 표현된 예술 작품
3	동그라미처럼
4	나는 동그라미처럼 너를 사랑해. 왜냐하면 동그라미는 절대 끝나지 않기에.
5	눈사람
6	바깥은 추워.
7	나는 밖으로 나가 놀고 싶지 않네.
8	하지만 엄마는 그래야 한다고 하시네.
9	눈이 오기 시작하고 나는 추워질 거야.
10	나는 이런 날에는 나가서 놀고 싶지 않아.
11	하지만 잠깐만, 나는 최고로 멋진 생각이 났어!
12	나는 눈으로 내 몸을 덮고 여기에 숨어야지!
13	손 글씨로 돌아보기
14	인생은 예술이다.
15	다양한 색깔로 살아라.
16	끝날 때까지 끝난 게 아니다.
17	나는 느리게 걷는 사람이지만 절대 물러서지는 않는다.
18	나는 네가 하는 작은 일들을 사랑해.
19	네 꿈을 좇아라.
20	나의 자전거
21	바퀴 두 개가 나를 데려가네 / 어느 곳으로든지 / 학교로 / 다시 집으로 / 산으로 / 강으로 / 나는 내 자전거가 아주 좋아 / 나는 그걸 매일 즐겨 타네
22	아낌없이 주는 나무
23	저곳 바깥은 – 젖어 있고
24	이곳 안쪽은 – 말라 있네
25	엄청 큰 우산이네

26 _____ me and the sky

27 _____ of This Year

28 _____ we lost the game, we had a lot of fun.

29 Look at the _____ we made.

30 Aren't they _____?

31 We made _____ _____ _____ for Mr. Han.

32 It _____ _____ _____.

33 _____ _____ _____ _____ a handsome Peter Pan like me?

34 _____ Do You Think of Your School _____?

35 The most uncomfortable _____

36 1. When I _____ _____

37 2. When I am really hungry and _____ _____ to eat

38 3. When I change clothes _____ and _____ P.E. class

39 4. others: When I am _____ in class

40 When the teacher doesn't finish classes _____ the bell _____

41 The most _____

42 1. _____ time

43 2. class with my _____ teacher

44 3. the _____ _____ on Friday

45 4. others: when I am sleeping _____ _____ _____

46 when I see _____ in the mirror

47 The most _____ news

48 1. I got better grades _____ _____

49 2. School _____ _____ today

50 3. I don't go to school _____ it _____ or _____ a lot

51 4. others: We eat delicious sweets _____ _____

52 My best friend and I are in the _____

53 The _____ _____ work to do

54 1. Washing _____ cans

---

26 나와 하늘 사이에 있는

27 올해의 셀피들

28 우리는 게임에 졌지만, 아주 즐거웠다.

29 우리가 만든 로봇들을 봐.

30 귀엽지 않니?

31 우리는 한 씨 할아버지께 드릴 큰 케이크를 만들었다.

32 그것은 할아버지를 행복하게 해 주었다.

33 나처럼 잘생긴 피터 팬을 본 적이 있니?

34 학교생활에 대해 어떻게 생각하니?

35 가장 불편한 순간

36 1. 시험을 칠 때

37 2. 정말 배가 고픈데 먹을 것이 없을 때

38 3. 체육 시간 전후에 옷을 갈아입을 때

39 4. 기타: 수업 중에 졸릴 때

40 종이 울렸는데 선생님이 수업을 끝내지 않을 때

41 가장 사랑스러운 시간

42 1. 점심시간

43 2. 가장 좋아하는 선생님의 수업 시간

44 3. 금요일의 마지막 수업 시간

45 4. 기타: 쉬는 시간에 잠잘 때

46 거울 속의 나를 볼 때

47 가장 멋진 뉴스

48 1. 전보다 좋은 성적을 받았다

49 2. 오늘 수업이 일찍 끝난다

50 3. 비나 눈이 많이 와서 학교에 가지 않는다

51 4. 기타: 후식으로 맛있는 단것을 먹는다

52 가장 친한 친구와 내가 같은 반이 되었다

53 가장 하기 힘든 일

54 1. 쓰레기통 씻기

55 2. _____

56 3. _____ _____ _____ in front of friends

57 4. others: Being _____ _____ every day

58 Group work

59 _____ We Love in Our _____

60 Daehan _____ Market

61 If you want to eat _____ _____, visit Daehan Market.

62 You can buy "*yeopjeon*" and use it to _____ your lunch box _____.

63 You can _____ many kinds of food and _____ them _____ your lunch box.

64 Saebom _____ Center

65 This is Saebom Youth Center _____ _____ _____ _____ our town.

66 We like this place because we can learn many things, _____ _____ dance and music.

67 We can also play board games and _____ _____ _____ here.

68 Mr. Kim's Bakery

69 This is a small bakery _____ the school.

70 We like to go there _____ school _____ we're always hungry!

71 It is good _____ _____ delicious bread with friends.

72 Let's _____ _____ with Puzzles!

73 _____ Puzzles

74 If you _____ the shape A _____ two same pieces, you can then make all the other shapes(B, C, D, E, F, G) _____ those two pieces.

75 Ten Balls in _____

76 Place 10 balls in 5 lines _____ _____ _____ _____ that each line has exactly 4 balls on it.

55 2. 공부하기

56 3. 친구들 앞에서 발표하기

57 4. 기타: 매일 제시간에 등교하기

58 모둠 활동

59 우리 마을에서 우리가 좋아하는 곳

60 대한 전통 시장

61 맛있는 것이 먹고 싶으면, 대한 시장을 방문하세요.

62 엽전을 사면 여러분의 점심 도시락을 가득 채우는 데 그걸 쓸 수 있어요.

63 많은 종류의 음식을 골라서 점심 도시락에 담을 수 있답니다.

64 새봄 청소년 센터

65 이곳은 우리 마을 한가운데에 있는 새봄 청소년 센터입니다.

66 춤과 음악 같은 많은 것을 배울 수 있어서 우리는 이곳을 좋아한답니다.

67 우리는 또한 이곳에서 보드게임도 하고 휴식도 취할 수 있어요.

68 김 씨네 빵집

69 이곳은 학교 근처의 작은 빵집입니다.

70 우리는 항상 배가 고파서 방과 후에 거기에 가는 것을 좋아해요!

71 친구들과 맛있는 빵을 즐기는 것이 좋아요.

72 퍼즐로 즐거운 시간을 보내자!

73 도형 퍼즐

74 A를 똑같은 두 개의 조각으로 자르면, 그 두 조각으로 다른 모든 형태(B, C, D, E, F, G)를 만들 수 있다.

75 5개의 선에 놓인 10개의 공

76 각각의 선 위에 정확하게 4개의 공이 놓이도록 10개의 공을 5개의 선에 놓아라.

77 You Are _____ Plastic Spoons!

78 1. A lot of plastic spoons _____ _____ _____ every year.

79 2. Most plastic _____ _____ smaller pieces in the ocean.

80 3. Very small pieces of plastic _____ into _____ .

81 4. If you eat the fish, you eat the plastic, too. _____ _____ 11,000 pieces each year!

82 _____ Make a Dream School!

83 We had a _____ _____ contest for our school last month.

84 Here are the _____ _____ .

85 1. When your hands _____ _____ , water comes out.

86 When you _____ your hands _____ , the water stops.

87 You don't _____ _____ turn or touch any parts.

88 We can _____ _____ _____ _____ with this. – by O Juyeon(1-3)

89 2. This is our school park _____ two buildings.

90 Anybody can go _____ and _____ _____ here.

91 Also we can sit and _____ _____ _____ here. – by Gim Jimin(3-5)

92 3. These are _____ desks and chairs for the classroom.

93 For group activities, you can get them _____ and make a wonderful group table _____ three, four, or five students. – by Choi Yumi(2-1)

94 LET'S _____

95 Funny Earth Day _____ Ha! Ha! Ha!

96 Why are recycle bins _____ ?

97 Because they're _____ _____ cans.

98 _____ can you tell the ocean is _____ ?

99 It waves.

100 _____ did the sun go to school?

101 _____ _____ brighter.

77 너는 플라스틱 숟가락을 먹고 있다!

78 1. 해마다 많은 플라스틱 숟가락이 버려진다.

79 2. 대부분의 플라스틱 숟가락은 바닷속에서 더 작은 조각으로 부서진다.

80 3. 아주 작은 플라스틱 조각들이 물고기의 몸속으로 들어간다.

81 4. 여러분이 그 물고기를 먹으면 여러분도 플라스틱을 먹게 되는 것이다. 해마다 11,000개의 조각까지!

82 꿈의 학교를 만들어 보자!

83 지난달에 우리는 우리 학교를 위한 유니버설 디자인 경시대회를 열었습니다.

84 여기 우승자들의 작품이 있습니다.

85 1. 손을 가까이 가져가면 물이 나옵니다.

86 손을 멀리 떨어뜨리면 물이 멈춥니다.

87 어떤 부분도 돌리거나 만질 필요가 없습니다.

88 우리는 이것으로 많은 물을 절약할 수 있답니다. — 오주연(1–3)

89 2. 이것은 두 개의 건물 사이에 있는 학교 정원입니다.

90 여기서는 누구라도 쉽게 위아래로 이동할 수 있습니다.

91 또한, 우리는 이곳에 앉아 휴식을 취할 수 있습니다. — 김지민 (3–5)

92 3. 교실용의 특별한 책상과 의자가 있습니다.

93 모둠 활동을 하기 위해 그것들을 함께 모아 3명, 4명, 또는 5명이 활동할 훌륭한 모둠 책상을 만들 수 있습니다. — 최유미 (2–1)

94 웃읍시다

95 재미있는 지구의 날 농담들 하! 하! 하!

96 재활용 통은 왜 희망적인가?

97 왜냐하면 '깡통[할 수 있다]'으로 가득 차 있기 때문이지.

98 바다가 다정하다는 것을 어떻게 알 수 있는가?

99 그것이 일렁이기[손을 흔들기] 때문이지.

100 태양은 왜 학교에 가는가?

101 더 밝아지기[똑똑해지기] 위해서지.

● 우리말을 참고하여 본문을 영작하시오.

1 십대들의 잡지
➡ _____

2 모양으로 표현된 예술 작품
➡ _____

3 동그라미처럼
➡ _____

4 나는 동그라미처럼 너를 사랑해. 왜냐하면 동그라미는 절대 끝나지 않기에.
➡ _____

5 눈사람
➡ _____

6 바깥은 추워.
➡ _____

7 나는 밖으로 나가 놀고 싶지 않네.
➡ _____

8 하지만 엄마는 그래야 한다고 하시네.
➡ _____

9 눈이 오기 시작하고 나는 추워질 거야.
➡ _____

10 나는 이런 날에는 나가서 놀고 싶지 않아.
➡ _____

11 하지만 잠깐만, 나는 최고로 멋진 생각이 났어!
➡ _____

12 나는 눈으로 내 몸을 완전히 덮고 여기에 숨어야지!
➡ _____

13 손 글씨로 돌아보기
➡ _____

14 인생은 예술이다.
➡ _____

15 다양한 색깔로 살아라.
➡ _____

16 끝날 때까지 끝난 게 아니다.
➡ _____

17 나는 느리게 걷는 사람이지만 절대 물러서지는 않는다.
➡ _____

18 나는 네가 하는 작은 일들을 사랑해.
➡ _____

19 네 꿈을 좇으라.
➡ _____

20 나의 자전거
➡ _____

21 바퀴 두 개가 나를 데려가네 / 어느 곳으로든지 / 학교로 / 다시 집으로 / 산으로 / 강으로 / 나는 내 자전거가 아주 좋아 / 나는 그걸 매일 즐겨 타네
➡ _____

22 아낌없이 주는 나무
➡ _____

23 저곳 바깥은 – 젖어 있고
➡ _____

24 이곳 안쪽은 – 말라 있네
➡ _____

25 엄청 큰 우산이네
➡ _____

26 나와 하늘 사이에 있는
➡ _____

27 올해의 셀피들
➡ _____

28 우리는 게임에 졌지만, 아주 즐거웠다.
➡ _____

29 우리가 만든 로봇들을 봐.
➡ _____

30 귀엽지 않니?
➡ _____

31 우리는 한 씨 할아버지께 드릴 큰 케이크를 만들었다.
➡ _____

32 그것은 할아버지를 행복하게 해 주었다.
➡ _____

33 나처럼 잘생긴 피터 팬을 본 적이 있니?
➡ _____

34 학교생활에 대해 어떻게 생각하니?
➡ _____

35 가장 불편한 순간
➡ _____

36 1. 시험을 칠 때
➡ _____

37 2. 정말 배가 고픈데 먹을 것이 없을 때
➡ _____

38 3. 체육 시간 전후에 옷을 갈아입을 때
➡ _____

39 4. 기타: 수업 중에 졸릴 때
➡ _____

40 종이 울렸는데 선생님이 수업을 끝내지 않을 때
➡ _____

41 가장 사랑스러운 시간
➡ _____

42 1. 점심시간
➡ _____

43 2. 가장 좋아하는 선생님의 수업 시간
➡ _____

44 3. 금요일의 마지막 수업 시간
➡ _____

45 4. 기타: 쉬는 시간에 잠잘 때
➡ _____

46 거울 속의 나를 볼 때
➡ _____

47 가장 멋진 뉴스
➡ _____

48 1. 전보다 좋은 성적을 받았다
➡ _____

49 2. 오늘 수업이 일찍 끝난다
➡ _____

50 3. 비나 눈이 많이 와서 학교에 가지 않는다
➡ _____

51 4. 기타: 후식으로 맛있는 단것을 먹는다
➡ _____

52 가장 친한 친구와 내가 같은 반이 되었다
➡ _____

53 가장 하기 힘든 일
➡ _____

54 1. 쓰레기통 씻기
➡ _____

55 2. 공부하기
➡ _____

56 3. 친구들 앞에서 발표하기
➡ _____

57 4. 기타: 매일 제시간에 등교하기
➡ _____

58 모둠 활동
➡ _____

59 우리 마을에서 우리가 좋아하는 곳
➡ _____

60 대한 전통 시장
➡ _____

61 맛있는 것이 먹고 싶으면, 대한 시장을 방문하세요.
➡ _____

62 엽전을 사면 여러분의 점심 도시락을 가득 채우는 데 그걸 쓸 수 있어요.
➡ _____

63 많은 종류의 음식을 골라서 점심 도시락에 담을 수 있답니다.
➡ _____

64 새봄 청소년 센터
➡ _____

65 이곳은 우리 마을 한가운데에 있는 새봄 청소년 센터입니다.
➡ _____

66 춤과 음악 같은 많은 것을 배울 수 있어서 우리는 이곳을 좋아한답니다.
➡ _____

67 우리는 또한 이곳에서 보드게임도 하고 휴식도 취할 수 있어요.
➡ _____

68 김 씨네 빵집
➡ _____

69 이곳은 학교 근처의 작은 빵집입니다.
➡ _____

70 우리는 항상 배가 고파서 방과 후에 거기에 가는 것을 좋아해요!
➡ _____

71 친구들과 맛있는 빵을 즐기는 것이 좋아요.
➡ _____

72 퍼즐로 즐거운 시간을 보내자!
➡ _____

73 도형 퍼즐
➡ _____

74 A를 똑같은 두 개의 조각으로 자르면, 그 두 조각으로 다른 모든 형태(B, C, D, E, F, G)를 만들 수 있다.
➡ _____

75 5개의 선에 놓인 10개의 공
➡ _____

76 각각의 선 위에 정확하게 4개의 공이 놓이도록 10개의 공을 5개의 선에 놓아라.
➡ _____

77 너는 플라스틱 숟가락을 먹고 있다!
➡ _____

78 1. 해마다 많은 플라스틱 숟가락이 버려진다.
➡ _____

79 2. 대부분의 플라스틱 숟가락은 바닷속에서 더 작은 조각으로 부서진다.
➡ _____

80 3. 아주 작은 플라스틱 조각들이 물고기의 몸속으로 들어간다.
➡ _____

81 4. 여러분이 그 물고기를 먹으면 여러분도 플라스틱을 먹게 되는 것이다. 해마다 11,000개의 조각까지!
➡ _____

82 꿈의 학교를 만들어 보자!
➡ _____

83 지난달에 우리는 우리 학교를 위한 유니버설 디자인 경시대회를 열었습니다.
➡ _____

84 여기 우승자들의 작품이 있습니다.
➡ _____

85 1. 손을 가까이 가져가면 물이 나옵니다.
➡ _____

86 손을 멀리 떨어뜨리면 물이 멈춥니다.
➡ _____

87 어떤 부분도 돌리거나 만질 필요가 없습니다.
➡ _____

88 우리는 이것으로 많은 물을 절약할 수 있답니다. ― 오주연(1-3)
➡ _____

89 2. 이것은 두 개의 건물 사이에 있는 학교 정원입니다.
➡ _____

90 여기서는 누구라도 쉽게 위아래로 이동할 수 있습니다.
➡ _____

91 또한, 우리는 이곳에 앉아 휴식을 취할 수 있습니다. ― 김지민(3-5)
➡ _____

92 3. 교실용의 특별한 책상과 의자가 있습니다.
➡ _____

93 모둠 활동을 하기 위해 그것들을 함께 모아 3명, 4명, 또는 5명이 활동할 훌륭한 모둠 책상을 만들 수 있습니다. ― 최유미(2-1)
➡ _____
_____

94 웃읍시다
➡ _____

95 재미있는 지구의 날 농담들 하! 하! 하!
➡ _____

96 재활용 통은 왜 희망적인가?
➡ _____

97 왜냐하면 '깡통[할 수 있다]'으로 가득 차 있기 때문이지.
➡ _____

98 바다가 다정하다는 것을 어떻게 알 수 있는가?
➡ _____

99 그것이 일렁이기[손을 흔들기] 때문이지.
➡ _____

100 태양은 왜 학교에 가는가?
➡ _____

101 더 밝아지기[똑똑해지기] 위해서지.
➡ _____

01 다음 문장에 공통으로 들어갈 말을 쓰시오.

(1) _____ we lost the game, we had a lot of fun.

(2) _____ Tim often annoyed Anne, she was fond of him.

➡ _____

02 다음 빈칸에 들어갈 말을 〈보기〉에서 찾아 쓰시오. (필요하면 변형하여 쓰시오.)

┌─ 보기 ─┐
throw away / such as / friend

(1) We like this place because we can learn many things, _____ dance and music.

(2) A lot of plastic spoons _____ every year.

(3) How can you tell that the ocean is _____?

03 영영풀이에 해당하는 단어를 〈보기〉에서 찾아 첫 번째 칸에 쓰고, 두 번째 칸에는 우리말 뜻을 쓰시오.

┌─ 보기 ─┐
grade / wheel / bread / circle

(1) _____: a circular object connected at the centre to a bar, used for making vehicles or parts of machines move: _____

(2) _____: a continuous curved line, the points of which are always the same distance away from a fixed central point: _____

(3) _____: a number or letter that shows how good someone's work or performance is: _____

(4) _____: a food made from flour, water, and usually yeast, mixed together and baked: _____

04 우리말과 같은 뜻이 되도록 빈칸을 채우시오.

(1) 여기에 우승자들의 작품이 있습니다.
➡ Here are the winners' _____.

(2) 교실용의 특별한 책상과 의자가 있습니다.
➡ There are _____ desks and chairs for the classroom.

05 어법상 어색한 것을 고쳐 바르게 쓰시오.

(1) I'll cover up myself with snow and I'll hide here!
➡ _____

(2) Her daughter was made for a cloth doll by her.
➡ _____

(3) When have you gone to Seoul?
➡ _____

06 주어진 어휘를 이용하여 영작하시오.

(1) 그는 젊지만 새치가 많다. (though, gray hair, 9 단어) (though로 시작할 것)
➡ _____

(2) 친구가 있는 것은 좋다. (it, good, have, to)
➡ _____

[07~09] 다음 글을 읽고 물음에 답하시오.

Snowman

It's cold outside.

I don't want to go out and play.

But Mom says I @have to.

It's starting to snow and I'm going to be cold.

I don't ___(A)___ playing outside on days __(B)__ these.

But wait a second, I have ⓑthe most wonderful idea!

I'll cover myself up with snow and I'll hide here!

brrr...

07 위 글의 빈칸 (A)와 (B)에 공통으로 들어갈 알맞은 말을 쓰시오.

➡ _____

중요
08 위 글의 밑줄 친 @have to 뒤에 생략된 말을 쓰시오.

➡ _____

09 위 글의 밑줄 친 ⓑ가 가리키는 것을 본문에서 찾아 쓰시오.

➡ _____

[10~12] 다음 글을 읽고 물음에 답하시오.

You Are Eating Plastic Spoons!

1. @A lot of plastic spoons are thrown away every year.

2. Most plastic breaks down into smaller pieces in the ocean.

3. Very small pieces of plastic go into fish.

4. ⓑIf you eat the fish, you eat the plastic, too. Up to ©11,000 pieces each year!

중요
10 위 글의 밑줄 친 @를 능동태로 고치시오.

➡ _____
_____

11 다음 빈칸에 알맞은 단어를 넣어, 위 글에서 밑줄 친 ⓑ처럼 말한 이유를 완성하시오.

> That's because when you eat the fish, you eat not only the fish _____ _____ the very small pieces of plastic that the fish ate.

12 위 글의 밑줄 친 ©를 읽는 법을 영어로 쓰시오.

➡ _____

고 난이도
[13~15] 다음 글을 읽고 물음에 답하시오.

LET'S LAUGH
Funny Earth Day Jokes Ha! Ha! Ha!

Why are recycle bins hopeful?

- Because they're full of @cans.

How can you tell the ocean is friendly?

- It ⓑwaves.

Why did the sun go to school?

- To get ©brighter.

13 위 글의 밑줄 친 @can의 중의적인 뜻을 우리말로 쓰시오.

➡ 본래의 뜻: _____ 숨어 있는 뜻: _____

14 위 글의 밑줄 친 ⓑwaves의 중의적인 뜻을 우리말로 쓰시오.

➡ 본래의 뜻: _____ 숨어 있는 뜻: _____

15 위 글의 밑줄 친 ©brighter의 중의적인 뜻을 우리말로 쓰시오.

➡ 본래의 뜻: _____ 숨어 있는 뜻: _____

출제율 95%

01 다음 단어에 대한 영어 설명이 <u>어색한</u> 것은?

① choose: to decide what you want from two or more things or possibilities
② youth: the period of your life when you are young, or the state of being young
③ shake hands: to raise your hand and move it from side to side as a way of greeting someone
④ friendly: behaving in a pleasant, kind way towards someone
⑤ save: to keep something, especially money, for use in the future

출제율 90%

02 다음 짝지어진 단어의 관계가 같도록 빈칸에 알맞은 말을 쓰시오.

exactly : accurately = such as : _____

출제율 95%

03 다음 주어진 글의 제목을 쓰고자 할 때 빈칸에 들어갈 단어로 알맞은 것은?

The most _____ moment
1. When I take tests
2. When I am really hungry and have nothing to eat
3. When I change clothes before and after P.E. class

① exciting　　　　② amazing
③ uncomfortable　④ lovely
⑤ friendly

출제율 100%

04 다음 〈보기〉의 단어를 활용하여 빈칸에 두 단어로 쓰시오.

┤ 보기 ├
break / up / lot

(1) Most plastic _____ into smaller pieces in the ocean.
(2) If you eat the fish, you eat the plastic, too. _____ 11,000 pieces each year!
(3) We can save _____ water with this invention.

출제율 95%

05 다음 우리말에 맞게 주어진 문장의 빈칸에 들어갈 말을 쓰시오.

(1) A를 똑같은 두 개의 조각으로 자르면, 그 두 조각으로 다른 모든 형태(B, C, D, E, F, G)를 만들 수 있다.
➡ If you _____ the shape A _____ two same pieces, you can then make all the other _____ (B, C, D, E, F, G) from those two pieces.
(2) 바퀴 두 개가 어느 곳으로든지 나를 데려간다.
➡ Two wheels _____ me _____ any place.

출제율 90%

06 다음 영영풀이에 해당하는 단어는?

sweet food eaten at the end of a meal

① dessert　　② batter
③ recipe　　　④ desert
⑤ cooker

출제율 90%

07 다음 중 짝지어진 단어의 관계가 <u>다른</u> 것은?

① push : pull　　　② handsome : ugly
③ outside : inside　④ sleepy : drowsy
⑤ close : far

08 다음 문장의 빈칸에 공통으로 들어갈 말을 쓰시오.

> • I'll cover myself _____ with snow and I'll hide here!
> • Anybody can go _____ and down easily here.

09 다음 중 어법상 적절한 것은?

① Place 10 balls in 5 lines in a such way that each line has exactly 4 balls on it.
② How can you tell is the ocean friendly?
③ Many kinds of food can be chosen for you.
④ If you eat the fish, you eat the plastic, either.
⑤ A little of plastic spoons are thrown away every year.

10 다음 중 밑줄 친 부분의 쓰임이 나머지 넷과 다른 것은?

① It is fun to play *tuho*.
② How long does it take from here to the station?
③ Was it interesting to play the game?
④ It's now safe to unplug your USB Disk.
⑤ It's no use shouting.

11 다음 문장을 주어진 문장의 빈칸을 채워 같은 뜻의 문장으로 바꿔 쓰시오.

> We like this place because we can learn many things.

➡ We can learn many things, _____
_____ .

12 다음 문장에서 어법상 어색한 것을 바르게 고쳐 쓰시오.

(1) We have had a universal design contest for our school last month.

➡ _____
_____

(2) That is good to enjoy delicious bread with friends.

➡ _____

[13~15] 다음 글을 읽고 물음에 답하시오.

Snowman

It's cold outside.
I don't want to go out and play.
But Mom says I have to.
It's ⓐstarting to snow and I'm going to be cold.
I don't like ⓑplaying outside on ⓒdays like these.
But wait a second, I have the most wonderful idea!
ⓓI'll cover me up with snow and I'll hide here!
brrr...
brrr...

13 다음 〈보기〉에서 위 글의 밑줄 친 ⓐstarting, ⓑplaying과 문법적 쓰임이 같은 것을 각각 고르시오.

> ① Getting up early in the morning is hard.
> ② Look at the flying bird.
> ③ She stopped smoking for the health.
> ④ Learning Japanese is very interesting.
> ⑤ She is walking to the park.

➡ ⓐ _____ ⓑ _____

14 위 글의 밑줄 친 ⓒdays like these는 어떤 날을 의미하는지 우리말로 쓰시오.

➡ _____

15 위 글의 밑줄 친 ⓓ에서 어법상 틀린 부분을 찾아 고치시오.

_____ ➡ _____

[16~18] 다음 글을 읽고 물음에 답하시오.

> **Selfies of This Year**
>
> ⓐ_____ we lost the game, we had a lot of fun. Look at the robots ⓑwe made. Aren't they cute?
>
> We made a big cake for Mr. Han. It made him happy.
>
> ⓒHave you ever seen a handsome Peter Pan like me?

16 위 글의 빈칸 ⓐ에 들어갈 알맞은 말을 고르시오.

① Because ② If ③ As
④ Though ⑤ While

17 위 글의 밑줄 친 ⓑwe made 앞에 생략된 말을 쓰시오.

➡ _____

18 아래 〈보기〉에서 위 글의 밑줄 친 ⓒ와 현재완료의 용법이 같은 것의 개수를 고르시오.

> ┤ 보기 ├
> ① How many times have you seen a monkey?
> ② He has gone to America.
> ③ I have just finished my work.
> ④ I have never met her before.
> ⑤ How long have you known Mrs. green?

① 1개 ② 2개 ③ 3개 ④ 4개 ⑤ 5개

[19~21] 다음 글을 읽고 물음에 답하시오.

Looking Back with Your ⓐHandwriting
Life is art. Live ⓑyours in COLOR.
IT ISN'T OVER UNTIL IT'S OVER.
I am a slow walker, but I never walk back.
I love the ⓒlittle things you do.
Follow your dream.

19 위 글의 밑줄 친 ⓐHandwriting과 바꿔 쓸 수 있는 말을 고르시오.

① Printout ② Calligraphy
③ Advertisement ④ Product
⑤ Catalog

20 위 글의 밑줄 친 ⓑyours가 가리키는 것을 영어로 쓰시오. (두 단어)

➡ _____

21 위 글의 밑줄 친 ⓒlittle과 같은 의미로 쓰인 것을 모두 고르시오.

① You still have a little time left.
② Look at the little bird.
③ I can speak English a little.
④ He lived in a little village.
⑤ She visited a little island last year.

[22~24] 다음 글을 읽고 물음에 답하시오.

The most lovely time

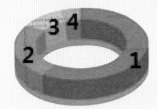

1. lunch time
2. class with my favorite teacher
3. the (A)[last / latest] class on Friday
4. others: when I am sleeping (B)[during / for]
   break time
   when I see (C)[me / myself] in the
   mirror

22 위 글의 괄호 (A)~(C)에서 문맥이나 어법상 알맞은 낱말을 골라 쓰시오.

➡ (A) _____ (B) _____ (C) _____

23 위 글의 종류로 알맞은 것을 고르시오.

① review   ② summary   ③ essay
④ article   ⑤ survey

24 위 글의 내용과 일치하지 <u>않는</u> 것은?

① The students like lunch time best.
② The students like class with their favorite teacher better than the last class on Friday.
③ The students like sleeping during break time better than eating lunch.
④ The students prefer lunch time to the last class on Friday.
⑤ The students prefer studying with their favorite teacher to sleeping during break time.

[25~27] 다음 글을 읽고 물음에 답하시오.

Places We Love in Our Village
Daehan Traditional Market -10 Likes

If you want to eat something delicious, visit Daehan Market. You can buy *"yeopjeon"* and use ⓐit ⓑto make your lunch box full. You can choose many kinds of food and add ⓒthem to your lunch box.

25 위 글의 밑줄 친 ⓐit과 ⓒthem이 가리키는 것을 본문에서 찾아 각각 쓰시오.

➡ ⓐ _____   ⓒ _____

26 위 글의 밑줄 친 ⓑto make와 to부정사의 용법이 다른 것을 <u>모두</u> 고르시오. (3개)

① To use the dictionary is necessary.
② I got up early to catch the train.
③ He grew up to be a doctor.
④ I am sorry to give you trouble.
⑤ There is no water to drink.

27 위 글의 내용과 일치하도록 다음 빈칸에 알맞은 단어를 쓰시오.

> If you want to make your lunch box full at Daehan Traditional Market, you can use "_____."

[28~30] 다음 글을 읽고 물음에 답하시오.

Selfies of This Year

Though we lost the game, we ⓐhad a lot of fun.

Look at the robots we made. Aren't ⓑthey cute?

We made a big cake for Mr. Han. ⓒIt made him happily.

Have you ever seen a handsome Peter Pan like me?

✏ 출제율 95%

28 위 글의 밑줄 친 ⓐ를 다음과 같이 바꿔 쓸 때 빈칸에 들어갈 알맞은 말을 쓰시오.

➡ had a great _____ = enjoyed _____ very much

✏ 출제율 85%

29 위 글의 밑줄 친 ⓑthey가 가리키는 것을 본문에서 찾아 쓰시오.

➡ _____

✏ 출제율 90%

30 위 글의 밑줄 친 ⓒ에서 어법상 틀린 부분을 찾아 고치시오.

_____ ➡ _____

[31~33] 다음 글을 읽고 물음에 답하시오.

The most (A)[awesome / awful] news

1. I got better grades than before
2. School finishes earlier today
3. I don't go to school ⓐbecause it rains or snows a lot
4. others: We eat delicious sweets for (B) [desert / dessert]
   My best friend and I are in (C) [different / the same] class

✏ 출제율 95%

31 위 글의 괄호 (A)~(C)에서 문맥상 알맞은 낱말을 골라 쓰시오.

➡ (A) _____ (B) _____ (C) _____

✏ 출제율 90%

32 위 글의 밑줄 친 ⓐ를 다음과 같이 바꿔 쓸 때 빈칸에 들어갈 알맞은 말을 쓰시오. (of를 이용할 것)

➡ _____ the heavy rain or snow

✏ 출제율 90%

33 다음 문장에서 위 글의 내용과 <u>다른</u> 부분을 찾아서 고치시오.

> To the students, the news that school finishes earlier than usual is the most wonderful news.

➡ _____
_____
_____

[34~36] 다음 글을 읽고 물음에 답하시오.

ⓐ _____

Saebom Youth Center - 12 Likes

This is Saebom Youth Center in the middle of our town. We like this place because we can learn many things, ⓑsuch as dance and music. We can also play board games and take a break here.

✏ 출제율 100%

34 위 글의 빈칸 ⓐ에 들어갈 제목으로 알맞은 것을 고르시오.

① What Do You Think of Your School Life?
② Places We Love in Our Village
③ Let's Have Fun with Puzzles!
④ Let's Make a Dream School!
⑤ Funny Earth Day Jokes Ha! Ha! Ha!

✏ 출제율 90%

35 위 글의 밑줄 친 ⓑsuch as와 바꿔 쓸 수 있는 한 단어를 쓰시오.

➡ _____

✏ 출제율 95%

36 위 글의 새봄 청소년 센터에서 할 수 있는 일로 언급되지 <u>않</u>은 것을 고르시오.

① 춤을 배울 수 있다.
② 음악을 배울 수 있다.
③ 보드 게임을 할 수 있다.
④ 하이킹을 갈 수 있다.
⑤ 휴식을 취할 수 있다.

INSIGHT
on the textbook
교과서 파헤치기

※ 다음 영어를 우리말로 쓰시오.

01 awesome

02 below

03 classical

04 actually

05 example

06 season

07 unique

08 widely

09 excellent

10 difference

11 express

12 fantasy

13 include

14 dynasty

15 wizard

16 tale

17 detective

18 craft

19 figure

20 artistic

21 performance

22 poem

23 foreign

24 creative

25 popular

26 monster

27 both

28 perfect

29 tool

30 imagine

31 handwriting

32 lightning

33 collect

34 sharp

35 be made of

36 lead to

37 build up

38 look like+명사

39 take a class

40 take+시간+to V

41 for free

42 dance to

43 at first

※ 다음 우리말을 영어로 쓰시오.

01 ~의 아래에 _____

02 탐정; 탐정의 _____

03 공예 _____

04 실제로 _____

05 완벽한 _____

06 글자, 성격 _____

07 공연 _____

08 판타지, 환상, 공상 _____

09 창의적인 _____

10 멋있는, 대단한, 굉장한 _____

11 손 글씨, 필적 _____

12 잡다 _____

13 훌륭한, 뛰어난 _____

14 (사람, 동물의) 상, 모형 _____

15 시 _____

16 왕조, 왕가 _____

17 차이 _____

18 예술의, 예술적인 _____

19 이야기 _____

20 공포 _____

21 널리 _____

22 인기 있는 _____

23 꼬리 _____

24 외국의 _____

25 배우다 _____

26 번개 _____

27 예, 사례 _____

28 ~의 사이에 _____

29 모으다 _____

30 괴물 _____

31 마법사 _____

32 날카로운 _____

33 표현하다 _____

34 독특한, 특별한 _____

35 ~에 맞춰 춤추다 _____

36 처음에 _____

37 만들다 _____

38 무료로 _____

39 ~에 관심이 있다 _____

40 ~로 이끌다, ~로 이어지다 _____

41 ~로 만들어지다 _____

42 수업을 듣다 _____

43 ~처럼 보이다 _____

※ 다음 영영풀이에 알맞은 단어를 <보기>에서 골라 쓴 후, 우리말 뜻을 쓰시오.

1 _____ : relating to any form of art: _____

2 _____ : in a lower place or position: _____

3 _____ : not the same as anything or anyone else: _____

4 _____ : a man in stories who has magic powers: _____

5 _____ : a series of rulers of a country who all belong to the same family:

_____

6 _____ : to show feeling or opinion: _____

7 _____ : to make someone or something part of a group: _____

8 _____ : the bright flashes of light that you see in the sky during a storm:

_____

9 _____ : at the present time: _____

10 _____ : the season between summer and winter: _____

11 _____ : liked by most people: _____

12 _____ : a story about imaginary events or people: _____

13 _____ : one of four periods of year that is based on the earth's position toward

the sun: _____

14 _____ : the name of a book, poem, movie, play, or other work of art: _____

15 _____ : a piece of equipment, usually one you hold in your hand, that is designed

to do a particular type of work: _____

16 _____ : a piece of writing using beautiful or unusual language arranged in fixed

lines that have a particular beat and often rhyme: _____

보기			
tale	title	unique	below
poem	autumn	season	express
wizard	artistic	dynasty	lightning
nowadays	tool	popular	include

※ 다음 우리말과 일치하도록 빈칸에 알맞은 말을 쓰시오.

Get Ready 2

(1) B: Do you like K-pop?
　 G: Yes. I _____ _____ to SJ's songs. I can _____ _____ his songs.
　 B: _____!

(2) B: _____ you _____ _____ _____ Korean dishes?
　 W: Yes. I _____ cook *bulgogi* _____ my family and they love it.

(3) B: _____ _____ _____ _____ _____ _____ *Hangeul*?
　 G: Yes. _____, I'm learning it in my _____ _____. Look! This is my _____.
　 B: _____!

Start Off Listen & Talk A

(1) B: _____ _____! Someone is _____ a cloud? _____ _____!
　 G: Thank you. Are you _____ _____ _____ _____ _____?
　 B: Yes, I am. Actually, I'm _____ an _____ _____ _____.
　 G: Oh, _____ _____ you.

(2) G: _____ work! I think your painting _____ the _____ of _____ well.
　 B: Thank you. _____ you _____ in painting?
　 G: Yes, I am. I started _____ a class _____ _____.
　 B: Oh, I _____ know _____.

Start Off Listen & Talk B

B: You _____ a good _____! It's _____.
G: Thanks.
B: What is it _____ _____? Glass?
G: Yes, it is. _____ you _____ _____ _____ _____ _____?
B: Yes, very much. _____ _____ did it _____ _____ _____ it?
G: _____ _____ one month.

Speak Up Look and talk

B: I _____ your _____. You did _____ _____ _____.
G: Thank you. Are you _____ in _____ _____ ukulele?
B: Sure. _____ _____ teach me?
G: No _____.

(1) B: 너는 K-pop을 좋아하니?
　 G: 응. 나는 SJ의 노래를 듣는 것을 즐겨. 그의 노래에 맞춰 춤을 출 수 있어.
　 B: 멋지다!

(2) B: 당신은 한국 음식을 요리하는 것에 관심이 있나요?
　 W: 네. 때때로 저는 가족을 위해 불고기를 요리하고 그들은 그것을 좋아해요.

(3) B: 너는 한글 배우는 것에 관심이 있니?
　 G: 응. 실제로, 나는 캘리그래피 수업에서 한글을 배우고 있어. 봐! 이게 나의 작품이야.
　 B: 훌륭하다!

(1) B: 잘했다! 누군가 구름을 잡고 있는 거야? 정말 창의적이구나!
　 G: 고마워. 너는 사진 찍는 것에 관심이 있니?
　 B: 응, 그래. 사실, 나는 무료 온라인 강좌를 듣고 있어.
　 G: 오, 잘됐구나.

(2) G: 잘했다! 네 그림은 가을 느낌을 잘 표현하고 있는 것 같아.
　 B: 고마워. 너는 그림에 관심이 있니?
　 G: 응, 그래. 나는 주말마다 수업을 듣기 시작했어.
　 B: 오, 몰랐어.

B: 너 정말 잘했구나! 정말 멋져.
G: 고마워.
B: 무엇으로 만든 거니? 유리?
G: 응, 그래. 너는 유리 공예에 관심이 있니?
B: 응, 많이 관심 있어. 그거 만드는 데 시간이 얼마나 걸렸니?
G: 한 달 걸렸어.

B: 너의 공연 즐거웠어. 정말 잘했어.
G: 고마워. 너는 우쿨렐레 연주하는 것에 관심이 있니?
B: 물론이야. 날 가르쳐 줄 수 있니?
G: 그럼.

Speak Up Mission

A: Are you _____ _____ _____ _____ movies?
B: Yes, I _____. I watch horror movies very often. / No, _____
_____. I'm _____ _____ _____ _____ stories.

A: 너는 공포 영화 보는 것에 관심이 있
니?
B: 응, 그래. 나는 공포 영화를 아주 자
주 봐. / 아니, 그렇지 않아. 나는 탐
정 소설 읽는 것에 관심이 있어.

Real-life Scene

James: What _____ you _____, Mina?
Mina: I'm _____ _____.
James: You're _____ with a brush. It _____ _____.
Mina: Are you _____ in _____?
James: Yes, very much.
Mina: Look at this! I just wrote it. _____ do you _____?
James: It _____ _____ a person _____ with _____ arms.
Mina: You _____ it. This Korean word _____ "dance."
James: You _____ a good _____! Can I _____ it?
Mina: _____ _____? Take this _____.

James: 미나야, 뭐 하고 있니?
미나: 캘리그래피를 연습하고 있어.
James: 너는 붓으로 쓰고 있구나. 재미
있어 보인다.
미나: 너는 캘리그래피에 관심이 있니?
James: 응, 무척.
미나: 이것 봐! 내가 방금 썼어. 어떻게
생각해?
James: 두 팔을 벌리고 춤을 추는 사
람처럼 보여.
미나: 바로 그거야. 이 한글 단어가 '춤'
이라는 뜻이거든.
James: 잘했다! 내가 해 봐도 되니?
미나: 물론이야. 이 붓을 잡아.

Your Turn

A: You're _____ _____. What's this?
B: It's my _____ _____. Do you like it?
A: Sure. I think you _____ a _____ job!

A: 너 뭔가 쓰고 있구나. 이게 뭐야?
B: 내 미술 숙제야. 마음에 드니?
A: 물론이야. 잘한 것 같아!

Express Yourself

(1) B: Look! Two girls are _____ Hangeul.
G: Are you _____ _____ Hangeul, Kevin?
B: Yes, very much. I want to _____ them and _____ it.

(2) B: Julie, are you _____ _____ hanbok?
G: _____ really.
B: Then, _____ are you _____ in?
G: Well, I'm _____ in taekwondo. It is a _____ Korean sport.
It's _____.

(3) G: _____ _____ the two men _____ pansori.
B: Are you _____ in pansori, Nancy?
G: Sure. I like the _____ of it. I _____ _____ _____ it.

(1) B: 봐! 두 여자아이가 한글을 배우고
있어.
G: 너는 한글에 관심이 있니,
Kevin?
B: 응, 무척. 나는 그들과 합류해서
그것을 배우고 싶어.

(2) B: Julie, 너 한복에 관심이 있니?
G: 사실은 관심이 없어.
B: 그럼, 너는 무엇에 관심이 있니?
G: 음, 나는 태권도에 관심이 있어.
그것은 한국 전통 스포츠야. 아주
멋져.

(3) G: 판소리를 배우고 있는 두 남자 좀
봐.
B: 너는 판소리에 관심이 있니,
Nancy?
G: 물론이야. 나는 그 소리가 좋아.
그것을 배우고 싶어.

Learning Diary Listen & Speak

B: Minji, are you _____ in animals?
G: Yes, I am. I'm _____ _____ _____ _____
them.
B: _____ _____ plants? Are you _____ in them, _____?
G: No, I'm not. I _____ _____ them well.

B: 민지야, 너는 동물에 관심이 있니?
G: 응, 그래. 나는 동물을 돌보는 것을
잘해.
B: 식물은 어떠니? 식물에도 관심이 있
니?
G: 아니, 없어. 식물은 잘 못 키워.

대화문 Test

※ 다음 우리말에 맞도록 대화를 영어로 쓰시오.

Get Ready 2

(1) B: _____
   G: _____
   B: _____

(2) B: _____
   W: _____

(3) B: _____
   G: _____
   B: _____

Start Off Listen & Talk A

(1) B: _____
   G: _____
   B: _____
   G: _____

(2) G: _____
   B: _____
   G: _____
   B: _____

Start Off Listen & Talk B

B: _____
G: _____
B: _____
G: _____
B: _____
G: _____

Speak Up Look and talk

B: _____
G: _____
B: _____
G: _____

해석

(1) B: 너는 K-pop을 좋아하니?
   G: 응. 나는 SJ의 노래를 듣는 것을 즐겨. 그의 노래에 맞춰 춤을 출 수 있어.
   B: 멋지다!

(2) B: 당신은 한국 음식을 요리하는 것에 관심이 있나요?
   W: 네. 때때로 저는 가족을 위해 불고기를 요리하고 그들은 그것을 좋아해요.

(3) B: 너는 한글 배우는 것에 관심이 있니?
   G: 응. 실제로, 나는 캘리그래피 수업에서 한글을 배우고 있어. 봐! 이게 나의 작품이야.
   B: 훌륭하다!

(1) B: 잘했다! 누군가 구름을 잡고 있는 거야? 정말 창의적이구나!
   G: 고마워. 너는 사진 찍는 것에 관심이 있니?
   B: 응, 그래. 사실, 나는 무료 온라인 강좌를 듣고 있어.
   G: 오, 잘됐구나.

(2) G: 잘했다! 네 그림은 가을 느낌을 잘 표현하고 있는 것 같아.
   B: 고마워. 너는 그림에 관심이 있니?
   G: 응, 그래. 나는 주말마다 수업을 듣기 시작했어.
   B: 오, 몰랐어.

B: 너 정말 잘했구나! 정말 멋져.
G: 고마워.
B: 무엇으로 만든 거니? 유리?
G: 응, 그래. 너는 유리 공예에 관심이 있니?
B: 응, 많이 관심 있어. 그거 만드는 데 시간이 얼마나 걸렸니?
G: 한 달 걸렸어.

B: 너의 공연 즐거웠어. 정말 잘했어.
G: 고마워. 너는 우쿨렐레 연주하는 것에 관심이 있니?
B: 물론이야. 날 가르쳐 줄 수 있니?
G: 그럼.

대화문 Test **07**

Speak Up Mission

A: _____

B: _____

_____

Real-life Scene

James: _____

Mina: _____

James: _____

Mina: _____

James: _____

Mina: _____

James: _____

Mina: _____

James: _____

Mina: _____

Your Turn

A: _____

B: _____

A: _____

Express Yourself

(1) B: _____

G: _____

B: _____

(2) B: _____

G: _____

B: _____

G: _____

(3) G: _____

B: _____

G: _____

Learning Diary Listen & Speak

B: _____

G: _____

B: _____

G: _____

A: 너는 공포 영화 보는 것에 관심이 있니?

B: 응, 그래. 나는 공포 영화를 아주 자주 봐. / 아니, 그렇지 않아. 나는 탐정 소설 읽는 것에 관심이 있어.

James: 미나야, 뭐 하고 있니?

미나: 캘리그래피를 연습하고 있어.

James: 너는 붓으로 쓰고 있구나. 재미있어 보인다.

미나: 너는 캘리그래피에 관심이 있니?

James: 응, 무척.

미나: 이것 봐! 내가 방금 썼어. 어떻게 생각해?

James: 두 팔을 벌리고 춤을 추는 사람처럼 보여.

미나: 바로 그거야. 이 한글 단어가 '춤'이라는 뜻이거든.

James: 잘했다! 내가 해 봐도 되니?

미나: 물론이야. 이 붓을 잡아.

A: 너 뭔가 쓰고 있구나. 이게 뭐야?

B: 내 미술 숙제야. 마음에 드니?

A: 물론이야. 잘한 것 같아!

(1) B: 봐! 두 여자아이가 한글을 배우고 있어.

G: 너는 한글에 관심이 있니, Kevin?

B: 응, 무척. 나는 그들과 합류해서 그것을 배우고 싶어.

(2) B: Julie, 너 한복에 관심이 있니?

G: 사실은 관심이 없어.

B: 그럼, 너는 무엇에 관심이 있니?

G: 음, 나는 태권도에 관심이 있어. 그것은 한국 전통 스포츠야. 아주 멋져.

(3) G: 판소리를 배우고 있는 두 남자 좀 봐.

B: 너는 판소리에 관심이 있니, Nancy?

G: 물론이야. 나는 그 소리가 좋아. 그것을 배우고 싶어.

B: 민지야, 너는 동물에 관심이 있니?

G: 응, 그래. 나는 동물을 돌보는 것을 잘해.

B: 식물은 어떠니? 식물에도 관심이 있니?

G: 아니, 없어. 식물은 잘 못 키워.

※ 다음 우리말과 일치하도록 빈칸에 알맞은 것을 골라 쓰시오.

1 ＿＿＿＿ Your ＿＿＿＿
A. Feelings　　　　B. Write

2 ＿＿＿＿ do you ＿＿＿＿ your ＿＿＿＿?
A. express　　　　B. feelings　　　　C. how

3 Do you ＿＿＿＿ or ＿＿＿＿?
A. dance　　　　B. sing

4 Do you ＿＿＿＿ a ＿＿＿＿ or ＿＿＿＿ a picture?
A. poem　　　　B. write　　　　C. draw

5 ＿＿＿＿, it is popular to ＿＿＿＿ feelings ＿＿＿＿ handwriting.
A. express　　　　B. nowadays　　　　C. through

6 Let's look ＿＿＿＿ some ＿＿＿＿ of ＿＿＿＿.
A. works　　　　B. at　　　　C. art

7 In the work of art on the right, the word ＿＿＿＿ an ＿＿＿＿ of a ＿＿＿＿ fruit, *hongsi*.
A. image　　　　B. delicious　　　　C. includes

8 It shows that ＿＿＿＿ is a ＿＿＿＿ of ＿＿＿＿.
A. season　　　　B. autumn　　　　C. fruit

9 The ＿＿＿＿ of art on the left shows a Korean ＿＿＿＿ and a ＿＿＿＿ ＿＿＿＿.
A. character　　　　B. word　　　　C. work　　　　D. Chinese

10 It ＿＿＿＿ ＿＿＿＿ a happy woman ＿＿＿＿ ＿＿＿＿ a road with autumn leaves.
A. like　　　　B. walking　　　　C. looks　　　　D. down

11 ＿＿＿＿ of these works ＿＿＿＿ the ＿＿＿＿ of autumn ＿＿＿＿ beautiful handwriting.
A. express　　　　B. through　　　　C. feeling　　　　D. both

12 This ＿＿＿＿ of art is ＿＿＿＿ ＿＿＿＿.
A. kind　　　　B. calligraphy　　　　C. called

13 Calligraphy is ＿＿＿＿ ＿＿＿＿.
A. new　　　　B. not

14 Many different ＿＿＿＿ of calligraphy ＿＿＿＿ from long ago can ＿＿＿＿ ＿＿＿＿ all around the world.
A. found　　　　B. works　　　　C. kinds　　　　D. be

15 Look ＿＿＿＿ the two ＿＿＿＿ from Korea and the UK ＿＿＿＿.
A. below　　　　B. examples　　　　C. at

16 Can you ＿＿＿＿ the ＿＿＿＿?
A. difference　　　　B. tell

17 The left one was ＿＿＿＿ ＿＿＿＿ Chusa in the ＿＿＿＿ of the Joseon Dynasty.
A. period　　　　B. created　　　　C. by

18 The characters were ＿＿＿＿ ＿＿＿＿ a soft ＿＿＿＿.
A. with　　　　B. painted　　　　C. brush

1 여러분의 느낌을 써라

2 여러분은 자신의 느낌을 어떻게 표현하는가?

3 노래를 부르거나 춤을 추는가?

4 시를 쓰거나 그림을 그리는가?

5 요즈음에는 손 글씨를 통해 감정을 표현하는 것이 인기다.

6 몇몇 작품을 살펴보자.

7 오른쪽 예술 작품에서는 단어가 맛있는 과일인 홍시의 이미지를 포함하고 있다.

8 그것은 가을이 결실의 계절임을 보여 준다.

9 왼쪽에 있는 예술 작품은 한글 단어와 한자를 보여 주고 있다.

10 그것은 마치 단풍잎이 깔린 길을 따라 걷고 있는 행복한 여인처럼 보인다.

11 이 두 작품은 아름다운 손 글씨를 통해 가을의 느낌을 표현한다.

12 이런 종류의 예술은 '캘리그래피'라고 불린다.

13 캘리그래피는 새로운 것이 아니다.

14 오래전의 다양한 종류의 많은 캘리그래피 작품들이 세계 곳곳에서 발견되고 있다.

15 아래에 있는 한국과 영국의 두 사례를 보라.

16 여러분은 그 차이를 구별할 수 있는가?

17 왼쪽 작품은 조선 왕조 시대에 추사에 의해 창작되었다.

18 그 글자들은 부드러운 붓으로 그려졌다.

19 The right one, *The Canterbury Tales*, was _____ _____ Chaucer in England _____ the _____ 1400s.

A. late   B. created   C. in   D. by

20 It _____ _____ _____ a pen.

A. written   B. with   C. was

21 _____ writing _____ led to different _____ of calligraphy.

A. styles   B. tools   C. different

22 _____ course, all calligraphers had to _____ _____ to make their _____ styles.

A. hard   B. of   C. unique   D. practice

23 Today calligraphy is _____ _____ _____ us.

A. around   B. widely   C. used

24 You can find designers' _____ _____ on movie posters, book covers, music CDs, and _____.

A. clothes   B. touches   C. artistic

25 _____ are some _____.

A. examples   B. below

26 Look _____ the _____ on the movie _____.

A. title   B. at   C. poster

27 _____ do you _____?

A. feel   B. how

28 Can you _____ the monster's big mouth, _____ teeth, and _____, long _____?

A. sharp   B. imagine   C. tail   D. ugly

29 _____ the title on the _____ novel?

A. fantasy   B. about   C. how

30 Do you see Harry's _____ and the _____ _____?

A. wizard   B. lightning   C. hats

31 _____ can start _____ calligraphy.

A. writing   B. anyone

32 It's not easy to write _____ _____ well at first, but _____ makes _____.

A. perfect   B. hand   C. practice   D. by

33 _____ _____ and make it _____ of your _____ life.

A. part   B. trying   C. everyday   D. keep

34 Write _____ your _____ on birthday cards, bookmarks, or _____.

A. feelings   B. with   C. gifts

35 Soon you will _____ _____ your _____ world of calligraphy.

A. up   B. own   C. build

---

19 오른쪽의 '캔터베리 이야기' 는 1400년대 후반 영국에서 Chaucer에 의해 창작되었다.

20 그것은 펜으로 쓰였다.

21 각기 다른 필기구가 각기 다른 캘리그래피의 스타일을 이끌었 다.

22 물론. 모든 캘리그래피 작가들 은 자신의 독특한 스타일을 만 들어 내기 위해 열심히 연습해 야 했다.

23 캘리그래피는 요즈음 우리 주변 에서 널리 쓰이고 있다.

24 여러분은 영화 포스터, 책 표지. 음악 CD, 그리고 의류에서 디자 이너들의 예술적인 손길을 발견 할 수 있다.

25 아래에 몇 가지 예가 있다.

26 영화 포스터의 제목을 보라.

27 어떤 느낌이 드는가?

28 괴물의 커다란 입. 날카로운 이 빨, 그리고 추하고 긴 꼬리를 상 상할 수 있는가?

29 공상 소설의 제목은 어떠한가?

30 Harry의 번개와 마술사 모자가 보이는가?

31 누구든지 캘리그래피를 쓰기 시 작할 수 있다.

32 처음부터 손으로 글씨를 잘 쓰 기는 쉽지 않지만, 연습하면 완 벽해진다.

33 계속해서 노력하고 자신의 일상 의 한 부분이 되게 하라.

34 생일 카드, 책갈피, 또는 선물에 느낌을 담아 써 보라.

35 곧 자신만의 캘리그래피 세계를 만들게 될 것이다.

※ 다음 우리말과 일치하도록 빈칸에 알맞은 말을 쓰시오.

1 _____ Your _____

2 _____ do you _____ your _____?

3 Do you _____ or _____?

4 Do you write a _____ or _____ _____ _____?

5 _____, it is _____ to express feelings _____ _____.

6 _____ _____ _____ _____ some _____ _____ _____ _____.

7 In the _____ _____ _____ on the right, the word _____ _____ _____ of a delicious fruit, *hongsi*.

8 It shows that autumn is _____ _____ _____ _____.

9 The work of art on the left shows a _____ _____ and a _____ _____.

10 It _____ _____ a happy woman _____ down a road with _____ _____.

11 Both of these works _____ _____ _____ of autumn _____ _____ _____.

12 This kind of art is _____ _____.

13 Calligraphy is _____ _____.

14 Many different kinds of calligraphy works from long ago _____ _____ _____ all _____ _____ _____ _____.

15 Look at the two _____ _____ Korea and the UK _____.

16 Can you _____ _____ _____?

17 The left one _____ _____ _____ Chusa in the _____ of the Joseon Dynasty.

18 The characters _____ _____ _____ a soft brush.

1 여러분의 느낌을 써라

2 여러분은 자신의 느낌을 어떻게 표현하는가?

3 노래를 부르거나 춤을 추는가?

4 시를 쓰거나 그림을 그리는가?

5 요즈음에는 손 글씨를 통해 감정을 표현하는 것이 인기다.

6 몇몇 작품을 살펴보자.

7 오른쪽 예술 작품에서는 단어가 맛있는 과일인 홍시의 이미지를 포함하고 있다.

8 그것은 가을이 결실의 계절임을 보여 준다.

9 왼쪽에 있는 예술 작품은 한글 단어와 한자를 보여 주고 있다.

10 그것은 마치 단풍잎이 깔린 길을 따라 걷고 있는 행복한 여인처럼 보인다.

11 이 두 작품은 아름다운 손 글씨를 통해 가을의 느낌을 표현한다.

12 이런 종류의 예술은 '캘리그래피'라고 불린다.

13 캘리그래피는 새로운 것이 아니다.

14 오래전의 다양한 종류의 많은 캘리그래피 작품들이 세계 곳곳에서 발견되고 있다.

15 아래에 있는 한국과 영국의 두 사례를 보라.

16 여러분은 그 차이를 구별할 수 있는가?

17 왼쪽 작품은 조선 왕조 시대에 추사에 의해 창작되었다.

18 그 글자들은 부드러운 붓으로 그려졌다.

19 The right one, *The Canterbury Tales*, _____ _____ _____ Chaucer in England _____ _____ _____ _____.

20 It _____ _____ _____ a pen.

21 _____ _____ _____ _____ led to _____ _____ of calligraphy.

22 _____ _____, all calligraphers had to _____ _____ to make their _____ _____.

23 Today calligraphy _____ _____ _____ _____ us.

24 You can find _____ _____ _____ on movie posters, book covers, music CDs, and _____.

25 Below _____ _____ _____.

26 Look at _____ _____ on the movie poster.

27 _____ do you _____?

28 Can you imagine the monster's big mouth, _____ _____, and _____, _____ _____?

29 _____ _____ the title on the _____ _____?

30 Do you see Harry's _____ and the _____ _____?

31 _____ can start _____ _____.

32 It's not easy _____ _____ _____ _____ well at first, but _____ _____ _____.

33 _____ _____ and make it _____ of your _____ life.

34 Write _____ _____ _____ on birthday cards, _____, or _____.

35 Soon you will _____ _____ your own world of calligraphy.

19 오른쪽의 '캔터베리 이야기'는 1400년대 후반 영국에서 Chaucer에 의해 창작되었다.

20 그것은 펜으로 쓰였다.

21 각기 다른 필기구가 각기 다른 캘리그래피의 스타일을 이끌었다.

22 물론, 모든 캘리그래피 작가들은 자신의 독특한 스타일을 만들어 내기 위해 열심히 연습해야 했다.

23 캘리그래피는 요즈음 우리 주변에서 널리 쓰이고 있다.

24 여러분은 영화 포스터, 책 표지, 음악 CD, 그리고 의류에서 디자이너들의 예술적인 손길을 발견할 수 있다.

25 아래에 몇 가지 예가 있다.

26 영화 포스터의 제목을 보라.

27 어떤 느낌이 드는가?

28 괴물의 커다란 입, 날카로운 이빨, 그리고 추하고 긴 꼬리를 상상할 수 있는가?

29 공상 소설의 제목은 어떠한가?

30 Harry의 번개와 마술사 모자가 보이는가?

31 누구든지 캘리그래피를 쓰기 시작할 수 있다.

32 처음부터 손으로 글씨를 잘 쓰기는 쉽지 않지만, 연습하면 완벽해진다.

33 계속해서 노력하고 자신의 일상의 한 부분이 되게 하라.

34 생일 카드, 책갈피, 또는 선물에 느낌을 담아 써 보라.

35 곧 자신만의 캘리그래피 세계를 만들게 될 것이다.

※ 다음 문장을 우리말로 쓰시오.

1 Write Your Feelings

➡ _____

2 How do you express your feelings?

➡ _____

3 Do you sing or dance?

➡ _____

4 Do you write a poem or draw a picture?

➡ _____

5 Nowadays, it is popular to express feelings through handwriting.

➡ _____

6 Let's look at some works of art.

➡ _____

7 In the work of art on the right, the word includes an image of a delicious fruit, *hongsi*.

➡ _____

8 It shows that autumn is a season of fruit.

➡ _____

9 The work of art on the left shows a Korean word and a Chinese character.

➡ _____

10 It looks like a happy woman walking down a road with autumn leaves.

➡ _____

11 Both of these works express the feeling of autumn through beautiful handwriting.

➡ _____

12 This kind of art is called calligraphy.

➡ _____

13 Calligraphy is not new.

➡ _____

14 Many different kinds of calligraphy works from long ago can be found all around the world.

➡ _____

15 Look at the two examples from Korea and the UK below.

➡ _____

16 Can you tell the difference?

➡ _____

17 The left one was created by Chusa in the period of the Joseon Dynasty.

➡ _____

18 The characters were painted with a soft brush.
➡ _____

19 The right one, *The Canterbury Tales*, was created by Chaucer in England in the late 1400s.
➡ _____

20 It was written with a pen.
➡ _____

21 Different writing tools led to different styles of calligraphy.
➡ _____

22 Of course, all calligraphers had to practice hard to make their unique styles.
➡ _____

23 Today calligraphy is widely used around us.
➡ _____

24 You can find designers' artistic touches on movie posters, book covers, music CDs, and clothes.
➡ _____

25 Below are some examples.
➡ _____

26 Look at the title on the movie poster.
➡ _____

27 How do you feel?
➡ _____

28 Can you imagine the monster's big mouth, sharp teeth, and ugly, long tail?
➡ _____

29 How about the title on the fantasy novel?
➡ _____

30 Do you see Harry's lightning and the wizard hats?
➡ _____

31 Anyone can start writing calligraphy.
➡ _____

32 It's not easy to write by hand well at first, but practice makes perfect.
➡ _____

33 Keep trying and make it part of your everyday life.
➡ _____

34 Write with your feelings on birthday cards, bookmarks, or gifts.
➡ _____

35 Soon you will build up your own world of calligraphy.
➡ _____

Step4

※ 다음 괄호 안의 단어들을 우리말에 맞도록 바르게 배열하시오.

1 (Your / Feelings / Write)
➡ _____

2 (do / how / express / you / feelings? / your)
➡ _____

3 (you / do / dance? / or / sing)
➡ _____

4 (you / do / a / write / poem / or / a / draw / picture?)
➡ _____

5 (nowadays, / is / it / to / popular / feelings / express / handwriting. / through)
➡ _____

6 (look / let's / some / at / art. / or / works)
➡ _____

7 (the / in / of / work / art / the / on / right, / word / the / an / includes / image / of / delicious / *hongsi*. / a / fruit,)
➡ _____

8 (shows / it / autumn / that / a / is / fruit. / of / season)
➡ _____

9 (work / the / art / of / the / on / shows / left / Korean / a / word / and / a / character. / Chinese)
➡ _____

10 (looks / it / a / like / happy / walking / woman / down / road / a / with / leaves. / autumn)
➡ _____

11 (of / both / works / these / express / feeling / the / autumn / of / through / handwriting. / beautiful)
➡ _____

12 (kind / this / art / of / is / calligraphy. / called)
➡ _____

13 (is / calligraphy / new. / not)
➡ _____

14 (different / many / of / kinds / calligraphy / from / works / ago / long / be / can / all / found / world. / the / around)
➡ _____

15 (at / look / two / the / examples / Korea / from / and / below. / UK / the)
➡ _____

16 (you / can / the / tell / difference?)
➡ _____

17 (left / the / was / one / by / created / Chusa / the / in / period / the / of / Dynasty. / Joseon)
➡ _____

18 (character / the / painted / were / with / brush. / soft / a)
➡ _____

1 여러분의 느낌을 써라

2 여러분은 자신의 느낌을 어떻게 표현하는가?

3 노래를 부르거나 춤을 추는가?

4 시를 쓰거나 그림을 그리는가?

5 요즈음에는 손 글씨를 통해 감정을 표현하는 것이 인기다.

6 몇몇 작품을 살펴보자.

7 오른쪽 예술 작품에서는 단어가 맛있는 과일인 홍시의 이미지를 포함하고 있다.

8 그것은 가을이 결실의 계절임을 보여 준다.

9 왼쪽에 있는 예술 작품은 한글 단어와 한자를 보여 주고 있다.

10 그것은 마치 단풍잎이 깔린 길을 따라 걷고 있는 행복한 여인처럼 보인다.

11 이 두 작품은 아름다운 손 글씨를 통해 가을의 느낌을 표현한다.

12 이런 종류의 예술은 '캘리그래피'라고 불린다.

13 캘리그래피는 새로운 것이 아니다.

14 오래전의 다양한 종류의 많은 캘리그래피 작품들이 세계 곳곳에서 발견되고 있다.

15 아래에 있는 한국과 영국의 두 사례를 보라.

16 여러분은 그 차이를 구별할 수 있는가?

17 왼쪽 작품은 조선 왕조 시대에 추사에 의해 창작되었다.

18 그 글자들은 부드러운 붓으로 그려졌다.

19 (right / the / one, *Canterbury* / *The* / *Tales*, / created / was / Chaucer / by / England / in / the / in / 1400s. / late)
➡ _____

20 (was / it / with / written / pen / a)
➡ _____

21 (writing / different / led / tools / to / styles / different / calligraphy. / of)
➡ _____

22 (course, / of / calligraphers / all / to / had / hard / practice / make / to / unique / their / styles.)
➡ _____

23 (calligraphy / today / widely / is / around / us. / used)
➡ _____

24 (can / you / designers' / find / touches / artistic / movie / on / book / posters, / covers, / CDs, / music / clothes. / and)
➡ _____

25 (are / examples. / below / some)
➡ _____

26 (at / look / title / the / the / on / poster. / movie)
➡ _____

27 (do / how / feel? / you)
➡ _____

28 (you / can / the / imagine / monster's / mouth, / big / teeth, / sharp / and / long / tail? / ugly,)
➡ _____

29 (about / how / title / the / the / on / novel? / fantasy)
➡ _____

30 (you / see / do / lightning / Harry's / and / hats? / wizard / the)
➡ _____

31 (can / anyone / start / calligraphy. / writing)
➡ _____

32 (not / it's / to / easy / by / write / hand / at / well / first, / but / makes / perfect. / practice)
➡ _____

33 (trying / keep / and / it / make / of / part / everyday / your / life.)
➡ _____

34 (with / write / feelings / your / birthday / on / cards, / gifts. / or / bookmarks,)
➡ _____

35 (you / soon / build / will / your / up / world / own / calligraphy. / of)
➡ _____

19 오른쪽의 '캔터베리 이야기'는 1400년대 후반 영국에서 Chaucer에 의해 창작되었다.

20 그것은 펜으로 쓰였다.

21 각기 다른 필기구가 각기 다른 캘리그래피의 스타일을 이끌었다.

22 물론, 모든 캘리그래피 작가들은 자신의 독특한 스타일을 만들어 내기 위해 열심히 연습해야 했다.

23 캘리그래피는 요즈음 우리 주변에서 널리 쓰이고 있다.

24 여러분은 영화 포스터, 책 표지, 음악 CD, 그리고 의류에서 디자이너들의 예술적인 손길을 발견할 수 있다.

25 아래에 몇 가지 예가 있다.

26 영화 포스터의 제목을 보라.

27 어떤 느낌이 드는가?

28 괴물의 커다란 입, 날카로운 이빨, 그리고 추하고 긴 꼬리를 상상할 수 있는가?

29 공상 소설의 제목은 어떠한가?

30 Harry의 번개와 마술사 모자가 보이는가?

31 누구든지 캘리그래피를 쓰기 시작할 수 있다.

32 처음부터 손으로 글씨를 잘 쓰기는 쉽지 않지만, 연습하면 완벽해진다.

33 계속해서 노력하고 자신의 일상의 한 부분이 되게 하라.

34 생일 카드, 책갈피, 또는 선물에 느낌을 담아 써 보라.

35 곧 자신만의 캘리그래피 세계를 만들게 될 것이다.

※ 다음 우리말을 영어로 쓰시오.

1 여러분의 느낌을 써라

➡ _____

2 여러분은 자신의 느낌을 어떻게 표현하는가?

➡ _____

3 노래를 부르거나 춤을 추는가?

➡ _____

4 시를 쓰거나 그림을 그리는가?

➡ _____

5 요즈음에는 손 글씨를 통해 감정을 표현하는 것이 인기다.

➡ _____

6 몇몇 작품을 살펴보자.

➡ _____

7 오른쪽 예술 작품에서는 단어가 맛있는 과일인 홍시의 이미지를 포함하고 있다.

➡ _____

8 그것은 가을이 결실의 계절임을 보여 준다.

➡ _____

9 왼쪽에 있는 예술 작품은 한글 단어와 한자를 보여 주고 있다.

➡ _____

10 그것은 마치 단풍잎이 깔린 길을 따라 걷고 있는 행복한 여인처럼 보인다.

➡ _____

11 이 두 작품은 아름다운 손 글씨를 통해 가을의 느낌을 표현한다.

➡ _____

12 이런 종류의 예술은 '캘리그래피'라고 불린다.

➡ _____

13 캘리그래피는 새로운 것이 아니다.

➡ _____

14 오래전의 다양한 종류의 많은 캘리그래피 작품들이 세계 곳곳에서 발견되고 있다.

➡ _____

15 아래에 있는 한국과 영국의 두 사례를 보라.

➡ _____

16 여러분은 그 차이를 구별할 수 있는가?

➡ _____

17 왼쪽 작품은 조선 왕조 시대에 추사에 의해 창작되었다.

➡ _____

18 그 글자들은 부드러운 붓으로 그려졌다.
➡ _____

19 오른쪽의 '캔터베리 이야기'는 1400년대 후반 영국에서 Chaucer에 의해 창작되었다.
➡ _____

20 그것은 펜으로 쓰였다.
➡ _____

21 각기 다른 필기구가 각기 다른 캘리그래피의 스타일을 이끌었다.
➡ _____

22 물론, 모든 캘리그래피 작가들은 자신의 독특한 스타일을 만들어 내기 위해 열심히 연습해야 했다.
➡ _____

23 캘리그래피는 요즈음 우리 주변에서 널리 쓰이고 있다.
➡ _____

24 여러분은 영화 포스터, 책 표지, 음악 CD, 그리고 의류에서 디자이너들의 예술적인 손길을 발견할 수 있다.
➡ _____

25 아래에 몇 가지 예가 있다.
➡ _____

26 영화 포스터의 제목을 보라.
➡ _____

27 어떤 느낌이 드는가?
➡ _____

28 괴물의 커다란 입, 날카로운 이빨, 그리고 추하고 긴 꼬리를 상상할 수 있는가?
➡ _____

29 공상 소설의 제목은 어떠한가?
➡ _____

30 Harry의 번개와 마술사 모자가 보이는가?
➡ _____

31 누구든지 캘리그래피를 쓰기 시작할 수 있다.
➡ _____

32 처음부터 손으로 글씨를 잘 쓰기는 쉽지 않지만, 연습하면 완벽해진다.
➡ _____

33 계속해서 노력하고 자신의 일상의 한 부분이 되게 하라.
➡ _____

34 생일 카드, 책갈피, 또는 선물에 느낌을 담아 써 보라.
➡ _____

35 곧 자신만의 캘리그래피 세계를 만들게 될 것이다.
➡ _____

※ 다음 우리말과 일치하도록 빈칸에 알맞은 말을 쓰시오.

After You Read B

1. These _____ _____ mean "Let's laugh."

2. This calligraphy shows two people _____ _____ _____.

3. These Korean _____ _____ "tree."

4. This calligraphy shows a tree _____ _____ _____ _____.

1. 이 한글 문자는 '웃자.'라는 뜻이다.
2. 이 캘리그래피는 큰 소리로 웃고 있는 두 사람을 보여 준다.
3. 이 한글 문자는 '나무'를 의미한다.
4. 이 캘리그래피는 화분에서 자라고 있는 나무를 보여 준다.

Express Yourself C

1. _____ _____ the two girls _____ taekwondo.

2. Taekwondo is a _____ _____ sport, and we _____ dobok _____ _____ it.

3. _____ is exciting _____ _____ taekwondo.

4. _____ you _____?

5. Please _____ and _____.

6. _____ _____ the two boys _____ yunnori.

7. Yunnori is a _____ _____ board game, and we use yuts and mals _____ _____ it.

8. _____ is exciting _____ _____ yunnori.

9. _____ you _____?

10. Please _____ and _____.

1. 태권도를 배우고[하고] 있는 두 여자아이를 보세요.
2. 태권도는 한국의 전통 스포츠이고, 우리는 그것을 하기 위해 도복을 입습니다.
3. 태권도를 배우는 것은 흥미진진합니다.
4. 관심이 있나요?
5. 와서 한번 해 보세요.
6. 윷놀이를 하는 두 남자아이를 보세요.
7. 윷놀이는 한국의 전통적인 말판 놀이고, 우리는 그것을 하기 위해 윷과 말을 사용합니다.
8. 윷놀이를 하는 것은 흥미진진합니다.
9. 관심이 있나요?
10. 와서 한번 해 보세요.

Link to the World

1. This is a set of _____ _____. It _____ _____ matryoshka.

2. _____ you open it, smaller dolls _____ _____ out of it.

3. _____ is interesting _____ _____ a smaller doll _____ _____.

4. _____ _____ _____ of matryoshka dolls was a mother doll _____ _____ _____.

5. Today, _____ _____ _____ of matryoshkas _____ _____ and _____ by many people.

1. 이것은 한 세트의 러시아 인형이다. 그것은 '마트료시카'라고 불린다.
2. 그것을 열면, 더 작은 인형들이 계속해서 나온다.
3. 각각의 인형 안에서 더 작은 인형을 보는 것은 재미있다.
4. 최초의 '마트료시카' 인형 세트는 여섯 아이를 둔 어머니 인형이었다.
5. 오늘날에는, 많은 새로운 스타일의 '마트료시카'가 제작되어 많은 사람에게 사랑을 받고 있다.

※ 다음 우리말을 영어로 쓰시오.

After You Read B

1. 이 한글 문자는 '웃자.'라는 뜻이다.
   ➡ _____

2. 이 캘리그래피는 큰 소리로 웃고 있는 두 사람을 보여 준다.
   ➡ _____

3. 이 한글 문자는 '나무'를 의미한다.
   ➡ _____

4. 이 캘리그래피는 화분에서 자라고 있는 나무를 보여 준다.
   ➡ _____

Express Yourself C

1. 태권도를 배우고[하고] 있는 두 여자아이를 보세요.
   ➡ _____

2. 태권도는 한국의 전통 스포츠이고, 우리는 그것을 하기 위해 도복을 입습니다.
   ➡ _____

3. 태권도를 배우는 것은 흥미진진합니다.
   ➡ _____

4. 관심이 있나요?
   ➡ _____

5. 와서 한번 해 보세요.
   ➡ _____

6. 윷놀이를 하는 두 남자아이를 보세요.
   ➡ _____

7. 윷놀이는 한국의 전통적인 말판 놀이고, 우리는 그것을 하기 위해 윷과 말을 사용합니다.
   ➡ _____

8. 윷놀이를 하는 것은 흥미진진합니다.
   ➡ _____

9. 관심이 있나요?
   ➡ _____

10. 와서 한번 해 보세요.
   ➡ _____

Link to the World

1. 이것은 한 세트의 러시아 인형이다. 그것은 '마트료시카'라고 불린다.
   ➡ _____

2. 그것을 열면, 더 작은 인형들이 계속해서 나온다.
   ➡ _____

3. 각각의 인형 안에서 더 작은 인형을 보는 것은 재미있다.
   ➡ _____

4. 최초의 '마트료시카' 인형 세트는 여섯 아이를 둔 어머니 인형이었다.
   ➡ _____

5. 오늘날에는, 많은 새로운 스타일의 '마트료시카'가 제작되어 많은 사람에게 사랑을 받고 있다.
   ➡ _____

※ 다음 영어를 우리말로 쓰시오.

01	bookshelf	_____
02	another	_____
03	uncomfortable	_____
04	dirty	_____
05	universal	_____
06	blind	_____
07	cotton	_____
08	tight	_____
09	hearing	_____
10	solution	_____
11	decide	_____
12	easily	_____
13	decorate	_____
14	add	_____
15	difficulty	_____
16	seat	_____
17	finally	_____
18	almost	_____
19	fountain	_____
20	handle	_____
21	product	_____

22	low	_____
23	crowded	_____
24	hang	_____
25	journey	_____
26	company	_____
27	bathtub	_____
28	moment	_____
29	locker	_____
30	thick	_____
31	view	_____
32	traffic	_____
33	flat	_____
34	bath	_____
35	go through	_____
36	put on	_____
37	watch out	_____
38	by oneself	_____
39	in danger	_____
40	tired of	_____
41	so+형용사/부사+that +주어+can't …	_____
42	get in	_____
43	more and more	_____

※ 다음 우리말을 영어로 쓰시오.

01 거의 _____

02 매달다, 걸다 _____

03 더러운 _____

04 지팡이 _____

05 해결책 _____

06 쿠션, 방석 _____

07 결심하다 _____

08 청력 _____

09 장식하다 _____

10 어려움 _____

11 쉽게 _____

12 평평한 _____

13 목욕 _____

14 욕조 _____

15 분수, 원천 _____

16 손잡이 _____

17 여행, 여정 _____

18 건너다 _____

19 붐비는 _____

20 방법 _____

21 눈이 먼 _____

22 책꽂이 _____

23 사물함 _____

24 견해, 관점 _____

25 불편한 _____

26 낮은 _____

27 두꺼운 _____

28 상품, 제품 _____

29 자리, 좌석 _____

30 회사 _____

31 꽉 조이는, 딱 붙는 _____

32 보편적인 _____

33 교통 _____

34 또 하나의 _____

35 ~을 타다 _____

36 위험에 처한 _____

37 혼자서 _____

38 점점 더 많은 _____

39 ~을 겪다 _____

40 ~을 입다 _____

41 ~에 지친, ~에 싫증 난 _____

42 ~할 것을 고려[생각] 중이다 _____

43 조심하다 _____

※ 다음 영영풀이에 알맞은 단어를 <보기>에서 골라 쓴 후, 우리말 뜻을 쓰시오.

1 _____ : unable to see: _____

2 _____ : having a lot of people or too many people: _____

3 _____ : in a lower place or position: _____

4 _____ : the answer to a problem: _____

5 _____ : to go across from one side of something to the other: _____

6 _____ : a long, thin wooden pole that especially old or injured people use to walk: _____

7 _____ : not having a part that is higher or lower than another: _____

8 _____ : a part that is designed especially to be held by the hand: _____

9 _____ : an act of traveling from one place to another: _____

10 _____ : small in height or smaller than the usual height: _____

11 _____ : something that is made or grown for selling: _____

12 _____ : not feeling comfortable and pleasant: _____

13 _____ : a personal opinion or belief about a situation or subject: _____

14 _____ : to add something to an object or place, especially in order to make it more attractive: _____

15 _____ : a business organization that makes money by producing or selling goods or services: _____

16 _____ : a cupboard, often tall and made of metal, in which you can keep your possessions, and leave them for a period of time: _____

보기

solution	low	crowded	cross
blind	handle	locker	stick
view	company	decorate	flat
journey	product	below	uncomfortable

※ 다음 우리말과 일치하도록 빈칸에 알맞은 말을 쓰시오.

Get Ready 2

(1) B: I'm _____ _____ _____ this _____. It's _____ _____ for some kids.

G: Well, I'_____ _____ _____ _____ _____ _____ fountains together with it.

B: That's a _____ _____.

(2) G: I _____ _____ the high steps here. People _____ _____ can't _____ _____.

B: Right. I'm _____ _____ _____ a new way _____ no _____.

(3) G: I'm not _____ about this swing. People _____ _____ can't _____ _____ it _____.

B: Right. I'm _____ _____ _____ a bigger and _____ _____ for them.

G: Good idea.

(1) B: 나는 이 음수대가 마음에 들지 않아. 몇몇 아이들에게는 너무 높아.

G: 음, 나는 그것과 함께 더 낮은 음수대들을 놓으려고 계획 중이야.

B: 좋은 생각이야.

(2) G: 나는 여기 높은 계단이 마음에 들지 않아. 휠체어를 탄 사람들은 들어설 수가 없잖아.

B: 맞아. 나는 계단 없는 새 길을 짓는 것을 생각 중이야.

(3) G: 나는 이 그네가 마음에 들지 않아. 휠체어를 탄 사람들은 그것을 쉽게 탈 수 없어.

B: 맞아. 나는 그들을 위해 더 크고 더 안전한 자리를 매달려고 계획 중이야.

G: 좋은 생각이야.

Start Off Listen & Talk A

(1) G: I'm _____ _____ _____ the button.

B: Why? What's _____ _____ it?

G: It's too high. Children or people in wheelchairs can't _____ it. _____ _____ _____ putting _____ switch for them.

(2) G: I'm not _____ _____ the sign. _____ _____ some people _____ can't see.

B: Right. Do you have _____ ideas?

G: Well, I'm _____ of _____ _____ on the sign.

B: That's a _____ _____.

(1) G: 나는 그 버튼이 마음에 들지 않아.

B: 왜? 뭐가 잘못됐니?

G: 그것은 너무 높아. 아이들이나 휠체어를 탄 사람들은 거기까지 닿을 수가 없어. 나는 그들을 위해 또 다른 스위치를 달까 생각 중이야.

(2) G: 나는 표지판이 마음에 들지 않아. 볼 수 없는 사람들도 좀 있잖아.

B: 맞아. 너는 어떤 아이디어라도 있니?

G: 음, 나는 표지판 위에 점자를 추가할까 생각 중이야.

B: 그거 좋은 생각이다.

Start Off Listen & draw

B: _____ _____ _____ _____ _____ the lights.

G: _____ _____ _____ them?

B: The _____ _____ look _____ _____ to some people _____ are _____ _____.

G: Oh, I see. _____ _____ _____ an image on each light?

B: A _____ man on the green light and a _____ man on the red light? Good idea!

B: 나는 불빛이 마음에 들지 않아.

G: 뭐가 잘못됐니?

B: 색맹인 사람들에게는 신호등이 똑같이 보일 거야.

G: 오, 알겠어. 각 불빛에 그림을 넣는 게 어떨까?

B: 파란불에는 걷는 사람을, 그리고 빨간불에는 서 있는 사람을? 좋은 생각이야!

Speak Up Look and talk

B: _____ _____ _____ _____ _____ _____ the desk. It's _____ _____.

G: Right. I'm _____ _____ _____ some pads on it.

B: Good idea.

B: 나는 책상이 마음에 들지 않아. 그것은 너무 낮아.

G: 맞아. 나는 그 위에 몇 장의 패드를 놓을까 생각 중이야.

B: 좋은 생각이야.

Speak Up Mission

A: I'm _____ _____ _____ the _____. It's too small.
B: I think so, _____. Do you have _____ _____?
A: I'm _____ _____ _____ _____ _____ on it.
B: That's a _____ _____.

Speak Up Real-life Scene

Dad: What _____ you _____ here?
Son: I'm _____ of _____ to _____ Miso.
Dad: What's _____?
Son: She can't _____ _____ the light _____ _____. This switch is _____ _____ for her.
Dad: That's right. I'm not _____ _____ it, _____. Do you have any good ideas _____ _____?
Son: I'm _____ _____ _____ a _____ _____ here _____ the switch.
Dad: Good idea. And I'll _____ the switch to a _____ _____.
Son: Great. Grandma will like it, too. She can _____ _____ the light _____ _____.

Express Yourself A

(1) G: _____ _____ _____ _____ my brother's chair. It's _____ _____ and _____ _____.
   B: Right. _____ _____ _____ _____ _____ this one. _____ do you _____?
   G: _____ _____. I think he can use it _____ _____ _____, even _____ he _____ _____.
(2) B: I'm _____ _____ _____ the door _____ in my house. They are not _____ _____ _____ for my grandma.
   G: _____ _____ _____ this one? She will pull it and open the door _____.
   B: That's good.
(3) G: _____ _____ _____ buying this spoon. It will _____ my grandma _____ soup easily.
   B: Right. She _____ _____ _____ hold it with her fingers.

Learning Diary Check Yourself

G: I'm _____ _____ about this _____ _____.
B: Why? What's _____?
G: It's _____ _____. Grandma can't use it easily.
B: Do you have _____ _____?
G: _____ _____ _____ _____ _____ it _____ a _____ one. That'll help her _____ _____ the light easily.
B: Good idea.

A: 나는 책꽂이가 마음에 들지 않아. 그것은 너무 작아.
B: 나도 그렇게 생각해. 어떤 아이디어라도 있니?
A: 나는 그 위에 또 다른 책꽂이를 놓을까 생각 중이야.
B: 그거 좋은 생각이다.

아빠: 너는 여기서 무엇을 하고 있니?
아들: 저는 미소를 도울 방법을 생각하고 있어요.
아빠: 뭐가 잘못됐니?
아들: 그녀는 혼자서 전등을 켤 수 없어요. 이 스위치는 그녀에게 너무 높아요.
아빠: 그렇구나. 나도 그것이 마음에 들지 않는구나. 그것에 대한 어떤 아이디어라도 있니?
아들: 저는 여기 스위치 아래에 디딤대를 놓을까 생각하고 있어요.
아빠: 좋은 생각이구나. 그럼 나는 스위치를 더 큰 것으로 바꾸마.
아들: 좋아요. 할머니께서도 그것을 좋아하실 거예요. 할머니께서는 전등을 더 쉽게 켜실 수 있어요.

(1) G: 나는 내 남동생의 의자가 마음에 안 들어. 그것은 너무 낮고 딱딱해.
   B: 맞아. 나는 이것을 살까 생각 중이야. 너는 어때?
   G: 좋아 보이네. 나는 그가 키가 더 자란 후에도 그것을 오랫동안 사용할 수 있을 거라고 생각해.
(2) B: 나는 우리 집의 문손잡이가 마음에 안 들어. 그것들은 우리 할머니께서 사용하시기에 쉽지 않아.
   G: 이것은 어때? 그녀는 그것을 당겨서 문을 쉽게 열 거야.
   B: 그것 좋네.
(3) G: 나는 이 숟가락을 살까 생각 중이야. 그것은 우리 할머니께서 국을 쉽게 드실 수 있도록 도와줄 거야.
   B: 맞아. 그녀는 그것을 손가락으로 잡으실 필요가 없어.

G: 나는 이 조명 스위치가 마음에 들지 않아.
B: 왜? 뭐가 잘못됐니?
G: 그것은 너무 작아. 할머니께서 그것을 쉽게 사용하실 수가 없어.
B: 어떤 아이디어라도 있니?
G: 나는 그것을 좀 더 큰 것으로 바꿀까 생각 중이야. 그것은 할머니께서 조명을 쉽게 켜실 수 있도록 도와줄 거야.
B: 좋은 생각이다.

※ 다음 우리말에 맞도록 대화를 영어로 쓰시오.

Get Ready 2

(1) B: _____

　G: _____

　B: _____

(2) G: _____

　B: _____

(3) G: _____

　B: _____

　G: _____

(1) B: 나는 이 음수대가 마음에 들지 않아. 몇몇 아이들에게는 너무 높아.
　G: 음, 나는 그것과 함께 더 낮은 음수대들을 놓으려고 계획 중이야.
　B: 좋은 생각이야.
(2) G: 나는 여기 높은 계단이 마음에 들지 않아. 휠체어를 탄 사람들은 들어설 수가 없잖아.
　B: 맞아. 나는 계단 없는 새 길을 짓는 것을 생각 중이야.
(3) G: 나는 이 그네가 마음에 들지 않아. 휠체어를 탄 사람들은 그것을 쉽게 탈 수 없어.
　B: 맞아. 나는 그들을 위해 더 크고 더 안전한 자리를 매달려고 계획 중이야.
　G: 좋은 생각이야.

Start Off Listen & Talk A

(1) G: _____

　B: _____

　G: _____

　　_____

(2) G: _____

　B: _____

　G: _____

　B: _____

(1) G: 나는 그 버튼이 마음에 들지 않아.
　B: 왜? 뭐가 잘못됐니?
　G: 그것은 너무 높아. 아이들이나 휠체어를 탄 사람들은 거기까지 닿을 수가 없어. 나는 그들을 위해 또 다른 스위치를 달까 생각 중이야.
(2) G: 나는 표지판이 마음에 들지 않아. 볼 수 없는 사람들도 좀 있잖아.
　B: 맞아. 너는 어떤 아이디어라도 있니?
　G: 음, 나는 표지판 위에 점자를 추가할까 생각 중이야.
　B: 그거 좋은 생각이다.

Start Off Listen & draw

B: _____

G: _____

B: _____

G: _____

B: _____

　_____

B: 나는 불빛이 마음에 들지 않아.
G: 뭐가 잘못됐니?
B: 색맹인 사람들에게는 신호등이 똑같이 보일 거야.
G: 오, 알겠어. 각 불빛에 그림을 넣는 게 어떨까?
B: 파란불에는 걷는 사람을, 그리고 빨간불에는 서 있는 사람을? 좋은 생각이야!

Speak Up Look and talk

B: _____

G: _____

B: _____

B: 나는 책상이 마음에 들지 않아. 그것은 너무 낮아.
G: 맞아. 나는 그 위에 몇 장의 패드를 놓을까 생각 중이야.
B: 좋은 생각이야.

Speak Up Mission

A: _____

B: _____

A: _____

B: _____

A: 나는 책꽂이가 마음에 들지 않아. 그것은 너무 작아.

B: 나도 그렇게 생각해. 어떤 아이디어라도 있니?

A: 나는 그 위에 또 다른 책꽂이를 놓을까 생각 중이야.

B: 그거 좋은 생각이다.

Speak Up Real-life Scene

Dad: _____

Son: _____

Dad: _____

Son: _____

Dad: _____

Son: _____

Dad: _____

Son: _____

아빠: 너는 여기서 무엇을 하고 있니?

아들: 저는 미소를 도울 방법을 생각하고 있어요.

아빠: 뭐가 잘못됐니?

아들: 그녀는 혼자서 전등을 켤 수 없어요. 이 스위치는 그녀에게 너무 높아요.

아빠: 그렇구나. 나도 그것이 마음에 들지 않구나. 그것에 대한 어떤 아이디어라도 있니?

아들: 저는 여기 스위치 아래에 디딤대를 놓을까 생각하고 있어요.

아빠: 좋은 생각이구나. 그럼 나는 스위치를 더 큰 것으로 바꾸마.

아들: 좋아요. 할머니께서도 그것을 좋아하실 거예요. 할머니께서는 전등을 더 쉽게 켜실 수 있어요.

Express Yourself A

(1) G: _____

B: _____

G: _____

(2) B: _____

_____

G: _____

B: _____

(3) G: _____

B: _____

(1) G: 나는 내 남동생의 의자가 마음에 안 들어. 그것은 너무 낮고 딱딱해.

B: 맞아. 나는 이것을 살까 생각 중이야. 너는 어때?

G: 좋아 보이네. 나는 그가 키가 더 자란 후에도 그것을 오랫동안 사용할 수 있을 거라고 생각해.

(2) B: 나는 우리 집의 문손잡이가 마음에 안 들어. 그것들은 우리 할머니께서 사용하시기에 쉽지 않아.

G: 이것은 어때? 그녀는 그것을 당겨서 문을 쉽게 여실 거야.

B: 그것 좋네.

(3) G: 나는 이 숟가락을 살까 생각 중이야. 그것은 우리 할머니께서 국을 쉽게 드실 수 있도록 도와줄 거야.

B: 맞아. 그녀는 그것을 손가락으로 잡으실 필요가 없어.

Learning Diary Check Yourself

G: _____

B: _____

G: _____

B: _____

G: _____

B: _____

G: 나는 이 조명 스위치가 마음에 들지 않아.

B: 왜? 뭐가 잘못됐니?

G: 그것은 너무 작아. 할머니께서 그것을 쉽게 사용하실 수가 없어.

B: 어떤 아이디어라도 있니?

G: 나는 그것을 좀 더 큰 것으로 바꿀까 생각 중이야. 그것은 할머니께서 조명을 쉽게 켜실 수 있도록 도와줄 거야.

B: 좋은 생각이다.

※ 다음 우리말과 일치하도록 빈칸에 알맞은 것을 골라 쓰시오.

1 Patricia Moore – _____ of _____ _____.
A. Universal   B. Mother   C. Design

2 In 1979, a _____ started a _____ to _____ in the U.S. and Canada.
A. cities   B. journey   C. woman

3 She _____ _____ 80.
A. over   B. looked

4 She _____ _____ or _____ well.
A. see   B. couldn't   C. hear

5 She couldn't _____ well _____ a _____.
A. without   B. walk   C. stick

6 _____ all these _____, the woman had to _____ stairs in subway stations and get on _____ buses.
A. climb   B. difficulties   C. crowded   D. with

7 She had to open _____ doors and use can openers _____ her _____ hands.
A. with   B. heavy   C. weak

8 Sometimes she _____ hurt or _____ herself _____ _____.
A. found   B. danger   C. got   D. in

9 Every _____ was very _____ for her, but she visited more _____ 115 cities and ended her _____ in 1982.
A. difficult   B. trip   C. moment   D. than

10 _____ was the woman and _____ made her _____ all this?
A. what   B. do   C. who

11 She was Patricia Moore, _____ _____ _____.
A. designer   B. 26-year-old   C. a

12 _____ the 1970's, she _____ for a big design _____.
A. worked   B. during   C. company

13 She often asked at _____, "How about _____ for old or _____ people?"
A. designing   B. meetings   C. weak

14 The _____ designers always answered, "We don't _____ for _____ people."
A. other   B. those   C. design

15 She _____ _____ of the _____ cold answer.
A. tired   B. same   C. became

16 _____, she decided to become one of "those people" and travel _____ many cities to _____ their _____ better.
A. around   B. difficulties   C. understand   D. finally

---

1 Patricia Moore – 유니버설 디자인의 어머니

2 1979년에, 한 여성이 미국과 캐나다의 도시로 여행을 시작했다.

3 그녀는 80세가 넘어 보였다.

4 그녀는 잘 보거나 잘 들을 수 없었다.

5 그녀는 지팡이가 없이는 잘 걸을 수 없었다.

6 이 모든 어려움을 가진 채, 그 여성은 지하철역에서 계단을 올라가거나 붐비는 버스에 올라타야 했다.

7 그녀는 무거운 문을 열거나 그녀의 약한 손으로 깡통 따개를 사용해야 했다.

8 때때로 그녀는 다치거나 위험에 처하기도 했다.

9 모든 순간이 그녀에게 매우 어려웠으나, 그녀는 115개 이상의 도시를 방문하였으며 1982년에 여행을 끝마쳤다.

10 그 여성은 누구였고 무엇이 그녀로 하여금 이 모든 것을 하게 만들었을까?

11 그녀는 26살의 디자이너인 Patricia Moore였다.

12 1970년대 동안, 그녀는 큰 디자인 회사에서 일했다.

13 그녀는 종종 회의에서 물었다. "나이 들거나 약한 사람들을 위해 디자인하는 게 어떨까요?"

14 다른 디자이너들은 항상 대답했다. "우리는 그런 사람들을 위해 디자인하지 않습니다."

15 그녀는 똑같은 냉담한 대답에 지쳤다.

16 마침내, 그녀는 '그런 사람들' 중의 하나가 되어 그들의 어려움을 더 잘 이해하기 위해 많은 도시를 여행하기로 결심했다.

17 For this, she put on her grandmother's _____, _____ shoes, and _____ _____.

    A. uncomfortable   B. glasses   C. thick   D. clothes

18 The shoes were _____ uncomfortable _____ she _____ walk well _____ a sick.

    A. that   B. without   C. couldn't   D. so

19 The glasses were so _____ that she _____ see well _____ them.

    A. with   B. couldn't   C. thick

20 She also _____ lots _____ cotton in her ears to _____ her _____ bad.

    A. hearing   B. make   C. put   D. of

21 _____ her journey, Patricia _____ the difficulties old people _____ _____.

    A. through   B. during   C. go   D. felt

22 _____ this experience, she designed _____ anybody could use _____ and _____.

    A. safely   B. products   C. easily   D. from

23 This was the _____ of " _____ _____," or "design for all."

    A. universal   B. design   C. beginning

24 One _____ of her _____ design ideas is _____ buses.

    A. low-floor   B. example   C. universal

25 They have no _____ and have _____ a low floor that even a person in a wheelchair can use them _____ any _____.

    A. without   B. steps   C. help   D. such

26 Of _____, this helps _____ people _____ on the bus more _____, too.

    A. other   B. comfortably   C. course   D. get

27 Today _____ and more designers are _____ Patricia's _____.

    A. way   B. following   C. more

28 Products like big _____ light switches, doors with _____ handles, and phones with _____ buttons are helping people live better _____.

    A. touch   B. lives   C. easy   D. flat

29 Look _____ you, feel the difficulties of people who are older or _____, and try to find solutions from their _____ of _____.

    A. view   B. around   C. weaker   D. point

30 You could be the _____ Patricia Moore and make the world a _____ _____ for _____.

    A. place   B. next   C. everybody   D. better

17 이를 위해, 그녀는 자신의 할머니 옷을 입고, 불편한 신발을 신고, 두꺼운 안경을 썼다.

18 신발은 너무 불편해서 그녀는 지팡이 없이는 잘 걸을 수 없었다.

19 안경은 너무 두꺼워서 그녀는 안경을 쓰고는 잘 볼 수 없었다.

20 그녀는 또한 그녀의 청력을 나쁘게 하려고 귀에 많은 솜을 넣었다.

21 여행 동안, Patricia는 나이 든 사람들이 겪는 어려움을 느꼈다.

22 이 경험으로부터, 그녀는 누구나 안전하고 쉽게 사용할 수 있는 제품들을 고안했다.

23 이것이 '유니버설 디자인' 또는 '모두를 위한 디자인'의 시작이었다.

24 그녀의 유니버설 디자인 아이디어의 한 가지 예는 저상 버스이다.

25 그것은 계단이 없고 낮은 바닥을 가지고 있어서 휠체어를 탄 사람조차 아무 도움 없이 이용할 수 있다.

26 물론, 이것은 다른 사람들도 버스를 더 편안하게 탈 수 있도록 도와준다.

27 오늘날 점점 더 많은 디자이너가 Patricia의 방식을 따르고 있다.

28 크고 평평한 조명 스위치, 편한 손잡이를 가진 문, 터치 버튼을 가진 전화기와 같은 제품들은 사람들이 더 나은 삶을 살도록 도와주고 있다.

29 여러분의 주위를 둘러보고, 더 나이 들거나 더 약한 사람들의 어려움을 느껴 보고, 그들의 관점에서 해결책을 찾으려고 노력해 봐라.

30 여러분은 다음의 Patricia Moore가 되어 세상을 모두에게 더 나은 곳으로 만들 수 있을 것이다.

※ 다음 우리말과 일치하도록 빈칸에 알맞은 말을 쓰시오.

1 Patricia Moore – Mother of _____ _____

2 In 1979, a woman _____ _____ _____ _____ _____ in the U.S. and Canada.

3 She _____ _____ _____.

4 She _____ _____ _____ _____ _____ well.

5 She _____ _____ well _____ _____.

6 _____ _____ _____ _____, the woman had to climb stairs in subway stations and _____ _____ _____ buses.

7 She had to open _____ _____ and use can openers _____ _____ _____ _____.

8 Sometimes she got hurt or _____ _____ _____ _____.

9 Every moment was _____ _____ _____ _____, but she visited _____ _____ 115 cities and ended her trip in 1982.

10 Who was the woman and _____ _____ _____ _____ all this?

11 She was Patricia Moore, _____ _____ _____.

12 _____ _____ _____, she _____ _____ a big design company.

13 She often asked at meetings, "_____ _____ _____ for old or _____ _____?"

14 The other designers always answered, "We don't design _____ _____ _____."

15 She _____ _____ _____ the same _____ _____.

16 _____, she decided to become one of "those people" and travel around many cities _____ _____ _____ _____ better.

1 Patricia Moore – 유니버설 디자인의 어머니

2 1979년에, 한 여성이 미국과 캐나다의 도시로 여행을 시작했다.

3 그녀는 80세가 넘어 보였다.

4 그녀는 잘 보거나 잘 들을 수 없었다.

5 그녀는 지팡이 없이는 잘 걸을 수 없었다.

6 이 모든 어려움을 가진 채, 그 여성은 지하철역에서 계단을 올라가거나 붐비는 버스에 올라타야 했다.

7 그녀는 무거운 문을 열거나 그녀의 약한 손으로 깡통 따개를 사용해야 했다.

8 때때로 그녀는 다치거나 위험에 처하기도 했다.

9 모든 순간이 그녀에게 매우 어려웠으나, 그녀는 115개 이상의 도시를 방문하였으며 1982년에 여행을 끝마쳤다.

10 그 여성은 누구였고 무엇이 그녀로 하여금 이 모든 것을 하게 만들었을까?

11 그녀는 26살의 디자이너인 Patricia Moore였다.

12 1970년대 동안, 그녀는 큰 디자인 회사에서 일했다.

13 그녀는 종종 회의에서 물었다. "나이 들거나 약한 사람들을 위해 디자인하는 게 어떨까요?"

14 다른 디자이너들은 항상 대답했다. "우리는 그런 사람들을 위해 디자인하지 않습니다."

15 그녀는 똑같은 냉담한 대답에 지쳤다.

16 마침내, 그녀는 '그런 사람들' 중의 하나가 되어 그들의 어려움을 더 잘 이해하기 위해 많은 도시를 여행하기로 결심했다.

17 _____ _____ , she _____ _____ her grandmother's clothes, _____ shoes, and _____ _____ .

18 The shoes were _____ uncomfortable _____ she _____ walk well _____ _____ _____ .

19 The glasses were _____ thick _____ she _____ see well _____ _____ .

20 She also put _____ _____ _____ in her ears _____ _____ _____ _____ _____ .

21 _____ her journey, Patricia _____ the _____ old people _____ _____ .

22 _____ _____ _____ , she designed products anybody could use _____ and _____ .

23 This was the _____ of " _____ _____ ," or " _____ _____ ."

24 _____ _____ of her universal design ideas is _____ _____ .

25 They have _____ _____ and have _____ _____ _____ that even a person _____ _____ _____ can use them _____ _____ _____ .

26 Of course, this _____ other people _____ _____ the bus _____ , too.

27 Today more and more designers are _____ _____ _____ .

28 Products _____ big flat light switches, doors _____ easy handles, and phones _____ touch buttons are helping people _____ _____ _____ .

29 _____ _____ you, feel the difficulties of people who are older or weaker, and try to find solutions _____ _____ _____ .

30 You could be the _____ Patricia Moore and make the world _____ _____ _____ _____ .

17 이를 위해, 그녀는 자신의 할머니 옷을 입고, 불편한 신발을 신고, 두꺼운 안경을 썼다.

18 신발은 너무 불편해서 그녀는 지팡이가 없이는 잘 걸을 수 없었다.

19 안경은 너무 두꺼워서 그녀는 안경을 쓰고는 잘 볼 수 없었다.

20 그녀는 또한 그녀의 청력을 나쁘게 하려고 귀에 많은 솜을 넣었다.

21 여행 동안, Patricia는 나이 든 사람들이 겪는 어려움을 느꼈다.

22 이 경험으로부터, 그녀는 누구나 안전하고 쉽게 사용할 수 있는 제품들을 고안했다.

23 이것이 '유니버설 디자인' 또는 '모두를 위한 디자인'의 시작이었다.

24 그녀의 유니버설 디자인 아이디어의 한 가지 예는 저상 버스이다.

25 그것은 계단이 없고 낮은 바닥을 가지고 있어서 휠체어를 탄 사람조차 아무 도움 없이 이용할 수 있다.

26 물론, 이것은 다른 사람들도 버스를 더 편안하게 탈 수 있도록 도와준다.

27 오늘날 점점 더 많은 디자이너가 Patricia의 방식을 따르고 있다.

28 크고 평평한 조명 스위치, 편한 손잡이를 가진 문, 터치 버튼을 가진 전화기와 같은 제품들은 사람들이 더 나은 삶을 살도록 도와주고 있다.

29 여러분의 주위를 둘러보고, 더 나이 들거나 더 약한 사람들의 어려움을 느껴 보고, 그들의 관점에서 해결책을 찾으려고 노력해 봐라.

30 여러분은 다음의 Patricia Moore가 되어 세상을 모두에게 더 나은 곳으로 만들 수 있을 것이다.

※ 다음 문장을 우리말로 쓰시오.

1 Patricia Moore – Mother of Universal Design

➡ _____

2 In 1979, a woman started a journey to cities in the U.S. and Canada.

➡ _____

3 She looked over 80.

➡ _____

4 She couldn't see or hear well.

➡ _____

5 She couldn't walk well without a stick.

➡ _____

6 With all these difficulties, the woman had to climb stairs in subway stations and get on crowded buses.

➡ _____

7 She had to open heavy doors and use can openers with her weak hands.

➡ _____

8 Sometimes she got hurt or found herself in danger.

➡ _____

9 Every moment was very difficult for her, but she visited more than 115 cities and ended her trip in 1982.

➡ _____

10 Who was the woman and what made her do all this?

➡ _____

11 She was Patricia Moore, a 26-year-old designer.

➡ _____

12 During the 1970's, she worked for a big design company.

➡ _____

13 She often asked at meetings, "How about designing for old or weak people?"

➡ _____

14 The other designers always answered, "We don't design for those people."

➡ _____

15 She became tired of the same cold answer.

➡ _____

16 Finally, she decided to become one of "those people" and travel around many cities to understand their difficulties better.

➡ _____

17 For this, she put on her grandmother's clothes, uncomfortable shoes, and thick glasses.

➡ _____

18 The shoes were so uncomfortable that she couldn't walk well without a stick.

➡ _____

19 The glasses were so thick that she couldn't see well with them.

➡ _____

20 She also put lots of cotton in her ears to make her hearing bad.

➡ _____

21 During her journey, Patricia felt the difficulties old people go through.

➡ _____

22 From this experience, she designed products anybody could use safely and easily.

➡ _____

23 This was the beginning of "universal design," or "design for all."

➡ _____

24 One example of her universal design ideas is low-floor buses.

➡ _____

25 They have no steps and have such a low floor that even a person in a wheelchair can use them without any help.

➡ _____

26 Of course, this helps other people get on the bus more comfortably, too.

➡ _____

27 Today more and more designers are following Patricia's way.

➡ _____

28 Products like big flat light switches, doors with easy handles, and phones with touch buttons are helping people live better lives.

➡ _____
_____

29 Look around you, feel the difficulties of people who are older or weaker, and try to find solutions from their point of view.

➡ _____
_____

30 You could be the next Patricia Moore and make the world a better place for everybody.

➡ _____

※ 다음 괄호 안의 단어들을 우리말에 맞도록 바르게 배열하시오.

1 (Moore / Patricia / — / Universal / of / Mother / Design)
➡ _____

2 (1979, / in / woman / a / started / journey / a / cities / to / the / in / Canada. / and / U.S.)
➡ _____

3 (she / over / looked / 80.)
➡ _____

4 (couldn't / she / hear / or / see / well.)
➡ _____

5 (she / walk / couldn't / well / a / stick. / without)
➡ _____

6 (all / with / difficulties, / these / woman / the / had / climb / to / stairs / subway / in / stations / and / on / get / buses. / crowded)
➡ _____

7 (had / she / open / to / doors / heavy / and / can / use / openers / her / with / hands. / weak)
➡ _____

8 (she / sometimes / got / or / hurt / found / in / herself / danger.)
➡ _____

9 (moment / every / very / was / for / difficult / her, / but / visited / she / than / more / cities / 115 / and / her / ended / in / trip / 1982.)
➡ _____

10 (was / who / woman / the / and / made / what / her / all / do / this?)
➡ _____

11 (was / she / Moore, / Patricia / 26-year-old / a / designer.)
➡ _____

12 (the / during / 1970's, / worked / she / a / for / design / big / company.)
➡ _____

13 (she / asked / often / meetings, / at / "how / designing / about / old / for / or / people?" / weak)
➡ _____

14 (other / the / always / designers / answered, / "we / design / don't / those / people." / for)
➡ _____

15 (became / she / of / tired / same / the / answer. / cold)
➡ _____

16 (she / finally, / decided / become / to / of / one / "those / and / people" / travel / many / around / to / cities / understand / difficulties / their / better.)
➡ _____

1 Patricia Moore – 유니버설 디자인의 어머니

2 1979년에, 한 여성이 미국과 캐나다의 도시로 여행을 시작했다.

3 그녀는 80세가 넘어 보였다.

4 그녀는 잘 보거나 잘 들을 수 없었다.

5 그녀는 지팡이 없이는 잘 걸을 수 없었다.

6 이 모든 어려움을 가진 채, 그 여성은 지하철역에서 계단을 올라가거나 붐비는 버스에 올라타야 했다.

7 그녀는 무거운 문을 열거나 그녀의 약한 손으로 깡통 따개를 사용해야 했다.

8 때때로 그녀는 다치거나 위험에 처하기도 했다.

9 모든 순간이 그녀에게 매우 어려웠으나, 그녀는 115개 이상의 도시를 방문하였으며 1982년에 여행을 끝마쳤다.

10 그 여성은 누구였고 무엇이 그녀로 하여금 이 모든 것을 하게 만들었을까?

11 그녀는 26살의 디자이너인 Patricia Moore였다.

12 1970년대 동안, 그녀는 큰 디자인 회사에서 일했다.

13 그녀는 종종 회의에서 물었다. "나이 들거나 약한 사람들을 위해 디자인하는 게 어떨까요?"

14 다른 디자이너들은 항상 대답했다. "우리는 그런 사람들을 위해 디자인하지 않습니다."

15 그녀는 똑같은 냉담한 대답에 지쳤다.

16 마침내, 그녀는 '그런 사람들' 중의 하나가 되어 그들의 어려움을 더 잘 이해하기 위해 많은 도시를 여행하기로 결심했다.

17 (this, / for / she / on / put / her / clothes, / grandmother's / shoes, / uncomfortable / and / glasses. / thick)

➡ _____

_____

18 (shoes / the / so / were / uncomfortable / she / that / couldn't / well / walk / a / without / stick.)

➡ _____

19 (glasses / the / so / were / thick / she / that / couldn't / well / see / them. / with)

➡ _____

20 (she / put / also / of / lots / cotton / her / in / ears / make / to / hearing / her / bad.)

➡ _____

21 (her / during / journey, / felt / Patricia / difficulties / the / people / old / through. / go)

➡ _____

22 (this / from / experience, / designed / she / anybody / products / use / could / easily. / and / safely)

➡ _____

_____

23 (was / this / beginning / the / "universal / of / design," / or / all." / for / "design)

➡ _____

24 (example / one / her / of / universal / ideas / design / low-floor / is / buses.)

➡ _____

25 (have / they / steps / no / and / such / have / low / a / floor / that / a / even / person / a / in / wheelchair / use / can / them / any / help. / without)

➡ _____

_____

26 (course, / of / helps / this / people / other / on / get / bus / the / more / too. / comfortably)

➡ _____

27 (more / today / more / and / designers / following / are / way. / Patricia's)

➡ _____

28 (like / products / big / light / flat / switches, / with / doors / handlers, / easy / and / with / phones / touch / buttons / helping / are / live / people / lives. / better)

➡ _____

_____

29 (around / look / you, / the / feel / difficulties / people / of / are / who / older / weaker, / or / try / and / to / solutions / find / their / from / view. / of / point)

➡ _____

_____

30 (could / you / the / be / next / Moore / Patricia / and / the / make / world / better / a / place / everybody. / for)

➡ _____

_____

17 이를 위해, 그녀는 자신의 할머니 옷을 입고, 불편한 신발을 신고, 두꺼운 안경을 썼다.

18 신발은 너무 불편해서 그녀는 지팡이가 없이는 잘 걸을 수 없었다.

19 안경은 너무 두꺼워서 그녀는 안경을 쓰고는 잘 볼 수 없었다.

20 그녀는 또한 그녀의 청력을 나쁘게 하려고 귀에 많은 솜을 넣었다.

21 여행 동안, Patricia는 나이 든 사람들이 겪는 어려움을 느꼈다.

22 이 경험으로부터, 그녀는 누구나 안전하고 쉽게 사용할 수 있는 제품들을 고안했다.

23 이것이 '유니버설 디자인' 또는 '모두를 위한 디자인'의 시작이었다.

24 그녀의 유니버설 디자인 아이디어의 한 가지 예는 저상 버스이다.

25 그것은 계단이 없고 낮은 바닥을 가지고 있어서 휠체어를 탄 사람조차 아무 도움 없이 이용할 수 있다.

26 물론, 이것은 다른 사람들도 버스를 더 편안하게 탈 수 있도록 도와준다.

27 오늘날 점점 더 많은 디자이너가 Patricia의 방식을 따르고 있다.

28 크고 평평한 조명 스위치, 편한 손잡이를 가진 문, 터치 버튼을 가진 전화기와 같은 제품들은 사람들이 더 나은 삶을 살도록 도와주고 있다.

29 여러분의 주위를 둘러보고, 더 나이 들거나 더 약한 사람들의 어려움을 느껴 보고, 그들의 관점에서 해결책을 찾으려고 노력해 봐라.

30 여러분은 다음의 Patricia Moore가 되어 세상을 모두에게 더 나은 곳으로 만들 수 있을 것이다.

※ 다음 우리말을 영어로 쓰시오.

1 Patricia Moore – 유니버설 디자인의 어머니

➡ _____

2 1979년에, 한 여성이 미국과 캐나다의 도시로 여행을 시작했다.

➡ _____

3 그녀는 80세가 넘어 보였다.

➡ _____

4 그녀는 잘 보거나 잘 들을 수 없었다.

➡ _____

5 그녀는 지팡이 없이는 잘 걸을 수 없었다.

➡ _____

6 이 모든 어려움을 가진 채, 그 여성은 지하철역에서 계단을 올라가거나 붐비는 버스에 올라타야 했다.

➡ _____

7 그녀는 무거운 문을 열거나 그녀의 약한 손으로 깡통 따개를 사용해야 했다.

➡ _____

8 때때로 그녀는 다치거나 위험에 처하기도 했다.

➡ _____

9 모든 순간이 그녀에게 매우 어려웠으나, 그녀는 115개 이상의 도시를 방문하였으며 1982년에 여행을 끝마쳤다.

➡ _____

10 그 여성은 누구였고 무엇이 그녀로 하여금 이 모든 것을 하게 만들었을까?

➡ _____

11 그녀는 26살의 디자이너인 Patricia Moore였다.

➡ _____

12 1970년대 동안, 그녀는 큰 디자인 회사에서 일했다.

➡ _____

13 그녀는 종종 회의에서 물었다. "나이 들거나 약한 사람들을 위해 디자인하는 게 어떨까요?"

➡ _____

14 다른 디자이너들은 항상 대답했다. "우리는 그런 사람들을 위해 디자인하지 않습니다."

➡ _____

15 그녀는 똑같은 냉담한 대답에 지쳤다.

➡ _____

16 마침내, 그녀는 '그런 사람들' 중의 하나가 되어 그들의 어려움을 더 잘 이해하기 위해 많은 도시를 여행하기로 결심했다.

➡ _____

_____

17 이를 위해, 그녀는 자신의 할머니 옷을 입고, 불편한 신발을 신고, 두꺼운 안경을 썼다.

➡ _____

18 신발은 너무 불편해서 그녀는 지팡이 없이는 잘 걸을 수 없었다.

➡ _____

19 안경은 너무 두꺼워서 그녀는 안경을 쓰고는 잘 볼 수 없었다.

➡ _____

20 그녀는 또한 그녀의 청력을 나쁘게 하려고 귀에 많은 솜을 넣었다.

➡ _____

21 여행 동안, Patricia는 나이 든 사람들이 겪는 어려움을 느꼈다.

➡ _____

22 이 경험으로부터, 그녀는 누구나 안전하고 쉽게 사용할 수 있는 제품들을 고안했다.

➡ _____

23 이것이 '유니버설 디자인' 또는 '모두를 위한 디자인'의 시작이었다.

➡ _____

24 그녀의 유니버설 디자인 아이디어의 한 가지 예는 저상 버스이다.

➡ _____

25 그것은 계단이 없고 낮은 바닥을 가지고 있어서 휠체어를 탄 사람조차 아무 도움 없이 이용할 수 있다.

➡ _____

_____

26 물론, 이것은 다른 사람들도 버스를 더 편안하게 탈 수 있도록 도와준다.

➡ _____

27 오늘날 점점 더 많은 디자이너가 Patricia의 방식을 따르고 있다.

➡ _____

28 크고 평평한 조명 스위치, 편한 손잡이를 가진 문, 터치 버튼을 가진 전화기와 같은 제품들은 사람들이 더 나은 삶을 살도록 도와주고 있다.

➡ _____

_____

29 여러분의 주위를 둘러보고, 더 나이 들거나 더 약한 사람들의 어려움을 느껴 보고, 그들의 관점에서 해결책을 찾으려고 노력해 봐라.

➡ _____

_____

30 여러분은 다음의 Patricia Moore가 되어 세상을 모두에게 더 나은 곳으로 만들 수 있을 것이다.

➡ _____

※ 다음 우리말과 일치하도록 빈칸에 알맞은 말을 쓰시오.

Express Yourself C1

1. The _____ _____ door in my house is _____ high _____
   my little brother _____ _____ clothes _____ into it.

2. _____, this machine has a _____ _____.

3. It'll _____ my brother _____ clothes in _____ _____.

1. 우리 집에 있는 세탁기 문은 너무 높아서 나의 남동생은 그 안에 옷을 쉽게 넣을 수 없다.
2. 그러나, 이 기계는 옆문을 가지고 있다.
3. 그것은 내 남동생이 옷을 더 쉽게 넣을 수 있도록 도와줄 것이다.

Project Step 3

1. The hole cover was _____ _____ _____ I _____ ride my
   bike on it.

2. So I want _____ _____ the cover _____ this.

3. The new cover will _____ people _____ a bike _____.

1. 맨홀 덮개가 너무 위험해서 나는 그 위에서 자전거를 탈 수 없었다.
2. 그래서 나는 덮개를 이처럼 바꾸고 싶다.
3. 새로운 덮개는 사람들이 자전거를 안전하게 타도록 도와줄 것이다.

Link to the World

1. Kim Mandeok _____ _____ _____ a poor family in Jeju.

2. She _____ _____ and _____ _____.

3. In 1794, lots of people in Jeju _____ _____ _____ hunger
   _____ _____ bad weather.

4. She _____ _____ _____ she had and _____ a lot of people.

5. King Jeongjo _____ _____ _____ _____ _____ to
   Mountain Geumgang.

1. 김만덕은 제주의 가난한 가정에서 태어났다.
2. 그녀는 열심히 일해서 부자가 되었다.
3. 1794년에 제주의 많은 사람이 나쁜 날씨로 인한 굶주림으로 죽어가고 있었다.
4. 그녀는 자신이 가진 거의 모든 것을 써서 많은 사람을 구했다.
5. 정조 임금은 그녀가 금강산으로 여행을 하도록 허락했다.

※ 다음 우리말을 영어로 쓰시오.

Express Yourself C1

1. 우리 집에 있는 세탁기 문은 너무 높아서 나의 남동생은 그 안에 옷을 쉽게 넣을 수 없다.

   ➡ _____

2. 그러나, 이 기계는 옆문을 가지고 있다.

   ➡ _____

3. 그것은 내 남동생이 옷을 더 쉽게 넣을 수 있도록 도와줄 것이다.

   ➡ _____

Project Step 3

1. 맨홀 덮개가 너무 위험해서 나는 그 위에서 자전거를 탈 수 없었다.

   ➡ _____

2. 그래서 나는 덮개를 이처럼 바꾸고 싶다.

   ➡ _____

3. 새로운 덮개는 사람들이 자전거를 안전하게 타도록 도와줄 것이다.

   ➡ _____

Link to the World

1. 김만덕은 제주의 가난한 가정에서 태어났다.

   ➡ _____

2. 그녀는 열심히 일해서 부자가 되었다.

   ➡ _____

3. 1794년에 제주의 많은 사람이 나쁜 날씨로 인한 굶주림으로 죽어가고 있었다.

   ➡ _____

4. 그녀는 자신이 가진 거의 모든 것을 써서 많은 사람을 구했다.

   ➡ _____

5. 정조 임금은 그녀가 금강산으로 여행을 하도록 허락했다.

   ➡ _____

※ 다음 영어를 우리말로 쓰시오.

01	activity		22	outside
02	slow		23	wet
03	winner		24	choose
04	delicious		25	ocean
05	second		26	close
06	wheel		27	place
07	youth		28	save
08	exactly		29	never
09	finish		30	change
10	break time		31	circle
11	bright		32	cute
12	sweet		33	mirror
13	friendly		34	P.E. class
14	though		35	cut A into B
15	clothes		36	wait a second
16	special		37	cover A up with B
17	grade		38	don't need to
18	handwriting		39	up and down
19	hopeful		40	take a break
20	trash can		41	such as
21	wave		42	add A to B
			43	be full of

※ 다음 우리말을 영어로 쓰시오.

01	느린		22	정확하게
02	대부분의		23	바다, 대양
03	결코 ~하지 않다		24	밝은, 똑똑한
04	활동		25	쓰레기 통
05	동그라미, 원		26	특별한
06	끝나다		27	체육 수업
07	친근한, 다정한		28	장소; 놓다, 두다
08	가까이; 닫다		29	바퀴
09	밖에		30	옷
10	절약하다		31	비록 ~일지라도
11	맛있는		32	파도치다, 손을 흔들다
12	젖은		33	단것, 단 음식
13	도형, 모양		34	젊음, 청춘
14	갈아입다, 바꾸다		35	휴식을 취하다
15	성적		36	~까지
16	손 글씨		37	~할 필요가 없다
17	희망적인		38	A를 B로 자르다
18	초, 짧은 시간, 두 번째		39	물러서다
19	쉬는 시간		40	A를 B에 더하다
20	승자		41	B로 A를 덮다
21	고르다		42	~로 가득 차다
			43	잠깐만

※ 다음 영영풀이에 알맞은 단어를 <보기>에서 골라 쓴 후, 우리말 뜻을 쓰시오.

1 _____ : containing, or tasting as if it contains, a lot of sugar: _____

2 _____ : behaving in a pleasant, kind way towards someone: _____

3 _____ : a food made from flour, water, and usually yeast, mixed together and baked: _____

4 _____ : to decide what you want from two or more things or possibilities: _____

5 _____ : the mass of salt water that covers most of the earth's surface: _____

6 _____ : writing that is done with a pen or pencil, not printed or typed: _____

7 _____ : covered with or containing liquid, especially water: _____

8 _____ : to keep something, especially money, for use in the future: _____

9 _____ : a person, a team, an animal, etc. that wins something: _____

10 _____ : a number or letter that shows how good someone's work or performance is: _____

11 _____ : to raise your hand and move it from side to side as a way of greeting someone: _____

12 _____ : the period of your life when you are young, or the state of being young: _____

13 _____ : a particular position, point or area: _____

14 _____ : a piece of special flat glass that reflects images, so that you can see yourself when you look in it: _____

15 _____ : a continuous curved line, the points of which are always the same distance away from a fixed central point: _____

16 _____ : a circular object connected at the centre to a bar, used for making vehicles or parts of machines move: _____

보기			
sweet	ocean	circle	grade
choose	friendly	wave	youth
place	wet	save	handwriting
bread	mirror	winner	wheel

※ 다음 우리말과 일치하도록 빈칸에 알맞은 것을 골라 쓰시오.

1 _____ _____
A. Magazine   B. Teens'

2 _____ of _____ in _____
A. Art   B. Works   C. Shapes

3 _____ a _____
A. Circle   B. Like

4 I love you _____ a circle _____ a circle never _____.
A. because   B. ends   C. like

5 Snowman

6 It's _____ _____.
A. outside   B. cold

7 I don't _____ to go _____ and _____.
A. out   B. play   C. want

8 But Mom _____ I _____ _____.
A. to   B. says   C. have

9 It's _____ to snow and I'm _____ to be _____.
A. going   B. starting   C. cold

10 I don't like playing _____ on _____ _____ these.
A. like   B. outside   C. days

11 But _____ a _____, I have the _____ wonderful idea!
A. wait   B. most   C. second

12 I'll _____ myself _____ with snow and I'll _____ here!
A. up   B. hide   C. cover

13 _____ _____ _____ Your Handwriting
A. with   B. Back   C. Looking

14 _____ is _____.
A. art   B. life

15 _____ _____ in COLOR.
A. yours   B. live

16 IT ISN'T OVER _____ IT'S _____.
A. OVER   B. UNTIL

17 I am a _____ walker, but I _____ walk _____.
A. slow   B. back   C. never

18 I love the _____ _____ you _____.
A. little   B. do   C. things

19 _____ your _____.
A. dream   B. follow

20 _____ _____
A. Bike   B. My

---

1 십대들의 잡지

2 모양으로 표현된 예술 작품

3 동그라미처럼

4 나는 동그라미처럼 너를 사랑해. 왜냐하면 동그라미는 절대 끝나지 않기에.

5 눈사람

6 바깥은 추워.

7 나는 밖으로 나가 놀고 싶지 않네.

8 하지만 엄마는 그래야 한다고 하시네.

9 눈이 오기 시작하고 나는 추워질 거야.

10 나는 이런 날에는 나가서 놀고 싶지 않아.

11 하지만 잠깐만, 나는 최고로 멋진 생각이 났어!

12 나는 눈으로 내 몸을 덮고 여기에 숨어야지!

13 손 글씨로 돌아보기

14 인생은 예술이다.

15 다양한 색깔로 살아라.

16 끝날 때까지 끝난 게 아니다.

17 나는 느리게 걷는 사람이지만 절대 물러서지는 않는다.

18 나는 네가 하는 작은 일들을 사랑해.

19 네 꿈을 좇으라.

20 나의 자전거

21 Two wheels _____ me / To any _____ / To school / _____ home / To the mountain / To the river / I love my bike / I enjoy _____ it every day

A. place   B. riding   C. take   D. back

22 _____ _____

A. Tree   B. Giving

23 _____ there – _____

A. wet   B. out

24 _____ here – _____

A. dry   B. in

25 _____ _____ umbrella

A. big   B. pretty

26 _____ me _____ the sky

A. and   B. between

27 _____ of This _____

A. Year   B. Selfies

28 _____ we _____ the game, we had a _____ of fun.

A. lot   B. lost   C. though

29 _____ _____ the robots we _____.

A. at   B. made   C. look

30 _____ they _____?

A. cute   B. aren't

31 We _____ a _____ cake _____ Mr. Han.

A. for   B. big   C. made

32 It _____ _____ _____.

A. him   B. made   C. happy

33 _____ you ever _____ a handsome Peter Pan _____ me?

A. seen   B. like   C. have

34 _____ Do You _____ of Your School _____?

A. Think   B. What   C. Life

35 The _____ uncomfortable _____

A. moment   B. most

36 1. When I _____

A. tests   B. take

37 2. _____ I am really _____ and have _____ to eat

A. nothing   B. when   C. hungry

21 바퀴 두 개가 나를 데려가네 / 어느 곳으로든지 / 학교로 / 다시 집으로 / 산으로 / 강으로 / 나는 내 자전거가 아주 좋아 / 나는 그걸 매일 즐겨 타네

22 아낌없이 주는 나무

23 저곳 바깥은 – 젖어 있고

24 이곳 안쪽은 – 말라 있네

25 엄청 큰 우산이네

26 나와 하늘 사이에 있는

27 올해의 셀피들

28 우리는 게임에 졌지만, 아주 즐거웠다.

29 우리가 만든 로봇들을 봐.

30 귀엽지 않니?

31 우리는 한 씨 할아버지께 드릴 큰 케이크를 만들었다.

32 그것은 할아버지를 행복하게 해 주었다.

33 나처럼 잘생긴 피터 팬을 본 적이 있니?

34 학교생활에 대해 어떻게 생각하니?

35 가장 불편한 순간

36 1. 시험을 칠 때

37 2. 정말 배가 고픈데 먹을 것이 없을 때

38 3. When I _____ clothes _____ and after P.E. _____

A. class   B. before   C. change

39 4. others: _____ I am _____ in _____

A. sleepy   B. class   C. when

40 _____ the teacher doesn't finish _____ after the bell _____

A. rings   B. when   C. classes

41 The most _____ _____

A. lovely   B. most

42 1. _____ _____

A. time   B. lunch

43 2. _____ _____ my _____ teacher

A. favorite   B. with   C. class

44 3. the _____ _____ on Friday

A. class   B. last

45 4. others: _____ I am sleeping _____ _____ time

A. during   B. when   C. break

46 _____ I see _____ in the _____

A. mirror   B. myself   C. when

47 The _____ _____ news

A. awesome   B. most

48 1. I _____ better _____ than _____

A. grades   B.before   C. got

49 2. School _____ _____ today

A. earlier   B. finishes

50 3. I don't go to school _____ _____ rains or snows a _____

A. because   B. lot   C. it

51 4. others: We eat _____ sweets _____ dessert

A. for   B. delicious

52 My _____ friend and I are _____ the _____ class

A. same   B. best   C. in

53 The _____ _____ work to _____

A. difficult   B. do   C. most

54 1. _____ trash _____

A. cans   B. washing

55 2. Studying

---

38 3. 체육 시간 전후에 옷을 갈아 입을 때

39 4. 기타: 수업 중에 졸릴 때

40 종이 울렸는데 선생님이 수업을 끝내지 않을 때

41 가장 사랑스러운 시간

42 1. 점심시간

43 2. 가장 좋아하는 선생님의 수업 시간

44 3. 금요일의 마지막 수업 시간

45 4. 기타: 쉬는 시간에 잠잘 때

46 거울 속의 나를 볼 때

47 가장 멋진 뉴스

48 1. 전보다 좋은 성적을 받았다

49 2. 오늘 수업이 일찍 끝난다

50 3. 비나 눈이 많이 와서 학교에 가지 않는다

51 4. 기타: 후식으로 맛있는 단것을 먹는다

52 가장 친한 친구와 내가 같은 반이 되었다

53 가장 하기 힘든 일

54 1. 쓰레기통 씻기

55 2. 공부하기

56 3. _____ a _____ in _____ of friends

　A. making　　　B. front　　　C. presentation

57 4. others: Being _____ time _____ day

　A. on　　　　　B. every

58 _____ _____

　A. work　　　　B. group

59 _____ We _____ in Our _____

　A. Village　　　B. Love　　　C. Places

60 Daehan _____ _____

　A. Market　　　B. Traditional

61 If you want to eat _____ _____, _____ Daehan Market.

　A. delicious　　B. something　C. visit

62 You can _____ "*yeopjeon*" and _____ it to _____ your lunch box _____.

　A. full　　　　B. use　　　C. make　　　D. buy

63 You can _____ many kinds of food and _____ them _____ your lunch box.

　A. add　　　　B. choose　　C. to

64 Saebom _____ _____

　A. Center　　　B. Youth

65 This is Saebom Youth Center in the _____ _____ our _____.

　A. of　　　　　B. town　　　C. middle

66 We like this place _____ we can _____ many things, _____ _____ dance and music.

　A. as　　　　　B. because　　C. such　　　D. learn

67 We can also _____ board games and _____ a _____ here.

　A. take　　　　B. play　　　C. break

68 _____ Kim's _____

　A. Bakery　　　B. Mr.

69 This is a _____ _____ _____ the school.

　A. near　　　　B. bakery　　C. small

---

70 We like to go there _____ school _____ we're always _____ !

A. because   B. hungry   C. after

71 _____ is good _____ enjoy delicious bread _____ friends.

A. to   B. with   C. it

72 _____ _____ _____ with Puzzles!

A. Have   B. Let's   C. Fun

73 _____ _____

A. Puzzles   B. Shape

74 If you _____ the shape A _____ two same pieces, you can then make all the other _____ (B, C, D, E, F, G) _____ those two pieces.

A. into   B. from   C. cut   D. shapes

75 Ten _____ in Five _____

A. Lines   B. Balls

76 Place 10 balls in 5 lines in _____ a _____ that each line has _____ 4 balls on it.

A. way   B. exactly   C. such

77 You Are _____ _____ _____ !

A. Eating   B. Spoons   C. Plastic

78 1. A _____ of plastic spoons are _____ _____ every year.

A. away   B. lot   C. thrown

79 2. Most plastic _____ _____ into smaller _____ in the ocean.

A. pieces   B. down   C. breaks

80 3. Very small _____ of plastic _____ _____ fish.

A. into   B. pieces   C. go

81 4. _____ you eat the fish, you eat the plastic, _____ . Up _____ 11,000 pieces _____ year!

A. each   B. too   C. to   D. if

82 _____ _____ a Dream School!

A. Make   B. Let's

83 We had a _____ design _____ for our school _____ month.

A. last   B. universal   C. contest

84 Here are the _____ _____ .

A. works   B. winners'

85 1. When your hands _____ _____ , water comes _____ .

A. close   B. out   C. come

70 우리는 항상 배가 고파서 방과 후에 거기에 가는 것을 좋아해요!

71 친구들과 맛있는 빵을 즐기는 것이 좋아요.

72 퍼즐로 즐거운 시간을 보내자!

73 도형 퍼즐

74 A를 똑같은 두 개의 조각으로 자르면, 그 두 조각으로 다른 모든 형태(B, C, D, E, F, G)를 만들 수 있다.

75 5개의 선에 놓인 10개의 공

76 각각의 선 위에 정확하게 4개의 공이 놓이도록 10개의 공을 5개의 선에 놓아라.

77 너는 플라스틱 숟가락을 먹고 있다!

78 1. 해마다 많은 플라스틱 숟가락이 버려진다.

79 2. 대부분의 플라스틱 숟가락은 바닷속에서 더 작은 조각으로 부서진다.

80 3. 아주 작은 플라스틱 조각들이 물고기의 몸속으로 들어간다.

81 4. 여러분이 그 물고기를 먹으면 여러분도 플라스틱을 먹게 되는 것이다. 해마다 11,000개의 조각까지!

82 꿈의 학교를 만들어 보자!

83 지난달에 우리는 우리 학교를 위한 유니버설 디자인 경시대회를 열었습니다.

84 여기 우승자들의 작품이 있습니다.

85 1. 손을 가까이 가져가면 물이 나옵니다.

86 When you _____ your hands _____, the water _____.

A. away   B. pull   C. stops

87 You don't _____ to _____ or _____ any parts.

A. need   B. touch   C. turn

88 We can _____ _____ of water _____ this. – by O Juyeon(1-3)

A. lots   B. with   C. save

89 2. This is _____ school park _____ two _____.

A. between   B. our   C. buildings

90 _____ can go _____ and down _____ here.

A. easily   B. anybody   C. up

91 Also we _____ sit and _____ some _____ here. – by Gim Jimin(3-5)

A. rest   B. get   C. can

92 3. These are _____ desks and _____ for the _____.

A. special   B. classroom   C. chairs

93 For group _____, you can get them _____ and make a _____ group table for three, four, or five students. – by Choi Yumi(2-1)

A. together   B. activities   C. wonderful

94 _____ _____.

A. LAUGH   B. LET'S

95 _____ Earth Day _____ Ha! Ha! Ha!

A. Jokes   B. Funny

96 Why are _____ bins _____?

A. hopeful   B. recycle

97 _____ they're _____ _____ cans.

A. full   B. because   C. of

98 _____ can you _____ the ocean is _____?

A. tell   B. how   C. friendly

99 _____ _____.

A. waves   B. it

100 _____ did the _____ go _____ school?

A. to   B. why   C. sun

101 To _____ _____.

A. brighter   B. get

---

86 손을 멀리 떨어뜨리면 물이 멈춥니다.

87 어떤 부분도 돌리거나 만질 필요가 없습니다.

88 우리는 이것으로 많은 물을 절약할 수 있답니다. — 오주연(1-3)

89 2. 이것은 두 개의 건물 사이에 있는 학교 정원입니다.

90 여기서는 누구라도 쉽게 위아래로 이동할 수 있습니다.

91 또한, 우리는 이곳에 앉아 휴식을 취할 수 있습니다. — 김지민(3-5)

92 3. 교실용의 특별한 책상과 의자가 있습니다.

93 모둠 활동을 하기 위해 그것들을 함께 모아 3명, 4명, 또는 5명이 활동할 훌륭한 모둠 책상을 만들 수 있습니다. — 최유미(2-1)

94 웃읍시다

95 재미있는 지구의 날 농담들 하! 하! 하!

96 재활용 통은 왜 희망적인가?

97 왜냐하면 '깡통[할 수 있다]'으로 가득 차 있기 때문이지.

98 바다가 다정하다는 것을 어떻게 알 수 있는가?

99 그것이 일렁이기[손을 흔들기] 때문이지.

100 태양은 왜 학교에 가는가?

101 더 밝아지기[똑똑해지기] 위해서지.

※ 다음 우리말과 일치하도록 빈칸에 알맞은 말을 쓰시오.

1 _____ _____

2 _____ of Art _____ _____

3 _____ a _____

4 I love you _____ a circle _____ a circle _____ _____.

5 _____

6 It's _____ _____.

7 I don't want to _____ _____ and _____.

8 But Mom says I _____ _____.

9 It's starting _____ _____ and I'm _____ _____ _____ _____.

10 I don't like playing outside _____ _____ _____.

11 But _____ _____ _____, I have _____ _____ _____ idea!

12 I'll _____ _____ _____ with snow and I'll _____ _____!

13 _____ _____ _____ Your _____

14 _____ is _____.

15 Live _____ in COLOR.

16 IT ISN'T OVER _____ IT'S _____.

17 I am a _____ _____, but I never _____ _____.

18 I love the _____ _____ you do.

19 _____ your dream.

20 _____ _____

21 Two wheels _____ me / _____ _____ _____ / To school / Back _____ / To the mountain / To the river / I love my bike / I _____ _____ it _____ _____

22 _____ Tree

23 Out _____ – _____

24 In _____ – _____

25 Pretty big _____

1 십대들의 잡지

2 모양으로 표현된 예술 작품

3 동그라미처럼

4 나는 동그라미처럼 너를 사랑해. 왜냐하면 동그라미는 절대 끝나지 않기에.

5 눈사람

6 바깥은 추워.

7 나는 밖으로 나가 놀고 싶지 않네.

8 하지만 엄마는 그래야 한다고 하시네.

9 눈이 오기 시작하고 나는 추워질 거야.

10 나는 이런 날에는 나가서 놀고 싶지 않아.

11 하지만 잠깐만. 나는 최고로 멋진 생각이 났어!

12 나는 눈으로 내 몸을 덮고 여기에 숨어야지!

13 손 글씨로 돌아보기

14 인생은 예술이다.

15 다양한 색깔로 살아라.

16 끝날 때까지 끝난 게 아니다.

17 나는 느리게 걷는 사람이지만 절대 물러서지는 않는다.

18 나는 네가 하는 작은 일들을 사랑해.

19 네 꿈을 좇으라.

20 나의 자전거

21 바퀴 두 개가 나를 데려가네 / 어느 곳으로든지 / 학교로 / 다시 집으로 / 산으로 / 강으로 / 나는 내 자전거가 아주 좋아 / 나는 그걸 매일 즐겨 타네

22 아낌없이 주는 나무

23 저곳 바깥은 – 젖어 있고

24 이곳 안쪽은 – 말라 있네

25 엄청 큰 우산이네

26 _____ me _____ the sky

27 _____ of _____ Year

28 _____ we _____ the game, we had a _____ of fun.

29 _____ _____ the _____ we made.

30 _____ they _____ ?

31 We made _____ _____ _____ for Mr. Han.

32 It _____ _____ _____ .

33 _____ _____ _____ _____ a handsome Peter Pan like me?

34 _____ Do You _____ _____ Your School _____ ?

35 The most _____ _____

36 1. When I _____ _____

37 2. When I am really hungry and _____ _____ to eat

38 3. When I _____ clothes _____ and _____ P.E. class

39 4. others: When I am _____ _____ _____

40 When the teacher doesn't finish classes _____ the bell _____

41 The _____ _____ _____

42 1. _____ time

43 2. _____ with my _____ teacher

44 3. the _____ _____ on Friday

45 4. others: when I am _____ _____ _____ _____

46 when I see _____ in the _____

47 The _____ _____ news

48 1. I got _____ _____ _____ _____ _____

49 2. School _____ _____ today

50 3. I don't go to school _____ it _____ or _____ a lot

51 4. others: We eat _____ sweets _____ _____

52 My best friend and I are _____ _____ _____

53 The _____ _____ work _____

54 1. Washing _____ _____

---

26 나와 하늘 사이에 있는

27 올해의 셀피들

28 우리는 게임에 졌지만, 아주 즐거웠다.

29 우리가 만든 로봇들을 봐.

30 귀엽지 않니?

31 우리는 한 씨 할아버지께 드릴 큰 케이크를 만들었다.

32 그것은 할아버지를 행복하게 해 주었다.

33 나처럼 잘생긴 피터 팬을 본 적이 있니?

34 학교생활에 대해 어떻게 생각하니?

35 가장 불편한 순간

36 1. 시험을 칠 때

37 2. 정말 배가 고픈데 먹을 것이 없을 때

38 3. 체육 시간 전후에 옷을 갈아 입을 때

39 4. 기타: 수업 중에 졸릴 때

40 종이 울렸는데 선생님이 수업을 끝내지 않을 때

41 가장 사랑스러운 시간

42 1. 점심시간

43 2. 가장 좋아하는 선생님의 수업 시간

44 3. 금요일의 마지막 수업 시간

45 4. 기타: 쉬는 시간에 잠잘 때

46 거울 속의 나를 볼 때

47 가장 멋진 뉴스

48 1. 전보다 좋은 성적을 받았다

49 2. 오늘 수업이 일찍 끝난다

50 3. 비나 눈이 많이 와서 학교에 가지 않는다

51 4. 기타: 후식으로 맛있는 단것을 먹는다

52 가장 친한 친구와 내가 같은 반이 되었다

53 가장 하기 힘든 일

54 1. 쓰레기통 씻기

55 2. _____

56 3. _____ _____ _____ in _____ of friends

57 4. others: Being _____ _____ every day

58 _____ _____

59 _____ We Love in Our _____

60 Daehan _____ _____

61 If you want to eat _____ _____, visit Daehan Market.

62 You can buy "*yeopjeon*" and use it _____ _____ your lunch box _____.

63 You can _____ many _____ _____ food and _____ them _____ your lunch box.

64 Saebom _____ _____

65 This is Saebom Youth Center _____ _____ _____ our town.

66 We like this place _____ we can learn many things, _____ _____ dance and music.

67 We can also play board games and _____ _____ _____ here.

68 Mr. Kim's _____

69 This is a small bakery _____ the school.

70 We like to go there _____ school _____ we're _____ _____!

71 _____ is good _____ _____ delicious bread with friends.

72 _____ _____ _____ with Puzzles!

73 _____ _____

74 If you _____ the shape A _____ two same pieces, you can then make all the _____ _____ (B, C, D, E, F, G) _____ those two pieces.

75 Ten Balls in _____ _____

76 Place 10 balls in 5 lines _____ _____ _____ that _____ _____ has exactly 4 balls on it.

55 2. 공부하기
56 3. 친구들 앞에서 발표하기
57 4. 기타: 매일 제시간에 등교하기
58 모둠 활동
59 우리 마을에서 우리가 좋아하는 곳
60 대한 전통 시장
61 맛있는 것이 먹고 싶으면, 대한 시장을 방문하세요.
62 엽전을 사면 여러분의 점심 도시락을 가득 채우는 데 그걸 쓸 수 있어요.
63 많은 종류의 음식을 골라서 점심 도시락에 담을 수 있답니다.
64 새봄 청소년 센터
65 이곳은 우리 마을 한가운데에 있는 새봄 청소년 센터입니다.
66 춤과 음악 같은 많은 것을 배울 수 있어서 우리는 이곳을 좋아한답니다.
67 우리는 또한 이곳에서 보드게임 도 하고 휴식도 취할 수 있어요.
68 김 씨네 빵집
69 이곳은 학교 근처의 작은 빵집 입니다.
70 우리는 항상 배가 고파서 방과 후에 거기에 가는 것을 좋아해요!
71 친구들과 맛있는 빵을 즐기는 것이 좋아요.
72 퍼즐로 즐거운 시간을 보내자!
73 도형 퍼즐
74 A를 똑같은 두 개의 조각으로 자르면, 그 두 조각으로 다른 모 든 형태(B, C, D, E, F, G)를 만 들 수 있다.
75 5개의 선에 놓인 10개의 공
76 각각의 선 위에 정확하게 4개의 공이 놓이도록 10개의 공을 5개 의 선에 놓아라.

77 You _____ _____ Plastic Spoons!

78 1. A lot of plastic spoons _____ _____ _____ every year.

79 2. Most plastic _____ _____ _____ smaller _____ in the ocean.

80 3. Very small pieces of plastic _____ _____ _____.

81 4. If you eat the fish, you eat the plastic, too. _____ _____ 11,000 pieces _____ _____!

82 _____ _____ a Dream School!

83 We had a _____ _____ contest for our school last month.

84 Here are the _____ _____.

85 1. When your hands _____ _____, water comes _____.

86 When you _____ your hands _____, the water stops.

87 You _____ _____ _____ turn or touch any parts.

88 We can _____ _____ _____ _____ _____ with this. – by O Juyeon(1-3)

89 2. This is our school park _____ two _____.

90 Anybody can go _____ and _____ here.

91 Also we can sit and _____ _____ _____ here. – by Gim Jimin(3-5)

92 3. These are _____ desks and chairs _____ the classroom.

93 For _____ _____, you can get them _____ and make a wonderful group table _____ three, four, or five students. – by Choi Yumi(2-1)

94 _____ _____

95 Funny Earth Day _____ Ha! Ha! Ha!

96 _____ are _____ bins _____?

97 _____ they're _____ cans.

98 _____ can you _____ the ocean is _____?

99 It _____.

100 _____ did the sun go to school?

101 _____ _____ brighter.

77 너는 플라스틱 숟가락을 먹고 있다!

78 1. 해마다 많은 플라스틱 숟가락이 버려진다.

79 2. 대부분의 플라스틱 숟가락은 바닷속에서 더 작은 조각으로 부서진다.

80 3. 아주 작은 플라스틱 조각들이 물고기의 몸속으로 들어간다.

81 4. 여러분이 그 물고기를 먹으면 여러분도 플라스틱을 먹게 되는 것이다. 해마다 11,000개의 조각까지!

82 꿈의 학교를 만들어 보자!

83 지난달에 우리는 우리 학교를 위한 유니버설 디자인 경시대회를 열었습니다.

84 여기 우승자들의 작품이 있습니다.

85 1. 손을 가까이 가져가면 물이 나옵니다.

86 손을 멀리 떨어뜨리면 물이 멈춥니다.

87 어떤 부분도 돌리거나 만질 필요가 없습니다.

88 우리는 이것으로 많은 물을 절약할 수 있습니다. — 오주연(1–3)

89 2. 이것은 두 개의 건물 사이에 있는 학교 정원입니다.

90 여기서는 누구라도 쉽게 위아래로 이동할 수 있습니다.

91 또한, 우리는 이곳에 앉아 휴식을 취할 수 있습니다. — 김지민(3–5)

92 3. 교실용의 특별한 책상과 의자가 있습니다.

93 모둠 활동을 하기 위해 그것들을 함께 모아 3명, 4명, 또는 5명이 활동할 훌륭한 모둠 책상을 만들 수 있습니다. — 최유미(2–1)

94 웃읍시다

95 재미있는 지구의 날 농담들 하! 하! 하!

96 재활용 통은 왜 희망적인가?

97 왜냐하면 '깡통[할 수 있다]'으로 가득 차 있기 때문이지.

98 바다가 다정하다는 것을 어떻게 알 수 있는가?

99 그것이 일렁이기[손을 흔들기] 때문이지.

100 태양은 왜 학교에 가는가?

101 더 밝아지기[똑똑해지기] 위해서지.

※ 다음 문장을 우리말로 쓰시오.

1 ▶ Teens' Magazine
➡ _____

2 ▶ Works of Art in Shapes
➡ _____

3 ▶ Like a Circle
➡ _____

4 ▶ I love you like a circle because a circle never ends.
➡ _____

5 ▶ Snowman
➡ _____

6 ▶ It's cold outside.
➡ _____

7 ▶ I don't want to go out and play.
➡ _____

8 ▶ But Mom says I have to.
➡ _____

9 ▶ It's starting to snow and I'm going to be cold.
➡ _____

10 ▶ I don't like playing outside on days like these.
➡ _____

11 ▶ But wait a second, I have the most wonderful idea!
➡ _____

12 ▶ I'll cover myself up with snow and I'll hide here!
➡ _____

13 ▶ Looking Back with Your Handwriting
➡ _____

14 ▶ Life is art.
➡ _____

15 ▶ Live yours in COLOR.
➡ _____

16 ▶ IT ISN'T OVER UNTIL IT'S OVER.
➡ _____

17 ▶ I am a slow walker, but I never walk back.
➡ _____

18 ▶ I love the little things you do.
➡ _____

19 ▶ Follow your dream.
➡ _____

20 ▶ My Bike
➡ _____

21 ▶ Two wheels take me / To any place / To school / Back home / To the mountain / To the river / I love my bike / I enjoy riding it every day
➡ _____
_____

22 ▶ Giving Tree
➡ _____

23 ▶ Out there – wet
➡ _____

24 In here – dry
➡

25 Pretty big umbrella
➡

26 Between me and the sky
➡

27 Selfies of This Year
➡

28 Though we lost the game, we had a lot of fun.
➡

29 Look at the robots we made.
➡

30 Aren't they cute?
➡

31 We made a big cake for Mr. Han.
➡

32 It made him happy.
➡

33 Have you ever seen a handsome Peter Pan like me?
➡

34 What Do You Think of Your School Life?
➡

35 The most uncomfortable moment
➡

36 1. When I take tests
➡

37 2. When I am really hungry and have nothing to eat
➡

38 3. When I change clothes before and after P.E. class
➡

39 4. others: When I am sleepy in class
➡

40 When the teacher doesn't finish classes after the bell rings
➡

41 The most lovely time
➡

42 1. lunch time
➡

43 2. class with my favorite teacher
➡

44 3. the last class on Friday
➡

45 4. others: when I am sleeping during break time
➡

46 when I see myself in the mirror
➡

47 The most awesome news
➡

48 1. I got better grades than before
➡

49 2. School finishes earlier today
➡

50 3. I don't go to school because it rains or snows a lot
➡

51 ▷ 4. others: We eat delicious sweets for dessert
➡ _____

52 ▷ My best friend and I are in the same class
➡ _____

53 ▷ The most difficult work to do
➡ _____

54 ▷ 1. Washing trash cans
➡ _____

55 ▷ 2. Studying
➡ _____

56 ▷ 3. Making a presentation in front of friends
➡ _____

57 ▷ 4. others: Being on time every day
➡ _____

58 ▷ Group work
➡ _____

59 ▷ Places We Love in Our Village
➡ _____

60 ▷ Daehan Traditional Market
➡ _____

61 ▷ If you want to eat something delicious, visit Daehan Market.
➡ _____

62 ▷ You can buy " *yeopjeon* " and use it to make your lunch box full.
➡ _____

63 ▷ You can choose many kinds of food and add them to your lunch box.
➡ _____

64 ▷ Saebom Youth Center
➡ _____

65 ▷ This is Saebom Youth Center in the middle of our town
➡ _____

66 ▷ We like this place because we can learn many things, such as dance and music.
➡ _____

67 ▷ We can also play board games and take a break here.
➡ _____

68 ▷ Mr. Kim's Bakery
➡ _____

69 ▷ This is a small bakery near the school.
➡ _____

70 ▷ We like to go there after school because we're always hungry!
➡ _____

71 ▷ It is good to enjoy delicious bread with friends.
➡ _____

72 ▷ Let's Have Fun with Puzzles!
➡ _____

73 ▷ Shape Puzzles
➡ _____

74 ▷ If you cut the shape A into two same pieces, you can then make all the other shapes(B, C, D, E, F, G) from those two pieces.
➡ _____

75 ▷ Ten Balls in Five Lines
➡ _____

76 ▷ Place 10 balls in 5 lines in such a way that each line has exactly 4 balls on it.
➡ _____

77 You Are Eating Plastic Spoons!
➡

78 1. A lot of plastic spoons are thrown away every year.
➡

79 2. Most plastic breaks down into smaller pieces in the ocean.
➡

80 3. Very small pieces of plastic go into fish.
➡

81 4. If you eat the fish, you eat the plastic, too. Up to 11,000 pieces each year!
➡

82 Let's Make a Dream School!
➡

83 We had a universal design contest for our school last month.
➡

84 Here are the winners' works.
➡

85 1. When your hands come close, water comes out.
➡

86 When you pull your hands away, the water stops.
➡

87 You don't need to turn or touch any parts.
➡

88 We can save lots of water with this. — by O Juyeon(1-3)
➡

89 2. This is our school park between two buildings.
➡

90 Anybody can go up and down easily here.
➡

91 Also we can sit and get some rest here.   by Gim Jimin(3-5)
➡

92 3. These are special desks and chairs for the classroom.
➡

93 For group activities, you can get them together and make a wonderful group table for three, four, or five students. — by Choi Yumi(2-1)
➡

94 LET'S LAUGH
➡

95 Funny Earth Day Jokes Ha! Ha! Ha!
➡

96 Why are recycle bins hopeful?
➡

97 Because they're full of cans.
➡

98 How can you tell the ocean is friendly?
➡

99 It waves.
➡

100 Why did the sun go to school?
➡

101 To get brighter.
➡

※ 다음 괄호 안의 단어들을 우리말에 맞도록 바르게 배열하시오.

1 (Magazine / Teens')
➡ _____

2 (Art / of / Works / Shapes / in)
➡ _____

3 (Circle / a / Like)
➡ _____

4 (you / love / I / like / circle / a / because / circle / a / ends. / never)
➡ _____

5 (snowman)
➡ _____

6 (cold / it's / outside.)
➡ _____

7 (don't / I / want / go / to / out / play. / and)
➡ _____

8 (Mom / but / I / says / to. / have)
➡ _____

9 (starting / it's / snow / to / and / going / I'm / cold. / be / to)
➡ _____

10 (I / like / don't / outside / playing / days / these. / like / on)
➡ _____

11 (wait / but / second, / a / have / I / most / the / idea! / wonderful)
➡ _____

12 (I'll / myself / cover / with / up / snow / and / hide / here! / I'll)
➡ _____

13 (Back / with / Looking / Handwriting / Your)
➡ _____

14 (art. / is / life)
➡ _____

15 (yours / live / COLOR / in)
➡ _____

16 (IT / OVER / ISN'T / IT'S / UNTIL / OVER)
➡ _____

17 (am / I / slow / a / walker, / I / but / walk / never / back.)
➡ _____

18 (love / I / little / the / you / things / do.)
➡ _____

19 (your / follow / dream)
➡ _____

20 (Bike / My)
➡ _____

21 (wheels / me / take / two / any / to / place // school / to // home / back // the / mountain / to // the / to / river // love / I / bike / my // enjoy / I / riding / day / it / every)
➡ _____

22 (Tree / Giving)
➡ _____

23 (there / out / — / wet)
➡ _____

24 (here / in / — / dry)
➡ _____

25 (big / pretty / umbrella)
➡ _____

1 십대들의 잡지

2 모양으로 표현된 예술 작품

3 동그라미처럼

4 나는 동그라미처럼 너를 사랑해. 왜냐하면 동그라미는 절대 끝나지 않기에.

5 눈사람

6 바깥은 추워.

7 나는 밖으로 나가 놀고 싶지 않네.

8 하지만 엄마는 그래야 한다고 하시네.

9 눈이 오기 시작하고 나는 추워질 거야.

10 나는 이런 날에는 나가서 놀고 싶지 않아.

11 하지만 잠깐만, 나는 최고로 멋진 생각이 났어!

12 나는 눈으로 내 몸을 덮고 여기에 숨어야지!

13 손 글씨로 돌아보기

14 인생은 예술이다.

15 다양한 색깔로 살아라.

16 끝날 때까지 끝난 게 아니다.

17 나는 느리게 걷는 사람이지만 절대 물러서지는 않는다.

18 나는 네가 하는 작은 일들을 사랑해.

19 네 꿈을 좇으라.

20 나의 자전거

21 바퀴 두 개가 나를 데려가네 / 어느 곳으로든지 / 학교로 / 다시 집으로 / 산으로 / 강으로 / 나는 내 자전거가 아주 좋아 / 나는 그걸 매일 즐겨 타네

22 아낌없이 주는 나무

23 저곳 바깥은 – 젖어 있고

24 이곳 안쪽은 – 말라 있네

25 엄청 큰 우산이네

26 (me / between / the / and / sky)

27 (of / Selfies / Year / This)

28 (we / though / lost / game, / the / had / we / lot / a / fun. / of)

29 (at / look / robots / the / made. / we)

30 (they / cute? / aren't)

31 (made / we / big / a / cake / Mr. / for / Han.)

32 (made / it / happy. / him)

33 (you / have / seen / ever / handsome / a / Pan / Peter / me? / like)

34 (Do / What / Think / You / of / School / Your / Life?)

35 (most / the / moment / uncomfortable)

36 (1. / I / tests / take / when)

37 (2. / I / when / really / am / and / hungry / nothing / have / eat / to)

38 (3. / I / when / clothes / change / before / and / P.E. / after / class)

39 (4. / others: / I / when / sleepy / am / class / in)

40 (the / when / doesn't / teacher / classes / finish / after / rings / bell / the)

41 (most / the / time / lovely)

42 (1. / time / lunch)

43 (2. / with / class / favorite / my / teacher)

44 (3. / last / the / class / Friday / on)

45 (4. / others: / I / when / am / sleeping / break / time / during)

46 (I / when / myself / see / the / mirror / in)

47 (most / the / news / awesome)

48 (1. / got / I / better / than / grades / before)

49 (2. / finishes / school / today / earlier)

50 (3. / don't / I / go / school / to / because / rains / it / snows / or / lot / a)

51 (4. / others: / eat / we / sweets / delicious / dessert / for)

52 (best / my / friend / and / are / I / the / in / class / same)

53 (the / difficult / most / do / to / work)

54 (1. / trash / washing / cans)

26 나와 하늘 사이에 있는

27 올해의 셀피들

28 우리는 게임에 졌지만, 아주 즐거웠다.

29 우리가 만든 로봇들을 봐.

30 귀엽지 않니?

31 우리는 한 씨 할아버지께 드릴 큰 케이크를 만들었다.

32 그것은 할아버지를 행복하게 해주었다.

33 나처럼 잘생긴 피터 팬을 본 적이 있니?

34 학교생활에 대해 어떻게 생각하니?

35 가장 불편한 순간

36 1. 시험을 칠 때

37 2. 정말 배가 고픈데 먹을 것이 없을 때

38 3. 체육 시간 전후에 옷을 갈아입을 때

39 4. 기타: 수업 중에 졸릴 때

40 종이 울렸는데 선생님이 수업을 끝내지 않을 때

41 가장 사랑스러운 시간

42 1. 점심시간

43 2. 가장 좋아하는 선생님의 수업 시간

44 3. 금요일의 마지막 수업 시간

45 4. 기타: 쉬는 시간에 잠잘 때

46 거울 속의 나를 볼 때

47 가장 멋진 뉴스

48 1. 전보다 좋은 성적을 받았다

49 2. 오늘 수업이 일찍 끝난다

50 3. 비나 눈이 많이 와서 학교에 가지 않는다

51 4. 기타: 후식으로 맛있는 단것을 먹는다

52 가장 친한 친구와 내가 같은 반이 되었다

53 가장 하기 힘든 일

54 1. 쓰레기통 씻기

55 (2. / studying)
➡ _____

56 (3. / a / making / presentation / of / front / in / friends)
➡ _____

57 (4. / others: / on / being / every / time / day)
➡ _____

58 (work / group)
➡ _____

59 (We / Places / in / Love / Village / Our)
➡ _____

60 (Traditional / Daehan / Market)
➡ _____

61 (you / if / to / want / something / eat / delicious, / Daehan / visit / Market.)
➡ _____

62 (can / you / buy / and / "yeopjeon" / use / to / it / make / your / box / full. / lunch)
➡ _____

63 (can / you / many / choose / kinds / food / of / and / them / to / add / your / box. / lunch)
➡ _____

64 (Youth / Saebom / Center)
➡ _____

65 (is / this / Youth / Saebom / Center / the / in / middle / our / town. / of)
➡ _____

66 (like / we / place / this / because / can / we / many / learn / things, / as / such / music. / and / dance)
➡ _____

67 (can / we / play / also / games / board / and / a / take / here. / break)
➡ _____

68 (Kim's / Mr. / Bakery)
➡ _____

69 (is / this / small / a / bakery / the / near / school.)
➡ _____

70 (like / we / go / to / there / school / after / because / always / we're / hungry!)
➡ _____

71 (is / it / to / good / delicious / enjoy / with / friends. / bread)
➡ _____

72 (Have / Let's / with / Fun / Puzzles!)
➡ _____

73 (Puzzles / Shape)
➡ _____

74 (you / if / the / cut / shape / A / two / into / pieces, / same / can / you / then / all / make / other / shapes(B, C, D, E, F, G) / those / from / pieces. / two)
➡ _____

75 (Balls / Ten / Five / in / Lines)
➡ _____

76 (10 / place / balls / 5 / in / lines / such / in / way / a / each / that / has / line / 4 / exactly / balls / it. / on)
➡ _____

---

55 2. 공부하기

56 3. 친구들 앞에서 발표하기

57 4. 기타: 매일 제시간에 등교하기

58 모둠 활동

59 우리 마을에서 우리가 좋아하는 곳

60 대한 전통 시장

61 맛있는 것이 먹고 싶으면, 대한 시장을 방문하세요.

62 엽전을 사면 여러분의 점심 도시락을 가득 채우는 데 그걸 쓸 수 있어요.

63 많은 종류의 음식을 골라서 점심 도시락에 담을 수 있답니다.

64 새봄 청소년 센터

65 이곳은 우리 마을 한가운데에 있는 새봄 청소년 센터입니다.

66 춤과 음악 같은 많은 것을 배울 수 있어서 우리는 이곳을 좋아한답니다.

67 우리는 또한 이곳에서 보드게임도 하고 휴식도 취할 수 있어요.

68 김 씨네 빵집

69 이곳은 학교 근처의 작은 빵집입니다.

70 우리는 항상 배가 고파서 방과 후에 거기에 가는 것을 좋아해요!

71 친구들과 맛있는 빵을 즐기는 것이 좋아요.

72 퍼즐로 즐거운 시간을 보내자!

73 도형 퍼즐

74 A를 똑같은 두 개의 조각으로 자르면, 그 두 조각으로 다른 모든 형태(B, C, D, E, F, G)를 만들 수 있다.

75 5개의 선에 놓인 10개의 공

76 각각의 선 위에 정확하게 4개의 공이 놓이도록 10개의 공을 5개의 선에 놓아라.

Step4

77 (Are / You / Plastic / Eating / Spoons!)
➡ _____

78 (1. / lot / a / plastic / of / are / spoons / away / thrown / year. / every)
➡ _____

79 (2. / plastic / most / down / breaks / smaller / into / in / pieces / ocean. / the)
➡ _____

80 (3. / small / very / of / pieces / go / plastic / fish. / into)
➡ _____

81 (4. / you / if / eat / fish, / the / eat / you / plastic, / the / too. // to / up / pieces / 11,000 / year! / each)
➡ _____

82 (Make / Let's / Dream / a / School!)
➡ _____

83 (had / we / universal / a / design / for / our / contest / school / month. / last)
➡ _____

84 (are / here / winner's / the / works.)
➡ _____

85 (your / when / come / hands / close, / comes / water / out.)
➡ _____

86 (you / when / your / pull / away, / hands / water / the / stops.)
➡ _____

87 (don't / you / to / need / turn / to / or / any / parts. / touch)
➡ _____

88 (can / we / lots / save / water / of / this. / with / — / O / by / Juyeon(1-3)
➡ _____

89 (is / this / school / our / between / park / buildings. / two)
➡ _____

90 (can / anybody / up / go / and / here. / easily / down)
➡ _____

91 (we / also / sit / can / and / some / get / here. / rest / — / Jimin(3-5) / Gim / by)
➡ _____

92 (are / these / desks / special / and / for / chairs / the / classroom.)
➡ _____

93 (group / for / activities, / can / you / get / together / them / and / a / make / group / wonderful / for / table / three, / or / four, / students. / five / — / Choi / Yumi(2-1) / by)
➡ _____

94 (LAUGH / LET'S)
➡ _____

95 (Earth / Funny / Jokes / Day / Ha! / Ha! / Ha!)
➡ _____

96 (are / recycle / why / hopeful? / bins)
➡ _____

97 (they're / because / cans. / of / full)
➡ _____

98 (can / how / tell / you / ocean / the / friendly? / is)
➡ _____

99 (waves. / it)
➡ _____

100 (did / why / sun / the / school? / to / go)
➡ _____

101 (get / to / brighter.)
➡ _____

77 너는 플라스틱 숟가락을 먹고 있다!

78 1. 해마다 많은 플라스틱 숟가락이 버려진다.

79 2. 대부분의 플라스틱 숟가락은 바닷속에서 더 작은 조각으로 부서진다.

80 3. 아주 작은 플라스틱 조각들이 물고기의 몸속으로 들어간다.

81 4. 여러분이 그 물고기를 먹으면 여러분도 플라스틱을 먹게 되는 것이다. 해마다 11,000개의 조각까지!

82 꿈의 학교를 만들어 보자!

83 지난달에 우리는 우리 학교를 위한 유니버설 디자인 경시대회를 열었습니다.

84 여기 우승자들의 작품이 있습니다.

85 1. 손을 가까이 가져가면 물이 나옵니다.

86 손을 멀리 떨어뜨리면 물이 멈춥니다.

87 어떤 부분도 돌리거나 만질 필요가 없습니다.

88 우리는 이것으로 많은 물을 절약할 수 있답니다. — 오주연(1-3)

89 2. 이것은 두 개의 건물 사이에 있는 학교 정원입니다.

90 여기서는 누구라도 쉽게 위아래로 이동할 수 있습니다.

91 또한, 우리는 이곳에 앉아 휴식을 취할 수 있습니다. — 김지민 (3-5)

92 3. 교실용의 특별한 책상과 의자가 있습니다.

93 모둠 활동을 하기 위해 그것들을 함께 모아 3명, 4명, 또는 5명이 활동할 훌륭한 모둠 책상을 만들 수 있습니다. — 최유미 (2-1)

94 웃읍시다

95 재미있는 지구의 날 농담들 하! 하! 하!

96 재활용 통은 왜 희망적인가?

97 왜냐하면 '깡통[할 수 있다]'로 가득 차 있기 때문이지.

98 바다가 다정하다는 것을 어떻게 알 수 있는가?

99 그것이 일렁이기[손을 흔들기] 때문이지.

100 태양은 왜 학교에 가는가?

101 더 밝아지기[똑똑해지기] 위해서지.

※ **다음 우리말을 영어로 쓰시오.**

1 십대들의 잡지
➡ _____

2 모양으로 표현된 예술 작품
➡ _____

3 동그라미처럼
➡ _____

4 나는 동그라미처럼 너를 사랑해. 왜냐하면 동그라미는 절대 끝나지 않기에.
➡ _____

5 눈사람
➡ _____

6 바깥은 추워.
➡ _____

7 나는 밖으로 나가 놀고 싶지 않네.
➡ _____

8 하지만 엄마는 그래야 한다고 하시네.
➡ _____

9 눈이 오기 시작하고 나는 추워질 거야.
➡ _____

10 나는 이런 날에는 나가서 놀고 싶지 않아.
➡ _____

11 하지만 잠깐만, 나는 최고로 멋진 생각이 났어!
➡ _____

12 나는 눈으로 내 몸을 완전히 덮고 여기에 숨어야지!
➡ _____

13 손 글씨로 돌아보기
➡ _____

14 인생은 예술이다.
➡ _____

15 다양한 색깔로 살아라.
➡ _____

16 끝날 때까지 끝난 게 아니다.
➡ _____

17 나는 느리게 걷는 사람이지만 절대 물러서지는 않는다.
➡ _____

18 나는 네가 하는 작은 일들을 사랑해.
➡ _____

19 네 꿈을 좇으라.
➡ _____

20 나의 자전거
➡ _____

21 바퀴 두 개가 나를 데려가네 / 어느 곳으로든지 / 학교로 / 다시 집으로 / 산으로 / 강으로 / 나는 내 자전거가 아주 좋아 / 나는 그걸 매일 즐겨 타네
➡ _____

22 아낌없이 주는 나무
➡ _____

23 저곳 바깥은 – 젖어 있고
➡ _____

24 이곳 안쪽은 – 말라 있네
➡ _____

25 엄청 큰 우산이네
➡ _____

26 나와 하늘 사이에 있는
➡ _____

27 올해의 셀피들
➡

28 우리는 게임에 졌지만, 아주 즐거웠다.
➡

29 우리가 만든 로봇들을 봐.
➡

30 귀엽지 않니?
➡

31 우리는 한 씨 할아버지께 드릴 큰 케이크를 만들었다.
➡

32 그것은 할아버지를 행복하게 해 주었다.
➡

33 나처럼 잘생긴 피터 팬을 본 적이 있니?
➡

34 학교생활에 대해 어떻게 생각하니?
➡

35 가장 불편한 순간
➡

36 1. 시험을 칠 때
➡

37 2. 정말 배가 고픈데 먹을 것이 없을 때
➡

38 3. 체육 시간 전후에 옷을 갈아입을 때
➡

39 4. 기타: 수업 중에 졸릴 때
➡

40 종이 울렸는데 선생님이 수업을 끝내지 않을 때
➡

41 가장 사랑스러운 시간
➡

42 1. 점심시간
➡

43 2. 가장 좋아하는 선생님의 수업 시간
➡

44 3. 금요일의 마지막 수업 시간
➡

45 4. 기타: 쉬는 시간에 잠잘 때
➡

46 거울 속의 나를 볼 때
➡

47 가장 멋진 뉴스
➡

48 1. 전보다 좋은 성적을 받았다
➡

49 2. 오늘 수업이 일찍 끝난다
➡

50 3. 비나 눈이 많이 와서 학교에 가지 않는다
➡

51 4. 기타: 후식으로 맛있는 단것을 먹는다
➡

52 가장 친한 친구와 내가 같은 반이 되었다
➡

53 가장 하기 힘든 일
➡

54 1. 쓰레기통 씻기
➡

55 2. 공부하기
➡

56 3. 친구들 앞에서 발표하기
➡

57 4. 기타: 매일 제시간에 등교하기
➡

58 모둠 활동
➡

59 우리 마을에서 우리가 좋아하는 곳
➡

60 대한 전통 시장
➡

61 맛있는 것이 먹고 싶으면, 대한 시장을 방문하세요.
➡

62 엽전을 사면 여러분의 점심 도시락을 가득 채우는 데 그걸 쓸 수 있어요.
➡

63 많은 종류의 음식을 골라서 점심 도시락에 담을 수 있답니다.
➡

64 새봄 청소년 센터
➡

65 이곳은 우리 마을 한가운데에 있는 새봄 청소년 센터입니다.
➡

66 춤과 음악 같은 많은 것을 배울 수 있어서 우리는 이곳을 좋아한답니다.
➡

67 우리는 또한 이곳에서 보드게임도 하고 휴식도 취할 수 있어요.
➡

68 김 씨네 빵집
➡

69 이곳은 학교 근처의 작은 빵집입니다.
➡

70 우리는 항상 배가 고파서 방과 후에 거기에 가는 것을 좋아해요!
➡

71 친구들과 맛있는 빵을 즐기는 것이 좋아요.
➡

72 퍼즐로 즐거운 시간을 보내자!
➡

73 도형 퍼즐
➡

74 A를 똑같은 두 개의 조각으로 자르면, 그 두 조각으로 다른 모든 형태(B, C, D, E, F, G)를 만들 수 있다.
➡

75 5개의 선에 놓인 10개의 공
➡

76 각각의 선 위에 정확하게 4개의 공이 놓이도록 10개의 공을 5개의 선에 놓아라.
➡

77 너는 플라스틱 숟가락을 먹고 있다!
➡

78 1. 해마다 많은 플라스틱 숟가락이 버려진다.
➡

79 2. 대부분의 플라스틱 숟가락은 바닷속에서 더 작은 조각으로 부서진다.
➡

80 3. 아주 작은 플라스틱 조각들이 물고기의 몸속으로 들어간다.
➡

81 4. 여러분이 그 물고기를 먹으면 여러분도 플라스틱을 먹게 되는 것이다. 해마다 11,000개의 조각까지!

82 꿈의 학교를 만들어 보자!
➡

83 지난달에 우리는 우리 학교를 위한 유니버설 디자인 경시대회를 열었습니다.
➡

84 여기 우승자들의 작품이 있습니다.
➡

85 1. 손을 가까이 가져가면 물이 나옵니다.
➡

86 손을 멀리 떨어뜨리면 물이 멈춥니다.
➡

87 어떤 부분도 돌리거나 만질 필요가 없습니다.
➡

88 우리는 이것으로 많은 물을 절약할 수 있답니다. — 오주연(1–3)

89 2. 이것은 두 개의 건물 사이에 있는 학교 정원입니다.
➡

90 여기서는 누구라도 쉽게 위아래로 이동할 수 있습니다.

91 또한, 우리는 이곳에 앉아 휴식을 취할 수 있습니다. — 김지민(3–5)
➡

92 3. 교실용의 특별한 책상과 의자가 있습니다.
➡

93 모둠 활동을 하기 위해 그것들을 함께 모아 3명, 4명, 또는 5명이 활동할 훌륭한 모둠 책상을 만들 수 있습니다. — 최유미(2–1)
➡

94 웃읍시다

95 재미있는 지구의 날 농담들 하! 하! 하!
➡

96 재활용 통은 왜 희망적인가?

97 왜냐하면 '깡통[할 수 있다]'으로 가득 차 있기 때문이지.
➡

98 바다가 다정하다는 것을 어떻게 알 수 있는가?
➡

99 그것이 일렁이기[손을 흔들기] 때문이지.

100 태양은 왜 학교에 가는가?
➡

101 더 밝아지기[똑똑해지기] 위해서지.
➡

MEMO

영어 기출 문제집

적중100

2학기

정답 및 해설

천재 | 정사열

중 2

적중100

A Step Inside the Culture

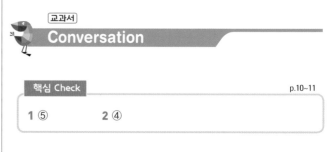

05 (1) '쓰이고 있다'는 동사를 수식하는 부사 'widely'가 적절하다. (2) light를 '번개' lightning으로 바꾸어 준다. (3) 진주어 역할을 하는 부정사 to express가 적절하다. (4) 동사 differ를 명사 'kind'를 수식하는 형용사 different로, many kinds of 뒤에 복수 명사 works를, find는 be동사와 함께 수동태를 만들어 과거분사 found로 쓴다.

시험대비 실력평가   p.08

01 ③	02 popular	03 ⑤	04 for free
05 ④	06 ②	07 character	
08 practice			

01 여러분은 자신의 느낌을 어떻게 표현하는가? 노래를 부르거나 춤을 추는가?

02 • 요즈음에는 손 글씨를 통해 감정을 표현하는 것이 인기다. <영영풀이> 대부분의 사람들이 좋아하는

03 'tale'은 '이야기'이고, '꼬리'는 'tail'이다.

04 '무료로'는 'for free'이다.

05 '누군가나 어떤 것을 그룹의 일부로 만들다'는 의미로 '포함하다'는 'include'가 적절하다.

06 '더 낮은 장소나 위치에'의 의미로 '… 아래에'라는 'below'가 적절하다.

07 '글자, 문자', '캐릭터, 역', '성격'의 의미를 가지는 단어는 character이다. • '한글은 한자보다 배우기에 훨씬 더 쉽다.' • '한국에서는, 초록색 공룡 둘리가 사랑 받는 캐릭터다.' • '관대함은 한국인의 성격의 일부이다.'

08 'practice'는 동사로 '연습하다'와 명사로 '연습'의 뜻을 갖는다. • 모든 캘리그래피 작가들은 자신의 독특한 스타일을 만들어 내기 위해 열심히 연습해야 했다. • 처음에는 손으로 글씨를 잘 쓰기가 쉽지 않지만, 연습하면 완벽해진다.

서술형 시험대비   p.09

01 (p)erformance   02 (a)utumn

03 (1) examples, below   (2) difference   (3) artistic touch   (4) imagine, monster

04 (1) fantasy, 판타지, 환상   (2) monster, 괴물   (3) dynasty, 왕조

05 (1) widely   (2) lightning   (3) to express   (4) different, works, found

01 B의 '고마워. 너는 우쿨렐레 연주하는 것에 관심이 있니?'라는 대답으로 보아 A는 공연을 즐겼다는 말이 적절하다.

02 '여름과 겨울 사이의 계절'은 '가을(autumn)'이다.

04 (1) 당신이 상상하는 즐겁고, 신나고, 특이한 경험이 당신에게 일어나는 것 (2) 크고 무서운 상상의 동물 (3) 모두 같은 가문에 속한 한 나라의 일련의 통치자들

Conversation (교과서)

핵심 Check   p.10~11

1 ⑤   2 ④

교과서 대화문 익히기

Check(√) True or False   p.12

1 T   2 F   3 T   4 F   5 T

교과서 확인학습   p.14~15

Get Ready 2

(1) enjoy listening, dance to / Great

(2) interested in cooking / sometimes, for

(3) Are you interested, Actually, calligraphy / Excellent

Start Off Listen & Talk A

(1) Good job, holding, How creative / in taking pictures / taking, for free / good for

(2) Good, expresses, feeling, autumn / Are, interested / taking / that

Start Off Listen & Talk B

did, awesome / made of / Are, interested in / How long, take to make / It took

Speak Up Look and talk

enjoyed, performance, a good job / interested, playing the / Can you

Speak Up Mission

interested, horror / am, I'm not, interested in, detective

Real-life Scene

practicing calligraphy / writing, looks fun / interested, calligraphy / What, think / looks like, dancing, open / got, means / did, job, try / Why not

---

시험대비 기본평가   p.16

01 ④   02 ①   03 I think you did a good job!   04 (B) → (C) → (D) → (A)

01 한글에 관심이 있다고 대답하고 있기 때문에 한글을 배우고 싶다는 말이 자연스럽다.

02 ①의 '판소리에 관심이 있니?'라는 물음이 자연스럽다. Nancy 의 마지막 말에 '판소리를 배우고 싶어.'라고 했기 때문에 ②의 물음은 자연스럽지 못하다.

03 자신의 생각을 표현하면서 상대방을 칭찬하는 말로, I think로 문장을 시작한다. '잘했다'는 표현은 'you did a good job'이다.

04 (B) 공연 즐거웠다는 말과 함께 잘했다는 칭찬을 하고 → (C) 칭찬의 말에 대해 고맙다는 답이 오고, 태권도에 관심 있는가의 물음에 → (D) 긍정의 답을 하고, 가르쳐 줄 수 있는지 묻고 → (A) 마지막으로 가르쳐 주겠다는 답이 오면 된다.

시험대비 실력평가   p.17~18

01 ③   02 ⑤

03 Are you interested in riding a bike?

04 ②   05 ④   06 awesome   07 ④

08 ④   09 ③   10 ①   11 ①

12 ②   13 ②

01 '…에 맞춰 춤추다'는 'dance to'를 사용한다.

02 나머지는 모두 상대방을 칭찬하는 말이고, ⑤는 '나도 K-pop에 빠져 있어.'라는 뜻이다.

03 관심을 묻는 표현은 'be interested in'을 이용하고, in은 전치사이기 때문에 뒤에 riding(동명사)을 사용해야 한다.

04 B가 G의 작품을 보고 '유리로 만들었니?'라고 묻는 말에 G가 B에게 '유리 공예에 관심이 있니?'라고 묻는 말이 자연스럽다.

05 G의 마지막 말에 '한 달 걸렸어.'라고 했기 때문에 (B)에는 얼마나 걸리는지 기간을 묻는 말이 적절하다.

06 '대단한 존경심과 걱정, 두려움을 느낄 정도로 매우 인상적이거

나 심각하거나 어려운', '매우 좋은, 훌륭한'의 의미를 가지는 단어는 awesome이다.

07 캘리그래피를 쓰기 시작하는 것이 쉬운지는 언급되어 있지 않다.

08 '…처럼 보이다'는 표현은 'look+형용사'나 'look like+명사'를 사용한다. look 뒤에 명사 'a person'이 있으므로 전치사 like가 필요하다.

09 G의 대답이 Yes, I am.이기 때문에 Be동사 의문문으로 시작하고 그림에 관심이 있는지 묻는 의문문이 적절하다.

10 빈칸 다음에 B가 '그렇다면 무엇에 관심이 있니?'라고 묻고 있으므로 G는 한복에 관심이 없다는 것을 알 수 있다.

11 ①: '사진을 찍는 데 관심이 있니?'라는 말에 '잘했어'라고 답하는 것은 어색하다.

12 '동물에 관심이 있니?'라는 물음에 Yes로 답하고 있기 때문에 빈칸에는 '동물을 돌보는 것을 잘해.'라는 말이 적절하다.

13 주어진 문장은 '식물은 어때?'라는 뜻으로 '식물에도 관심이 있니?'라고 묻는 말의 앞인 ②가 적절하다.

서술형 시험대비   p.19

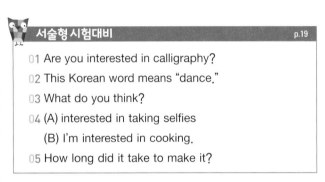

01 Are you interested in calligraphy?

02 This Korean word means "dance."

03 What do you think?

04 (A) interested in taking selfies

    (B) I'm interested in cooking.

05 How long did it take to make it?

01 상대방이 관심이 있는지 묻는 표현은 'be interested in'을 이용하여 의문문을 만든다.

03 What do you think?가 '어떻게 생각해?'라는 표현이다.

04 B가 'No, I'm not.'으로 답한 것으로 보아 주어진 그림에서 take selfies는 관심이 없기 때문에 (A)는 셀피 찍는 데 관심이 있는지 묻는 것이 적절하다. (B)는 요리에 관심이 있기 때문에 I am interested in cooking.이 오는 것이 자연스럽다.

05 시간을 묻는 표현은 'How long ~?'으로 문장을 시작하고, '시간이 걸리다'라는 동사는 'take'를 사용한다. 그리고 비인칭 주어 it과 glass art를 가리키는 대명사 it을 사용한다.

교과서

Grammar

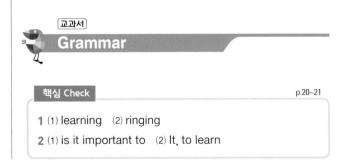

핵심 Check   p.20~21

1 (1) learning   (2) ringing

2 (1) is it important to   (2) It, to learn

01 ③

02 (1) kick → kicking (2) the playing the piano man
   → the man playing the piano
   (3) stars shining → shining stars
   (4) live → to live (5) That → It (6) to not → not to

03 (1) The girls singing on the street are my
   students.
   (2) It is a good idea to provide various programs.
   (3) Look at the sleeping baby.

01 it을 가주어로 하고 to부정사를 진주어로 이용할 수 있는 ③번이
적절하다.

02 (1) 현재분사가 뒤에서 the boy를 수식하도록 하는 것이 적절
하다. (2) 현재분사가 목적어나 어구를 수반할 때에는 명사 뒤에
와서 앞의 명사를 수식한다. (3) 현재분사가 단독으로 쓰일 때는
명사 앞에 와서 명사를 수식한다. (4) 진주어로 to부정사가 적절
하다. (5) 가주어로는 That이 아니라 It을 쓴다. (6) to부정사의
부정은 to부정사 앞에 not[never]을 써서 'not[never]+to V'
로 나타낸다.

03 (1) '거리에서 노래를 부르고 있는'이 '소녀들'을 수식하도록 현
재분사의 후치 수식을 이용한다. (2) 가주어 it을 추가하여 to부
정사를 진주어로 하여 영작한다. (3) '자고 있는'이 '아기'를 수
식하도록 현재분사를 이용한다. 목적어나 다른 어구를 수반하고
있지 않으므로 명사 앞에 와서 명사를 수식하도록 한다.

01 ④   02 ③   03 ②   04 ①

05 ⑤   06 (1) carrying (2) written (3) sleeping
cat (4) to listen (5) It   07 ④   08 ②

09 ③   10 It is important to learn a foreign
language. 11 ⑤   12 ①   13 ①

14 (1) For me to do this work would be really stupid.
   또는 It would be really stupid for me to do this
   work.
   (2) It is easy to solve the puzzle.
   (3) It was amazing to see such an old house there.
   (4) There was a girl eating ice cream.
   (5) A boy carrying a box got on the bus.
   (6) Last week I read *Harry Potter* written by JK
   Rowling.

15 (1) beginning (2) dancing (3) frightened
   (4) taken 16 ④   17 ③   18 ②, ⑤

01 The baby sleeping in the bed is really cute. 현재분사가
목적어나 부사구를 수반할 때에는 명사 뒤에 와서 앞의 명사를
수식한다.

02 ① It is common knowledge that swimming is a
good exercise. ② It's kind of you to ask me some
questions. ④ It's good to own your own business. ⑤
It's necessary to say no.

03 현재분사가 뒤에서 앞의 명사를 수식하도록 한다. It이 나와 있
으므로 It을 가주어로 하고 빈칸에는 진주어로 이용할 수 있는
to부정사가 적절하다.

04 가주어로 It이 적절하다.

05 ⑤번은 동명사이고 나머지는 다 현재분사이다.

06 (1) 현재분사가 뒤에서 앞의 명사를 수식하도록 한다. (2) e-mail
이 쓰여지는 것이므로 과거분사가 적절하다. (3) 현재분사가 단독
으로 쓰일 때는 명사 앞에 와서 명사를 수식한다. (4) 진주어로 to
부정사가 적절하다. (5) 가주어로 It이 적절하다.

07 ① The person running fastest in our class is Angie.
② Look at the men singing pansori. ③ His dream is
helping[to help] the poor. ⑤ The boy is washing the
dog.

08 ②번은 비인칭 주어(날씨)이지만 나머지는 모두 가주어로 쓰인
It이다.

09 현재분사가 뒤에서 명사를 수식하는 경우, 명사와 현재분사 사
이에 '관계대명사+be동사'가 생략되어 있다고 볼 수 있다.

10 '외국어를 배우는 것(to learn a foreign language)'을 진주어
로 하고 가주어 It을 이용하여 'It ~ to …' 형식으로 쓴다.

11 두 문장을 관계대명사로 한 문장으로 만든 후 '주격 관계대명사
+be동사'를 생략하면 ⑤번과 같은 문장이 된다.

12 가주어로 it을 쓰고 진주어로 to부정사를 쓰는 것이 적절하다.

13 ① 축구를 하는 것이므로 '수동, 완료'의 의미로 쓰이는 과거분
사가 아니라 '능동, 진행'을 나타내는 현재분사를 쓰는 것이 적절
하다.

14 (1) For me가 의미상의 주어로 나와 있으므로 to do가 주어
가 되도록 하거나 가주어 it을 사용하고 진주어로 to do를 쓴다.
(2) 가주어로는 that이 아니라 it을 쓴다. (3) 진주어로 to부정
사를 쓴다. (4) 분사가 목적어나 부사를 수반할 때에는 명사 뒤
에 와서 앞의 명사를 수식한다. (5) 박스를 나르는 것이므로 현
재분사가 적절하다. (6) *Harry Potter*라는 책이 JK Rowling
에 의해 쓰여진 것이므로 과거분사가 적절하다.

15 (1), (2) 분사가 목적어나 부사구를 수반할 때에는 명사 뒤에 와
서 앞의 명사를 수식한다. (3) 뉴스에 놀라는 것이므로 과거분사
가 적절하다. (4) 사진이 찍히는 것이므로 과거분사가 적절하다.

16 '태권도를 배우고 있는 여자아이'이므로 현재분사를 이용하여 뒤
에서 명사를 수식하도록 해야 한다.

17 '가주어(It) ~ 진주어(to부정사: to eat fast food often) …'
구문으로 쓰는 것이 적절하다.

18 ② 문장에 쓰인 형용사가 사람의 성향, 성격을 나타내는 말일 때
는 to부정사의 의미상의 주어로 'of+목적격'을 쓴다. ⑤ 현재분
사가 목적어나 어구를 수반할 때에는 명사 뒤에 와서 앞의 명사
를 수식한다.

01 (1) Jack gave his wife a necklace made of pearls.

   (2) Who is the man cutting the beef sandwiches with a knife?

   (3) It is awesome to find a good book.

   (4) It is easy to start writing calligraphy.

   (5) Is it dangerous to look at the sun directly?

02 • (1) To kick a jegi is interesting.

    (2) It is interesting to kick a *jegi*.

   • (1) To do paragliding looks dangerous.

    (2) It looks dangerous to do paragliding.

03 (1) enjoying, It, to do   (2) playing, It, to play

04 (1) The business woman running a big company is Sophie.

   (2) The bridge built long time ago is a connection to the past.

05 (1) It is silly to meet trouble halfway.

   (2) It was great to get your e-mail this morning.

   (3) It is safe to wear a helmet while riding a bike.

   (4) It was difficult for the police to calm down the angry crowd.

   (5) It is quite true that blood is thicker than water.

06 (1) The two girls wearing *hanbok* are my friends.

   (2) The man had the roof of his house painted blue.

   (3) It is interesting to talk about the past.

   (4) It's lucky for you to have a kind neighbor.

07 (1) sending → sent   (2) played → playing

   (3) two laughing out loud people → two people laughing out loud

   (4) Buy → To buy[Buying], 또는 전체 문장 → It is not so hard to buy a ticket at the subway station.

   (5) This → It

   (6) for her eats → for her to eat

08 (1) for me to write letters in English

   (2) for her to watch the horror movie

01 (1) 목걸이가 진주로 만들어진 것이므로 과거분사로 쓴다. (2) 칼로 샌드위치를 자르는 것이므로 현재분사로 쓴다. (3)~(5) '가주어(It) ~ 진주어(to부정사) …' 구문을 이용한다.

02 to부정사가 문장의 주어로 쓰일 때 주어 자리에 가주어 it을 두고 to부정사 부분(진주어)을 문장 뒤로 보낸다.

03 현재분사의 '후치 수식'을 이용하고 '가주어(It) ~ 진주어(to부정사) …' 구문을 이용하여 쓴다.

04 분사가 목적어나 부사구를 수반할 때에는 명사 뒤에 와서 앞의 명사를 수식한다. 이때 명사와 분사 사이에 '관계대명사+be동사'가 생략되어 있다고 볼 수 있다.

05 (1)~(4) 문장의 주어로 쓰인 to부정사를 뒤로 보내고 대신 주어

자리에 가주어 it을 쓴다. (5) 주어로 쓰인 that절의 경우에도 긴 that절을 뒤로 보내고 주어 자리에 가주어 it을 쓴다. (4)번의 경우 For the police는 to부정사의 의미상의 주어이다.

06 (1) 분사의 '후치 수식'을 이용한다. (2) 파랗게 칠해지는 것이므로 과거분사를 쓴다. (3), (4) '가주어(it) ~ 진주어(to부정사) …' 구문을 이용한다. (4) 당신이 운이 좋은 것이므로 의미상의 주어 for you를 써 주어야 한다.

07 (1) email이 보내지는 것이므로 과거분사가 적절하다. (2) 소년들이 축구를 하는 것이므로 현재분사가 적절하다. (3) 분사가 목적어나 부사구를 수반할 때에는 명사 뒤에 와서 앞의 명사를 수식한다. (4) to부정사나 동명사를 주어로 하거나 전체 문장을 '가주어(it) ~ 진주어(to부정사) …' 구문으로 고쳐 쓴다. (5) 가주어로 it을 쓰는 것이 적절하다. (6) for her가 to eat의 의미상의 주어가 되도록 고쳐야 한다.

08 (1) '영어로 편지를 쓰는 데 어려움이 있다'는 것을 '영어로 편지를 쓰는 것은 어렵다'는 문장으로, (2) Watching을 to watch로 바꾸고 for her를 to watch의 의미상의 주어로 하는 '가주어(it) ~ 진주어(to부정사) …' 구문을 이용하여 쓴다.

교과서
Reading

확인문제   p.28

1 T   2 F   3 F   4 T

확인문제   p.29

1 T   2 F   3 T   4 F   5 T   6 F

교과서 확인학습 A   p.30~31

01 Write   02 How, feelings

03 sing, dance   04 draw a picture

05 Nowadays, through handwriting

06 works of art

07 includes an image   08 a season of fruit

09 Korean word, Chinese character

10 looks like, walking

11 express the feeling, through   12 calligraphy

13 not new   14 can be found

15 from, below   16 tell the difference

17 was created by   18 were painted with

19 in the late 1400s   20 was written with

21 Different writing tools, different styles

22 practice hard, unique styles   23 is widely used

24 designers' artistic touches

25 are some examples　　　26 the title

27 How

28 sharp teeth, ugly

29 How about

30 lightning, wizard hats　　31 Anyone, writing

32 by hand, practice makes perfect

33 Keep trying, part, everyday　34 with your feelings

35 build up

교과서 확인학습 B
p.32~33

1 Write Your Feelings

2 How do you express your feelings?

3 Do you sing or dance?

4 Do you write a poem or draw a picture?

5 Nowadays, it is popular to express feelings through handwriting.

6 Let's look at some works of art.

7 In the work of art on the right, the word includes an image of a delicious fruit, *hongsi*.

8 It shows that autumn is a season of fruit.

9 The work of art on the left shows a Korean word and a Chinese character.

10 It looks like a happy woman walking down a road with autumn leaves.

11 Both of these works express the feeling of autumn through beautiful handwriting.

12 This kind of art is called calligraphy.

13 Calligraphy is not new.

14 Many different kinds of calligraphy works from long ago can be found all around the world.

15 Look at the two examples from Korea and the UK below.

16 Can you tell the difference?

17 The left one was created by Chusa in the period of the Joseon Dynasty.

18 The characters were painted with a soft brush.

19 The right one, *The Canterbury Tales*, was created by Chaucer in England in the late 1400s.

20 It was written with a pen.

21 Different writing tools led to different styles of calligraphy.

22 Of course, all calligraphers had to practice hard to make their unique styles.

23 Today calligraphy is widely used around us.

24 You can find designers' artistic touches on movie posters, book covers, music CDs, and clothes.

25 Below are some examples.

26 Look at the title on the movie poster.

27 How do you feel?

28 Can you imagine the monster's big mouth, sharp teeth, and ugly, long tail?

29 How about the title on the fantasy novel?

30 Do you see Harry's lightning and the wizard hats?

31 Anyone can start writing calligraphy.

32 It's not easy to write by hand well at first, but practice makes perfect.

33 Keep trying and make it part of your everyday life.

34 Write with your feelings on birthday cards, bookmarks, or gifts.

35 Soon you will build up your own world of calligraphy.

시험대비 실력평가
p.34~37

01 ②　　　02 ②, ④　　　03 ④　　　04 ①

05 some examples are → are some examples

06 ②, ⑤　　　07 ②

08 interesting → interested

09 (A) Chusa　(B) Joseon Dynasty　(C) soft brush

10 Different writing tools led to different styles of calligraphy.　　　11 ③　　　12 ②, ⑤

13 writing calligraphy 또는 calligraphy

14 with your feelings　　　15 before / Before

16 We use *yuts* and *mals*.

17 (A) board　(B) to play　(C) interested

18 ③　　　19 a soft brush, a pen　　　20 ③

21 ⑤　　　22 ②　　　23 looks → looks like

24 ①　　　25 ②, ⑤ / ①, ③, ④

01 단어가 홍시의 '이미지'를 포함하고 있다고 하는 것이 적절하다. ① 현장, 장면, ③ 상상력, 상상, ④ 수치, 인물, 사람, 모습, ⑤ 경치

02 ⓑ와 ①, ③, ⑤: 앞의 명사를 뒤에서 수식하는 현재분사의 후치 수식, ②, ④: 동명사

03 ④ '그림'이 아니라 아름다운 '손 글씨'를 통해 가을의 느낌을 표현하고 있다.

04 ⓐ와 ①: (명사) 손길, 솜씨, (마무리) 손질, ② 마음을 움직이다, 감동시키다, ③ (명사) 만지기, 건드리기, ④ ~에 (손·손가락 등으로) 대다, 건드리다, ⑤ (음식물 따위에) 손을 대다, 먹다, 마시다

05 부사 'below'가 맨 앞에 왔기 때문에 '부사+동사(+대명사가 아닌) 주어'의 어순으로 도치시키는 것이 적절하다.

06 ②와 ⑤는 '영화 포스터의 제목'이 아니라 '공상 소설의 제목'에서 볼 수 있다.

07 ② 위 글은 '홍보 전단'이다. PR: 홍보(public relations), leaflet: (광고나 선전용) 전단, ① 요약, 개요, ③ (책·연극·영

화 등에 대한) 논평[비평], 감상문, ④ (신문·잡지의) 글, 기사, ⑤ 수필

08 사람의 감정을 나타내므로 과거분사로 고치는 것이 적절하다.

09 그것은 오래전의 캘리그래피 작품들의 한 예이다. 그것은 '조선 왕조' 시대에 '추사'가 '부드러운 붓'으로 그 글자들을 그려서 창작하였다.

10 lead to: ~로 이끌다, ~로 이어지다

11 '줄거리'는 알 수 없다. ① Chaucer, ② 영국, ④ 1400년대 후반, ⑤ 펜

12 ② That이 아니라 가주어 It을 쓰는 것이 적절하다. ⑤ by hand: (기계가 아닌) 사람 손으로, by the hand: 손을 잡고

13 '캘리그래피를 쓰는 것' 또는 '캘리그래피'를 가리킨다.

14 전치사 'with'를 사용하는 것이 적절하다.

15 Soon = It will not be long before = Before long: 곧

16 우리는 윷놀이를 하기 위해 '윷'과 '말'을 사용한다.

17 (A) 전통적인 '말판' 놀이라고 해야 하므로 board가 적절하다. board: 널빤지, (게임) 판, broad: 넓은, (B) 그것을 '하기 위해'라고 해야 하므로 to부정사의 부사적 용법(목적)을 나타내는 to play가 적절하다. (C) 감정을 나타내는 동사는 수식받는 명사가 감정을 느끼게 되는 경우에 과거분사를 써야 하므로 interested가 적절하다.

18 주어진 문장의 the difference에 주목한다. ③번 다음부터 '차이'가 설명되기 시작하므로 ③번이 적절하다.

19 '부드러운 붓'과 '펜'을 가리킨다.

20 이 글은 캘리그래피는 새로운 것이 아니고 오래전의 다양한 종류의 많은 캘리그래피 작품들이 세계 곳곳에서 발견되고 있다는 것을 다루고 있는 글이다.

21 (A) on the right[left]: 오른[왼]쪽의, (B) through: [수단·매체] ~을 통하여

22 ⓐ와 ③, ⑤번: 가주어, ① 그것(앞에 이미 언급되었거나 현재 이야기되고 있는 사물·동물을 가리킴), ② 가목적어, ④ 비인칭 주어(거리)

23 look+형용사, look like+명사: ~처럼 보이다

24 이 글은 한국 문화 체험을 '홍보하는' 글이다. ① promote: 홍보하다, ② 비교하다, ③ (설문) 조사하다, ④ 알리다, 발표하다, ⑤ 연락을 주고받다, 의사소통을 하다

25 ⓐ와 ②, ⑤: 현재분사, ⓑ와 ①, ③, ④: 동명사

서술형 시험대비
p.38~39

01 (1) 노래를 부른다. (2) 춤을 춘다. (3) 시를 쓴다.
   (4) 그림을 그린다. (5) 손 글씨를 통해 감정을 표현한다.

02 It looks like a happy woman walking down a road with autumn leaves.

03 (A) handwriting (B) calligraphy

04 be found

05 (1) Chusa's work (2) brush
   (3) *The Canterbury Tales* (4) pen

06 fourteen hundreds

07 They had to practice hard.

08 artistic touches

09 (A) movie poster (B) fantasy novel.

10 (A) How (B) includes (C) handwriting

11 (A) fruit (B) autumn (C) happy

12 We call this kind of art calligraphy.

01 첫 단락의 내용을 쓰는 것이 적절하다.

02 look like: ~처럼 보이다, 현재분사 walking이 이끄는 어구 전체가 뒤에서 앞의 명사 woman을 수식하는 것이 적절하다.

03 요즈음에는 '손 글씨'를 통해 감정을 표현하는 것이 인기이고, 이런 종류의 예술을 '캘리그래피'라고 부른다.

04 조동사가 포함된 수동태는 '조동사+be동사의 원형+과거분사'이다.

05 (1) 추사의 작품, (2) 붓, (3) 캔터베리 이야기, (4) 펜

06 1400s: 1400년대

07 모든 캘리그래피 작가들은 자신의 독특한 스타일을 만들어 내기 위해 열심히 연습해야 했다.

08 캘리그래피를 사용한 영화 포스터, 책 표지, 음악 CD, 그리고 의류들의 몇 가지 예들이고, 여러분은 그것들에서 디자이너들의 '예술적인 손길'을 발견할 수 있다.

09 캘리그래피 제목을 포함하고 있는 두 가지 상업적인 제품이 있다. 하나는 '영화 포스터'의 제목이고 다른 하나는 '공상 소설'의 제목이다.

10 (A) 느낌을 '어떻게' 표현하는가라고 해야 하므로 How가 적절하다. (B) 홍시의 이미지를 '포함하고 있다'고 해야 하므로 includes가 적절하다. exclude: 제외[배제]하다, (C) 아름다운 '손 글씨'를 통해 가을의 느낌을 표현한다고 해야 하므로 handwriting이 적절하다. drawing: 그림, 소묘, 데생

12 We나 They 등 일반인을 주어로 하여 능동태로 고치는 것이 적절하다.

영역별 핵심문제
p.41~45

01 (e)xcellent   02 ③   03 ⑤
04 ②   05 ④   06 ③
07 Look at the two men learning *pansori*. 08 ④
09 Do you have an interest in learning Hangeul?
10 ⑤   11 ②   12 ③   13 ①
14 ⑤   15 ③   16 ④   17 ④
18 ⑤
19 (1) Kate climbed the mountain covered with snow
   (2) When are you going to fix the broken window?
   (3) Mariko looked at her daughter playing in the park.
   (4) It is dangerous to ride a bike without a helmet.
   (5) It was very wise of Laura to learn how to speak Chinese.

01 반의어 관계다. 포함하다 : 제외하다 = 형편없는 : 훌륭한

02 • 그림을 잘 그리기 위해서는 예술적 기교가 필요하다. • 가을이 오면, 나뭇잎들은 색이 변한다. • 그 여행은 루브르 박물관 방문을 포함했다.

03 다른 어떤 것 또는 누구와도 같지 않은

04 • 외국어를 배우는 것은 쉽지 않다. • 이 편지에 쓰여 있는 그의 필체(손 글씨)를 알아볼 수 없다.

05 ⓐ는 마트료시카 인형은 그것을 열면, 더 작은 인형들이 계속해서 나온다는 의미가 적절하므로 'keep –ing'가 오고, ⓑ는 각각의 인형 안에 더 작은 인형이 있기 때문에 inside가 적절하다.

06 'sharp'는 '날카로운'의 뜻이다.

07 '~을 봐'라는 명령문으로 동사원형으로 문장을 시작한다. 그리고 현재분사구인 learning pansori가 명사 men을 뒤에서 수식하는 구조다.

08 (D) 공연을 즐겼다는 말과 함께 상대방을 칭찬하고 → (A) 칭찬에 대해 감사의 답을 하고, 탈춤에 관심이 있는지 묻는다 → (B) 긍정의 답과 함께 가르쳐 줄 수 있는지 묻고 → 마지막으로 (C)의 승낙의 답이 오는 것이 자연스럽다.

09 일반동사 have를 이용한 의문문 'Do you have ~?'로 문장을 시작한다. 'an interest'는 명사로 have의 목적어 역할을 한다.

10 '이것이 나의 작품이야.'라고 한 말에 대해 칭찬하는 말이 오는 것이 자연스럽다.

11 쇼핑을 가는 데 관심이 있냐는 말에 부정의 답을 하고 있으므로 빈칸에는 관심 있는 다른 것을 언급하는 것이 자연스럽다.

12 예술 전시회에서 물을 수 있는 질문으로 ③이 가장 적절하다.

13 it을 가주어로 하고 의미상의 주어로 for students가 있으므로 to부정사를 진주어로 쓰는 것이 적절하다.

14 ⑤번은 동명사이지만 나머지는 모두 현재분사이다.

15 ③에는 사람의 성격이나 성질을 나타내는 형용사(foolish)가 왔으므로 의미상의 주어 앞에 of가 들어가야 한다. 나머지는 모두 for가 들어간다.

16 ④번은 인칭대명사로 쓰인 It이지만 나머지는 모두 가주어 It이다. 인칭대명사는 '그것'이라고 해석하지만 가주어는 해석하지 않는다.

17 in this town이라는 부사구를 수반하고 있으므로 현재분사가 뒤에서 앞의 명사 Everyone을 수식하도록 한다.

18 for me라는 의미상의 주어가 나왔으므로 to부정사를 진주어로 쓰는 것이 적절하다.

19 (1) 눈으로 덮인 것이므로 과거분사를 쓴다. (2) 창문이 깨진 것이므로 과거분사를 쓴다. (3) 놀고 있는 것이므로 현재분사를 쓴다. (4) to가 있으므로 '가주어(It) ~ 진주어(to부정사) …' 구문

을 이용하여 영작한다. (5) wise라는 사람의 성질을 나타내는 형용사가 나왔으므로 의미상의 주어로 'of+목적격'을 써야 한다.

20 calligraphy: 캘리그래피, 서도, 서예, 붓이나 특별한 펜을 사용하여 아름다운 손 글씨를 만드는 예술

21 본문에서 언급된 두 예술 작품은 아름다운 손 글씨를 통해 가을의 '전통 문화'가 아니라 '느낌'을 표현한다.

22 ⓐ와 ①, ⑤: 명사적 용법, ②: 형용사적 용법, ③, ④부사적 용법

23 부드러운 붓과 펜이라는 '각기 다른 필기구'가 각기 다른 캘리그래피의 스타일을 이끌었다고 하는 것이 적절하다. ① subject: (그림·사진 등의) 대상[소재]

24 tell the difference = distinguish: (차이를) 분간하다, 구별하다 ① 다르다, ② (~해야 한다고) 고집하다[주장하다], ④ (크기·모양 등에서) 서로[각기] 다르다, ⑤ (~하도록) 설득하다

25 왼쪽 작품은 '1400년대 후반'이 아니라 '조선 왕조 시대'에 창작되었다. 참고로 추사(秋史) 김정희(金正喜, 1786~1856)는 조선 후기의 문인이자 추사체를 만들어낸 명필가이며 실학자이다.

26 주어진 문장의 some examples에 주목한다. ②번 앞 문장의 예들에 해당하므로 ②번이 적절하다.

27 ③ 디자이너들이 캘리그래피 제목에 예술적인 손길을 어떻게 더하는지는 대답할 수 없다. ① Yes. ② It is used in movie posters, book covers, music CDs, and clothes. ④ We can imagine the monster's big mouth, sharp teeth, and ugly, long tail. ⑤ We see Harry's lightning and the wizard hats.

28 (A) '누구든지'라고 해야 하므로 Anyone이 적절하다. 긍정문의 any: 어떤 ~이라도, (B) '손으로' 글씨를 잘 쓰는 것이라고 해야 하므로 by hand가 적절하다. by hand: (기계가 아닌) 사람 손으로, on a keyboard: 키보드로, (C) '곧'이라고 해야 하므로 Soon이 적절하다. before long = soon: 곧, long before: 훨씬 이전에, 오래 전에

29 'everyday'를 보충하면 된다.

01 망치와 톱은 목수의 도구이다. hammers and saws가 복수 명사이기 때문에 복수형 tools가 적절하다.

02 (A) period: 시대 (B) title: 제목

03 B의 마지막 질문 'How long did it take to make it?'은 '그거 만드는 데 시간이 얼마나 걸렸니?'라는 뜻이므로 빈칸에는 걸린 시간이 오는 것이 자연스럽다.

04 상상의 사건이나 사람에 관한 이야기

05 미나는 캘리그래피를 연습하고 있다.

06 위 대화는 캘리그래피 작품에 대해 이야기하면서 James가 미나의 작품을 칭찬하고 자신도 한 번 해볼 수 있는지 묻고 미나가 한 번 그려 보라고 하는 내용으로 ⑤의 '캘리그래피와 함께 즐겁게'가 적절하다.

07 미나의 작품은 두 팔을 벌리고 춤을 추는 사람처럼 보인다고 했으므로 실제로 춤추는 사람을 그린 것은 아니다.

08 B의 대답이 '그것이 먹고 싶어.'라고 했으므로 ②가 적절하다.

09 ④는 '무엇에 관심이 있니?'라는 의미로 'Yes / No'로 답할 수 없는 의문문이다.

10 ③번 A가 '책을 읽는 것을 좋아하니?'라는 말에 '응, 그래. 책을 읽는 것은 지겨워!'라는 대답은 어색하다.

11 ⓐ It is fun to read books. ⓒ This calligraphy shows a tree growing in a pot. ⓔ Who was the man playing the piano on the stage? ⓗ It is a lot of fun to dance talchum.

12 ③번은 동명사이고 나머지는 모두 현재분사이다.

13 ① It is important to keep your teeth clean. ② It was boring to wait for her. ③ It was impossible to estimate the flood damage this year. ⑤ It is nice of you to help that old man.

14 '가주어(It) ~ 진주어(to부정사) …' 구문을 이용한다.

15 주어진 문장의 It에 주목한다. ②번 앞 문장의 the word를 받고 있으므로 ②번이 적절하다.

16 ⓐ와 ④: 문자, ① 성격, 기질, ② 특징, ③ (책·영화 등의) 등장인물, ⑤ 인격

17 느낌을 표현하는 가장 좋은 방법이 무엇인지는 대답할 수 없다. ② It includes an image of a delicious fruit, hongsi. ③ It shows a Korean word and a Chinese character. ④ It looks like a happy woman walking down a road with autumn leaves. ⑤ It is called calligraphy.

18 one은 앞에 이미 언급했거나 상대방이 알고 있는 사람이나 사물을 가리킬 때 명사의 반복을 피하기 위해 씀.

19 dynasty: 왕조, (동일 가문이 다스리는) 시대, 동일 가문에 속하는 한 나라의 일련의 통치자들

20 '시를 인용한 이유'는 알 수 없다. 참고: 추사 김정희의 묵란도 '山上蘭花'는 추사가 난을 치고 화제(畫題)로 중국 청나라 판교(板橋) 정섭(鄭燮)의 시를 쓴 작품이다. ① 추사, ② 한국, ③ 조선 왕조 시대, ④ 부드러운 붓

21 우리 주변에서 널리 쓰이고 있는 캘리그래피의 예들에 관한 글이므로, 제목으로는 ③번이 적절하다.

22 (A) 디자이너들의 '예술적인' 손길이라고 해야 하므로 artistic이 적절하다. artistic: 예술의, awkward: 어색한, (B) 괴물의 긴 '꼬리'라고 해야 하므로 tail이 적절하다. tale: 이야기, 소설, (C) Harry의 '번개'라고 해야 하므로 lightning이 적절하다.

lightening: lighten(가볍게 해주다[덜어 주다])의 현재분사[동명사] 형태

23 공상 소설의 제목에서 'Harry의 번개'와 '마술사 모자'를 볼 수 있다.

24 처음부터 손으로 글씨를 잘 쓰기는 쉽지 않지만, '연습하면 완벽해진다'고 하는 것이 적절하다. ① 신중하게 행동하라.(돌다리도 두드려 보고 건너라.) ③ 두 사람의 지혜는 한 사람의 지혜보다 낫다.(백지장도 맞들면 낫다.) ④ 해가 있을 때 건초를 만들어라.(기회를 놓치지 마라.) ⑤ 서두르면 일을 그르친다.

25 처음부터 손으로 글씨를 잘 쓰기는 '쉽지 않다'고 해야 하므로 not easy 또는 difficult로 고치는 것이 적절하다.

서술형 실전문제
p.50~51

01 Are you interested in taking pictures?

02 How long did it take to make it?

03 calligraphy, practicing, brush, dance, good, writing

04 (1) for Dick to be sent to hospital because of his illness

   (2) for her to eat lots of vegetables

05 She bought a smartphone made in Korea.

06 it is popular to express feelings through handwriting.

07 (A) feeling   (B) Korean word
   (C) Chinese character .

08 (A) handwriting   (B) feelings

09 (A) new   (B) hard   (C) unique

10 Chusa created the left one in the period of the Joseon Dynasty.

11 (A) Chaucer   (B) a pen

01 'be interested in'을 사용하고, 전치사 in 뒤에 동사 'take'를 동명사 'taking'으로 바꾸어 쓴다.

02 '~하는 데 시간이 걸리다'라는 표현은 'take+시간+to부정사' 구문을 이용한다.

03 미나와 James는 미나의 캘리그래피 작품에 대해 이야기 중이다. 미나는 붓으로 캘리그래피를 연습하고 있다. 그녀는 "춤"을 의미하는 한국어를 쓰고 있다. James는 미나가 잘 했다고 생각한다. 그는 캘리그래피를 써보려고 한다.

04 '~해야 한다'는 의미를 가주어 it을 이용하여 '~할 필요가 있다'라고 쓰려면 진주어로 to부정사를 이용한다. 이때 의미상의 주어를 빠뜨리지 않도록 주의한다.

05 분사가 명사 뒤에서 명사를 꾸며줄 때, 분사 앞에는 '주격 관계대명사+be동사'가 생략되었다고 볼 수 있다.

06 to부정사가 진주어 역할을 하도록 영작하는 것이 적절하다.

07 그것은 가을의 '느낌'을 표현하는 캘리그래피이고, '한글 단어'와 '한자'를 보여 주고 있다. 그것은 단풍잎이 깔린 길을 따라 걷고 있는 행복한 여인처럼 보인다.

9

08 캘리그래피는 '감정'을 표현할 수 있는 '손 글씨'이다.

09 (A) 오래 전의 다양한 종류의 많은 캘리그래피 작품들이 세계 곳곳에서 발견되고 있다고 했으므로 캘리그래피는 '새로운' 것이 아니라고 하는 것이 적절하다. (B) '열심히' 연습해야 했다고 해야 하므로 hard가 적절하다. hardly: 거의 ~ 아니다, (C) 자신의 '독특한' 스타일을 만들어 내기 위해라고 해야 하므로 unique가 적절하다. common: 흔한, 공통의, 보통의

10 Chusa를 주어로 해서 고치는 것이 적절하다.

11 1400년대 후반 영국에서 'Chaucer'가 그것을 창작했다. Chaucer는 '펜'으로 그것을 썼다.

창의사고력 서술형 문제
p.52

|모범답안|

01 (1) A: Are you interested in going shopping?
    B: Yes, I am. I go shopping very often. / No, I'm not. I'm interested in riding a bike.
  (2) A: Are you interested in cooking?
    B: Yes, I am. I cook very often. / No, I'm not. I'm interested in collecting figures.

02 (1) It is not easy to learn English.
  (2) It is exciting to play yunnori.
  (3) It is important to keep promises.
  (4) It is interesting to study history.
  (5) It's dangerous to swim in this river.
  (6) It's awesome to see his art collection.

03 (A) kicking (B) traditional Korean game
  (C) one of our feet (D) exciting

단원별 모의고사
p.53~56

01 ①   02 led to   03 ③
04 (A) interested (B) taking   05 ④
06 ⑤   07 ⓐYou did a good job ⓑ Are you interested in glass art 08 ③   09 ④
10 ①   11 ⑤   12 It looks like a person dancing with open arms.   13 sitting
14 (1) It is easy to use knives and forks.
  (2) It is important to read books.
15 (1) said → saying (2) That's → It's
16 ②   17 ③   18 ⑤
19 (A) image (B) autumn
20 ⓐ Chaucer created the right one, *The Canterbury Tales*, in England in the late 1400s.
  ⓑ Chaucer wrote it with a pen.
21 ①, ③   22 ③   23 Today calligraphy is widely used around us.   24 ⑤

---

01 ①번은 'widely'에 대한 영어 설명이다. 'wildly'에 대한 영어 설명은 'in an uncontrolled or extreme way'로 '난폭하게, 미친 듯이'의 뜻이다.

02 '…을 이끌다'는 'lead to …'를 사용하고 과거시제이므로 'led to'가 적절하다.

03 특별한 펜이나 붓으로 만들어지는 아름다운 글씨

04 (A) 관심이 있는지 묻는 말로 be동사와 함께 사용되는 interested가 적절하다. (B)는 전치사 at 뒤에서 '~을 돌보다'는 의미로 'taking care of ~'가 적절하다.

05 '위의 예술 작품은 한글 단어와 한자를 보여 주고 있다. 그것은 마치 단풍잎이 깔린 길을 따라 걷고 있는 행복한 여인처럼 보인다.'

06 한글에 관심이 있느냐는 물음에. 배우고 싶다고 했으므로 관심이 있다는 긍정의 답이 적절하다.

07 ⓐ 칭찬을 할 때 'did a good job'을 이용한다. ⓑ be동사로 관심을 묻는 표현은 'Are you interested in ~?'을 사용한다.

08 '어떻게 생각하니?'라는 뜻으로 캘리그래피를 쓰고 나서 상대방의 의견을 묻는 말이기 때문에 ③이 적절하다.

09 '내가 해 봐도 되니?'라는 James의 말에 미나가 '이 붓을 잡아.'라고 말한 것으로 보아 승낙한 것을 알 수 있다.

10 '마음에 드니?'라는 물음에 'Sure.'라고 답했으므로 빈칸에는 미술 숙제에 대한 긍정의 말이나 칭찬의 말이 오는 것이 적절하다.

11 한복에 관심이 있느냐는 물음에 별로라고 말하고 있으므로 그렇다면 무엇에 관심이 있는지 물어보는 것이 자연스럽다.

12 '~처럼 보이다'는 'look like+명사'를 사용하고 '춤추고 있는'은 앞의 명사 a person을 수식하는 현재분사 dancing으로 바꾸어 준다. 'with open arms'는 '두 팔을 벌리고'의 의미이다.

13 현재분사가 목적어나 부사구를 수반할 때에는 명사 뒤에 와서 앞의 명사를 수식한다.

14 (1) It을 가주어로 하고 to use를 진주어로 쓴다. to use의 목적어로 knives and forks를 쓴다. (2) It을 가주어로 하고 to부정사를 진주어로 쓴다.

15 (1) say는 '~라고 쓰여지다'라는 의미로 sign이 알려주고 있는 것이므로 현재분사가 적절하다. (2) 가주어로는 it을 사용한다.

16 It is not wise of you to put all your eggs in one basket.

17 이 글은 '손 글씨로 감정을 표현하는 것'에 관한 글이다.

18 ⓐ와 ⑤: 작품, ① (어떤 직장에서) 일하다, ② (기계 장치 등이) 작동되다, ③ 공장, 제작소, ④ (약 따위가) 작용하다

19 그것은 맛있는 과일인 홍시의 '이미지'를 포함하고 있는 캘리그래피이고, '가을'이 결실의 계절임을 보여 준다.

20 둘 다 Chaucer를 주어로 해서 고치는 것이 적절하다.

21 lead to: ~로 이끌다, ~로 이어지다, ⓒ와 ②, ④, ⑤: ~을 야기하다, 가져오다, ① ~로부터 생기다, ~이 원인이다, ③ ~이 생기다, 일어나다

22 ⓓ와 ②, ③, ⑤: 부사적 용법, ①: 명사적 용법, ④: 형용사적 용법

23 수동태로 쓰는 것이 적절하다.

24 ⑤ 공상 소설의 제목은 우리 주변에서 쓰이고 있는 '그림'이 아니라 '캘리그래피'의 좋은 예이다.

Design for All

일반적인 높이보다 더 작은 (3) 어떤 상황이나 주제에 관한 개인적인 의견이나 믿음 (4) 어떤 것의 한쪽 편에서 반대편으로 가로질러 가다

시험대비 실력평가   p.60

01 ④	02 universal	03 by herself	04 ⑤
05 ②	06 ②	07 switch	
08 (f)ountain			

01 그녀가 잘 보거나 들을 수 없고, 지팡이 없이는 잘 걸을 수 없는 것으로 미루어 보아 빈칸에는 '어려움'이 적절하다.

02 • 그녀의 유니버설 디자인 아이디어의 한 가지 예는 저상 버스이다. <영영풀이> 세상의 모든 사람과 관련된.

03 '혼자서'는 'by oneself'를 사용한다. 주어가 'she'이기 때문에 재귀대명사는 herself로 바꾸어 준다.

04 'difficult'는 '어려운'의 뜻이다. '다른'은 'different'이다.

05 '노인들이나 부상당한 사람들이 걷기 위해 사용하는 길고 가는 나무로 된 막대'

06 '(…보다) 더 낮은 장소나 위치에'의 의미로 '… 아래에'라는 'below'가 적절하다.

07 'switch'는 명사로 '스위치', 동사로 '교대하다, 바꾸다'라는 의미로 사용된다. • 그것을 끄려면 어느 스위치를 눌러야 하나요? • 내가 다음 주말에 근무를 할 수가 없는데 당신이 나와 좀 바꿔 줄 수 있나요?

08 '분수'는 'fountain'이다.

서술형 시험대비   p.61

01 (j)ourney   02 (1) crowded   (2) tired of
   (3) uncomfortable   03 f(lat)
04 (1) view   (2) tight   (3) example, wheelchair,
   without   (4) During, company
05 (1) product, 제품   (2) low, 낮은   (3) view, 관점,
   견해   (4) cross, 건너다

01 글의 마지막에 1982년에 여행(trip)을 끝마쳤다고 했으므로 1979년에 여행(journey)을 시작한 것을 알 수 있다.

02 (1) 동사 'crowd(가득 메우다)'를 명사 'buses'를 수식하는 형용사 'crowded'로 바꾸어야 한다. (2) 동사 'tire'를 형용사 'tired'로 고친다. (3) 주어진 단어 'comfortable'은 '편안한'의 뜻이므로 반의어인 'uncomfortable'로 고친다.

03 '다른 부분보다 더 높거나 더 낮은 부분을 가지지 않은' 즉, '평평한'의 뜻을 가진 'flat'이 적절하다.

05 (1) 팔기 위해 만들어지거나 재배되는 것 (2) 높이가 작은 또는

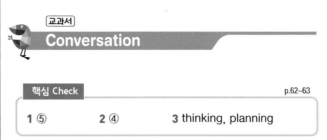

Conversation

핵심 Check   p.62~63

1 ⑤	2 ④	3 thinking, planning

교과서 대화문 익히기

Check(√) True or False   p.64

1 T   2 F   3 T   4 F   5 T

교과서 확인학습   p.66~67

Get Ready 2
(1) not happy about, fountain, too high / m planning to put / good idea
(2) don't like, in wheelchairs, get in / thinking of building, with, steps
(3) happy, get on, easily / planning to hang

Start Off Listen & Talk A
(1) not happy about / wrong / reach, I'm thinking of, another
(2) happy about, who / any / thinking, adding / good idea

Start Off Listen & draw
I'm not happy about / What's wrong with / the same, who, blind to colors / How about putting / walking, standing

Speak Up Look and talk
I'm not happy about, too low / thinking of putting

Speak Up Mission
not happy about, bookshelf / any ideas / thinking of putting

Speak Up Real-life Scene
doing / thinking, ways / wrong / turn on, by herself, too high / happy about, either, about that / thinking, step box, below / change, bigger one / turn on, easily

(1) I'm not happy about, too low, too hard / I'm thinking of buying, What, think / Looks great, so long, grows taller

(2) not happy about, handles, easy to use / How about

(3) I'm thinking of / doesn't have to

not happy, light switch / wrong / too small / any ideas / I'm thinking of changing, with, turn on

---

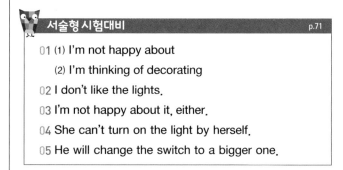

시험대비 기본평가　　　　　　p.68

01 ⑤　　　　02 ②　　　　03 I'm not happy about the shirt.　　04 (C) → (D) → (B) → (A)

01　몇몇 아이들에게 너무 높다고 했기 때문에 음수대가 마음에 들지 않는다는 말이 적절하다.

02　빈칸 뒤에 동명사 'building'이 있기 때문에 전치사 of가 있는 ②가 적절하다. 나머지 표현도 의도를 나타내는 말이지만 모두 동사원형이 뒤에 온다.

03　"I'm not happy about ..."은 '나는 …이 마음에 들지 않는다.'라는 의미로, 만족스럽지 못한 것에 대해 불평하는 표현이다.

04　(C) 책꽂이가 마음에 들지 않는다는 말이 오고 → (D) 나도 그렇게 생각한다는 동의의 말과 함께 어떤 아이디어가 있는지 묻고 → (B) '나는 …을 할까 생각 중이다'라는 뜻으로, 의도나 계획을 나타내는 말을 하고 → (A) 좋은 생각이라고 동의하는 말이 오는 것이 자연스럽다.

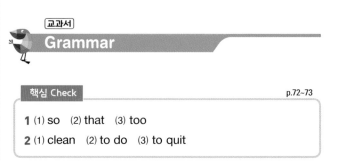

시험대비 실력평가　　　　　p.69~70

01 ⑤　　　　02 ②　　　　03 What's wrong with it?
04 ③　　　　05 ④　　　　06 ⑤
07 She doesn't have to hold it with her fingers.
08 ④　　　　09 That'll help her turn[to trun] on the light easily.　　10 ①　　　11 ③　　　12 ③
13 I want to complain about the shirt.

01　대화의 내용상 그녀에 만족하지 못한다는 의미가 적절하다. ⑤는 불평하지 않는다는 의미다.

02　'I'm planning to …'는 의도나 계획을 나타낼 때 쓰는 표현이다.

03　'무슨 일이야?' 또는 '뭐가 문제니?'의 의미로 'the button'을 가리키는 인칭대명사 'it'을 사용한 'What's wrong with it?'이 적절하다.

04　색깔을 못 보는 사람들(색맹인 사람들)에게 교통 신호등이 똑같아 보이는 것이 문제여서 각 불빛에 그림을 넣자고 제안하고 있다. 'different'를 'the same'으로 바꾸어야 한다.

05　④는 '너는 왜 각 불빛에 그림을 넣고 있니?'라는 뜻이다.

06　'할머니께서 국을 쉽게 드실 수 있도록 도움이 된다.'고 했으므로 이 숟가락을 살 거라는 의도를 말하는 표현이 적절하다.

07　have to를 이용하여 '…할 필요가 없다'는 뜻을 나타낼 때는 'don't have to'를 사용한다.

08　G의 마지막 말에서 '더 큰 것으로 바꿀 생각이야.'라고 말하고 있으므로 스위치가 너무 작다는 것을 알 수 있다.

09　'help+목적어+동사원형/to부정사' 형태로 사용된다.

10　①의 'be happy with ...'는 '…이 마음에 들다'라는 뜻이다. A의 '나는 이 전등이 마음에 들어.'라는 말에 B가 '왜? 뭐가 문제니?'라고 말하는 것은 어색하다.

11　"I'm not happy about ..."은 '나는 …이 마음에 들지 않는다'라는 의미로, 만족스럽지 못한 것에 대해 불평하는 표현이다.

12　셔츠가 마음에 들지 않는다고 했기 때문에 빈칸에는 셔츠가 가지고 있는 문제점이 언급되는 것이 자연스럽다.

13　불평하는 표현으로 'I want to complain about ...'을 사용한다.

서술형 시험대비　　　　　　p.71

01 (1) I'm not happy about
　　(2) I'm thinking of decorating
02 I don't like the lights.
03 I'm not happy about it, either.
04 She can't turn on the light by herself.
05 He will change the switch to a bigger one.

01　(1)번은 happy를 이용해 사물함에 대한 불평을 나타내는 표현을 (2)는 'think of'를 이용하여 앞으로의 계획이나 의도를 말하는 표현을 사용한다. 전치사 of 뒤에 동명사를 사용해야 한다.

02　'I don't like ...'를 이용해서 불평을 표현한다.

03　'happy'를 이용하여 불평하는 표현은 'I'm not happy about ...'이다. 부정문에서 동의를 하는 '또한, 역시'는 'either'를 사용한다.

04　'…을 켜다'는 'turn on'을 사용하고 '…할 수 없다'는 부정의 의미로 can't turn on을 쓴다. '혼자서'는 재귀대명사를 이용하면 'by herself'가 적절하다.

05　아빠의 마지막 말에서 'I'll change the switch to a bigger one'이라고 했다.

Grammar

핵심 Check　　　　　　　　p.72~73

1 (1) so　(2) that　(3) too
2 (1) clean　(2) to do　(3) to quit

---

01 (1) to wash → wash   (2) swimming → swim

    (3) very → so   (4) so → too

02 (1) draw   (2) thrown   (3) to drop

    (4) win(또는 to win)

03 ②

04 He hid himself so that no one could find him.

01 (1), (2) 사역동사의 목적어와 목적격보어의 관계가 능동일 경우 목적격보어로 원형부정사를 쓰는 것이 적절하다. (3) 'so+형용사[부사]+that+주어+동사'의 형태로 '매우 ~해서 …하다'라는 의미를 나타낸다. (4) so+형용사/부사+that+주어+can't … = too ~ to …

02 (1) 사역동사의 목적격보어는 목적어와의 관계가 능동일 경우 원형부정사가 쓰인다. (2) 사역동사의 목적격보어는 목적어와의 관계가 수동일 경우 과거분사가 쓰인다. (3) get이 '~하게 하다'라는 사역동사의 뜻으로 쓰일 때에는 목적격보어로 to부정사를 쓴다. (4) help는 목적격보어로 동사원형이나 to부정사가 나오며 뜻의 차이는 없다.

03 'so+형용사[부사]+that+주어+can't …'의 형태로 '너무 ~해서 …할 수 없다'

04 'so that+주어+동사' 구문으로 쓴다. 'so that+주어+동사'는 목적을 나타내어 '~하기 위해서' 혹은 '~하도록'이라는 의미로 쓰인다.

01 ⑤   02 ④, ⑤   03 ①

04 You speak so fast that I can't get you. 05 ③

06 (1) do   (2) watch   (3) painted   (4) help   (5) that

    (6) so   (7) too   (8) smart enough   07 ③

08 tall so that → so tall that   09 ③, ④

10 ③, ⑤   11 ①   12 ②, ④   13 ⑤

14 (1) The window is so heavy that I can't open it.

    (2) My brother's chair is too low for him to sit on comfortably.

    (3) These walls are thick enough to shut out outside sounds.

    (4) I finished my homework, so Mom let me watch TV.

    (5) The P.E. teacher had the boy bring the ball.

15 (1) repairing → to repair   (2) to wear → wear

    (3) too strong → strong enough

16 ③   17 ④

18 (1) so heavy that I can't move it

    (2) because it is very heavy

01 목적어와의 관계가 능동이므로 사역동사의 목적격보어로 원형부정사가 적절하고 원인과 결과를 나타내는 'so+형용사[부사]+that+주어+can't …' 구문이 적절하다.

02 help는 준사역동사로 목적어와 목적격보어의 관계가 능동일 경우 목적격보어로 원형부정사 또는 to부정사를 받는다.

03 '너무 ~해서 …할 수 없다'는 결과를 나타내는 'so+형용사[부사]+that+주어+can't …' 구문이 적절하다.

04 '너무 ~해서 …할 수 없다'는 의미의 'so+형용사[부사]+that+주어+can't …' 구문이 적절하다.

05 목적어와의 관계가 능동이므로 사역동사 have의 목적격보어로 원형부정사가 적절하다.

06 (1) 사역동사 have의 목적격보어로 원형부정사가 적절하다. (2) 사역동사 let의 목적격보어로 원형부정사가 적절하다. (3) 의자가 칠해지는 것이므로 목적격보어로 수동의 의미를 갖는 과거분사가 적절하다. (4) help는 준사역동사로 목적격보어로 원형부정사 또는 to부정사를 받는다. (5), (6) 'so+형용사[부사]+that+주어+can't …' 구문이다. (7) 'so+형용사[부사]+that+주어+can't ~'는 'too+형용사[부사]+to 동사원형'으로 바꿔 쓸 수 있다. (8) 'so+형용사[부사]+that+주어+can …'은 '형용사[부사]+enough+to 동사원형'으로 바꿔 쓸 수 있다.

07 물이 무엇을 끓이는 것이 아니라 주어가 물이 끓도록 하는 것이므로 사역동사 have의 목적격보어로 과거분사 boiled를 쓰는 것이 적절하다.

08 'so+형용사[부사]+that+주어+동사'는 원인과 결과를 나타내지만 'so that+주어+동사'는 목적을 나타낸다.

09 목적어와의 관계가 능동이므로 사역동사 help의 목적격보어로 원형부정사 혹은 to부정사가 적절하다.

10 'so+형용사[부사]+that+주어+can …'은 '형용사[부사]+enough+to 동사원형'으로 바꿔 쓸 수 있다.

11 want는 목적격보어로 to부정사가 나와야 한다.

12 ① Emily had her daughters take care of her dogs. ③ This rock is so heavy that I can't lift it. ⑤ It was such a nice concert that the $15 for the ticket seemed cheap.

13 (A) 사역동사의 목적어와 목적격보어의 관계가 능동이므로 원형부정사가 적절하다. (B) 동사 get의 목적어와 목적격보어의 관계가 능동이므로 to부정사가 적절하다. (C) 사역동사의 목적어와 목적격보어의 관계가 수동이므로 과거분사가 적절하다.

14 (1) 'so+형용사[부사]+that+주어+can[can't] …' 구문으로 영작한다. (2)~(3) 'so+형용사[부사]+that+주어+can …' = '형용사[부사]+enough+to 동사원형', 'so+형용사[부사]+that+주어+can't …' = 'too+형용사[부사]+to …' (4), (5) 사역동사의 목적격보어로 원형부정사를 이용한다.

15 (1) 목적어와의 관계가 능동이므로 get의 목적격보어로 to부

정사가 적절하다. (2) 사역동사의 목적격보어로 원형부정사가 적절하다. (3) 내용상 '너무 ~해서 …할 수 있다'는 '형용사[부사]+enough+to 동사원형' 구문이 적절하다.

16 'so ... that ~'은 so 뒤의 형용사나 부사가 원인을 나타내며, 접속사 that 뒤에는 그에 따른 결과를 나타낸다.

17 주어진 문장과 ④번의 make는 사역동사로 그 쓰임이 같다.

18 too ... to ~ = so ... that 주어 can't ~. 이때 to부정사 앞에 for 목적격으로 쓰인 것은 to부정사의 의미상의 주어로 that 이하의 절로 바꿀 때는 주격으로 바꿔야 하며, to부정사로 썼을 때 생략된 동사의 목적어는 써 주어야 한다.

01 (1) They made the students wear school uniforms.

(2) She doesn't let her kids watch TV late at night.

(3) I had my puppy get me the ball.

(4) My sister asked me to have her computer repaired.

(5) I helped my cousin bake[to bake] some cookies.

(6) He got his sister to help him with his homework.

02 Patricia had Benjamin repair her broken computer.

03 (1) My brother is too young to understand the words.

(2) Sam was smart enough to understand what the scientist said.

(3) This coffee is too hot for me to drink.

(4) The bookshelf is low enough for my little brother to reach.

04 (1) carry   (2) repaired   (3) to wait   (4) do[to do]

05 (1) The storm was so strong that we couldn't go out.

(2) I was so tired that I didn't go there.

(3) The bus is so noisy that I can't hear the music.

(4) The fog was so thick that driving became really dangerous.

06 The button is so high that people in wheelchairs can't reach it.

07 (1) Eve allowed him to use her pen.

(2) She made Dan follow her advice.

08 because[as, since] the button is very high /
so high that the boy can't push it /
too high for the boy to push

09 take

01 (1)~(3) 사역동사의 목적어와 목적격보어의 관계가 능동이므로 목적격보어로 원형부정사가 적절하다. (4) 사역동사의 목적어와 목적격보어의 관계가 수동이므로 과거분사가 적절하다. (5) help는 목적격보어로 동사원형이나 to부정사가 나온다. (6) get이 '~하게 하다'라는 사역동사의 뜻으로 쓰일 때 목적격보어로 to부정사를 쓴다.

02 사역동사의 목적어와 목적격보어의 관계가 능동일 경우 목적격보어로 원형부정사를 쓴다.

03 (1) so ~ that 주어 can't ... = too ~ to ... (2) so ~ that 주어 can ... = ~ enough to ... (3), (4) 'so ~ that can[can't] ...' 구문에서 주절의 주어와 that 절의 주어가 서로 다를 경우 'too ~ to ...'나 '~ enough to ...'로 바꿔 쓸 때 'for+목적격'으로 의미상의 주어를 나타낸다. drink와 reach의 목적어가 문장의 주어와 같으므로 목적어를 쓰지 않음에 주의한다.

04 (1) 사역동사의 목적어와 목적격보어의 관계가 능동이므로 목적격보어로 원형부정사가 적절하다 (2) 목적어와 목적격보어의 관계가 수동이므로 목적격보어로 과거분사가 적절하다. (3) get은 사역동사의 의미로 쓰일 수 있지만 목적격보어로 to부정사가 나온다. (4) help는 준사역동사로 목적격보어로 원형부정사 또는 to부정사가 나온다.

05 (1), (3) 'so+형용사[부사]+that+주어+can't ...'의 형태로 '너무 ~해서 …할 수 없다'라는 의미를 나타낸다. (2), (4) 'so+형용사[부사]+that+주어+동사'의 형태로 '매우 ~해서 …하다'는 의미를 나타낸다. so 뒤의 형용사[부사]는 원인을, that 뒤에 나오는 내용은 그에 따른 결과를 나타낸다.

06 '너무 ~해서 …할 수 없다'라는 의미를 나타내는 'so+형용사[부사]+that+주어+can't …' 구문을 이용한다.

07 사역동사 have, let, make는 목적격보어로 동사원형을 취한다. get, allow, force는 목적격보어로 to부정사를 취한다.

08 'so+형용사[부사]+that+주어+(can't) ...' 구문은 기본적으로 '원인과 결과'를 나타낸다.

09 사역동사 let의 목적어와 목적격보어의 관계가 능동이므로 목적격보어로 원형부정사가 적절하다.

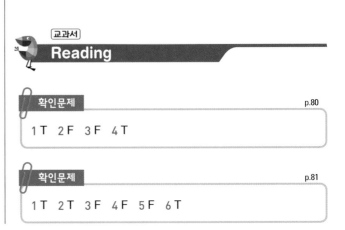

교과서
Reading

확인문제   p.80

1 T   2 F   3 F   4 T

확인문제   p.81

1 T   2 T   3 F   4 F   5 F   6 T

01 Universal Design
02 started a journey
03 looked over 80
04 couldn't see or hear
05 without a stick
06 With all these difficulties
07 with her weak hands
08 found herself in danger
09 very difficult for her, more than
10 what made her do
11 a 26-year-old designer
12 During the 1970's
13 How about designing
14 for those people
15 became tired of
16 Finally, to understand their difficulties
17 For this, uncomfortable, thick glasses
18 so, that, couldn't, without a stick
19 so, that, couldn't, with them
20 to make her hearing bad
21 During, go through
22 From, safely, easily
23 universal design, design for all
24 One example, buses
25 no steps, such a low floor, in a wheelchair, without any help
26 more comfortably
27 following Patricia's way
28 like, live better lives
29 from their point of view
30 next, a better place for everybody

1 Patricia Moore – Mother of Universal Design

2 In 1979, a woman started a journey to cities in the U.S. and Canada.

3 She looked over 80.

4 She couldn't see or hear well.

5 She couldn't walk well without a stick.

6 With all these difficulties, the woman had to climb stairs in subway stations and get on crowded buses.

7 She had to open heavy doors and use can openers with her weak hands.

8 Sometimes she got hurt or found herself in danger.

9 Every moment was very difficult for her, but she visited more than 115 cities and ended her trip in 1982.

10 Who was the woman and what made her do all this?

11 She was Patricia Moore, a 26-year-old designer.

12 During the 1970's, she worked for a big design company.

13 She often asked at meetings, "How about designing for old or weak people?"

14 The other designers always answered, "We don't design for those people."

15 She became tired of the same cold answer.

16 Finally, she decided to become one of "those people" and travel around many cities to understand their difficulties better.

17 For this, she put on her grandmother's clothes, uncomfortable shoes, and thick glasses.

18 The shoes were so uncomfortable that she couldn't walk well without a stick.

19 The glasses were so thick that she couldn't see well with them.

20 She also put lots of cotton in her ears to make her hearing bad.

21 During her journey, Patricia felt the difficulties old people go through.

22 From this experience, she designed products anybody could use safely and easily.

23 This was the beginning of "universal design," or "design for all."

24 One example of her universal design ideas is low-floor buses.

25 They have no steps and have such a low floor that even a person in a wheelchair can use them without any help.

26 Of course, this helps other people get on the bus more comfortably, too.

27 Today more and more designers are following Patricia's way.

28 Products like big flat light switches, doors with easy handles, and phones with touch buttons are helping people live better lives.

29 Look around you, feel the difficulties of people who are older or weaker, and try to find solutions from their point of view.

30 You could be the next Patricia Moore and make the world a better place for everybody.

01 (A) 26-year-old   (B) The other   (C) them
02 ②
03 We don't design for those people.
04 ③
05 difficulties
06 ②
07 (A) journey 또는 trip   (B) 115 cities
08 ①, ④
09 (A) safely and easily   (B) such   (C) comfortably
10 low-floor buses
11 ②, ⑤
12 ⓐ such as   ⓑ viewpoint

13 여러분의 주위를 둘러보고, 더 나이 들거나 더 약한 사람들의 어려움을 느껴 보고, 그들의 관점에서 해결책을 찾으려고 노력해야 한다.

14 ④　　　　　15 too, for, to

16 세탁기 문이 너무 높아서 남동생이 그 안에 옷을 쉽게 넣을 수 없다. / 이 세탁기는 옆문을 가지고 있어서 남동생이 옷을 더 쉽게 넣을 수 있도록 도와줄 것이다.

17 ⓓ　　　　　18 over　　　19 ⑤　　　　20 ②

21 experience

22 she designed products anybody could use safely and easily

23 ①　　　　24 ②, ③　　　25 the glasses

26 easily　　　　　　　27 special legs

28 too high, to use

---

01 (A) 수사가 명사를 수식할 때는 단수로 써야 하므로 26-year-old가 적절하다. (B) Patricia Moore를 제외한 '다른' 디자이너들을 지칭하는 것이므로 The other가 적절하다. (C) 'The glasses'를 가리키므로 them이 적절하다.

02 ②We: The other designers, 나머지는 다 '나이 들거나 약한 사람들'을 지칭한다.

03 '우리는 그런 사람들을 위해 디자인하지 않습니다.'를 가리킨다.

04 이 글은 Patricia가 나이 들거나 약한 사람들의 어려움을 더 잘 이해하기 위해 스스로 늙어 보이도록 분장을 하고 여행을 하는 내용의 글이므로, 제목으로는 'Patricia는 나이든 사람들을 직접 이해하려고 노력했다'가 적절하다. in person: 직접[몸소], ④ for one's age: 나이에 비해서는, 그 나이로는

05 'difficult'의 명사형을 써야 하고, these가 있기 때문에 복수 형태로 쓰는 것이 적절하다.

06 ② rarely: 드물게, 좀처럼 ~하지 않는, 나머지는 다 '가끔'

07 1979년에, 한 여성이 미국과 캐나다의 도시로 '여행'을 시작했고, '115개 이상'의 도시를 방문한 뒤 1982년에 그녀는 여행을 끝마쳤다.

08 help+목적어+원형부정사 또는 to부정사

09 (A) 동사 use를 수식하므로 부사인 'safely and easily'가 적절하다. (B) 'such+a+형용사+명사'이므로 such가 적절하다. (C) 동사 get을 수식하므로 부사인 comfortably가 적절하다.

10 '저상 버스'를 가리킨다.

11 선행사인 people을 수식하는 주격 관계대명사 who나 that이 적절하다.

12 ⓐ like = such as: ~와 같은, ⓑ point of view = viewpoint: 관점[시각]

13 바로 앞 문장의 내용을 쓰는 것이 적절하다.

14 앞에 나오는 내용과 상반되는 내용이 뒤에 이어지므로 However가 가장 적절하다. ① 그러므로, ② 예를 들어, ③ 게다가, ⑤ 즉, 다시 말해

15 so+형용사/부사+that+주어+can't ... = too ~ to ...

16 세탁기 문에 관한 단점과 개선된 점을 쓰는 것이 적절하다.

17 ⓓ 'for', 나머지는 다 'in'이 적절하다.

18 more than = over: ~ 이상

19 모든 순간이 그녀에게 매우 어려웠으나, 그녀는 1982년에 여행을 '끝마쳤다'.

20 (A) From this experience: 이 경험으로부터, (B) in a wheelchair: 휠체어를 탄

21 go through = experience: 겪다

22 긍정문의 any: '어떤 ~이라도'

23 ①번 다음 문장의 this에 주목한다. 주어진 문장의 내용을 받고 있으므로 ①번이 적절하다.

24 ②, ③ so+형용사/부사+that+주어+can't ... = too ~ to ... = very ~, so+주어+can't ..., ① such 뒤에는 명사가 있어야 한다. ④ so ~ that can ... = ~ enough to, ⑤ in order that ... couldn't ~: ~하지 않기 위해서

25 '안경'을 가리킨다.

26 easily = with ease, 전치사+추상명사 = 부사

27 '특별한 다리'를 가지고 있는 책상을 가리킨다.

28 집에 있는 책상은 '너무 높아서' 그 여동생은 그것을 쉽게 '사용'할 수 없다.

---

01 (A) looked　(B) crowded　(C) herself

02 ⓐ nineteen seventy-nine　ⓓ one hundred (and) fifteen　ⓔ nineteen eighty-two

03 ⓑ with → without　ⓒ Without → With

04 (1) 그녀는 자신의 할머니 옷을 입고, 불편한 신발을 신고, 두꺼운 안경을 썼다.
(2) 그녀는 또한 그녀의 청력을 나쁘게 하려고 귀에 많은 솜을 넣었다.

05 too / for / to

06 (A) old or weak　(B) those people

07 use them → use　　　08 comfortably.

09 (1) 크고 평평한 조명 스위치　(2) 편한 손잡이를 가진 문　(3) 터치 버튼을 가진 전화기

10 living → live[to live]　　11 older / weaker

12 safely　　13 very / so

---

01 (A) look+형용사, look like+명사: ~처럼 보이다, 80은 형용사(기수사)이므로 looked가 적절하다. (B) '붐비는' 버스라고 해야 하므로 crowded가 적절하다. crowded: 붐비는, 복잡한, crowding: 가득 메우는, 밀려오는, 떼 지어 모이는, (C) 주어와 목적어가 같을 때는 재귀대명사를 써야 하므로 herself가 적절하다.

02 ⓐ와 ⓔ: 연도는 두 자리씩 끊어 읽는다. 21에서 99까지는 십 단위와 단 단위 사이에 hyphen(-)을 붙인다. ⓓ: hundred 다음에는 and를 넣어 읽는데, 생략도 가능하다.

03 ⓑ 지팡이 '없이'는 잘 걸을 수 없었다고 하는 것이 적절하다. ⓒ 이 모든 어려움을 '가진 채'라고 하는 것이 적절하다.

04 뒤에 이어지는 내용을 쓰는 것이 적절하다.

05 so+형용사/부사+that+주어+can't ... = too ~ to ..., for her: to부정사의 의미상의 주어

06 Patricia는 '그들'(나이 들거나 약한 사람들) 중의 하나가 되어 많은 도시를 여행함으로써 '나이 들거나 약한 사람들'의 어려움을 더 잘 이해하려고 노력했다.

07 use 다음의 them은 선행사인 products를 수식하는 목적격 관계대명사 that[which]으로 바꾼 다음 생략하는 것이므로, 또 them을 쓰는 것은 부적절하다.

08 부사형이 되어야 한다.

09 (1) big flat light switches, (2) doors with easy handles, (3) phones with touch buttons

10 help+목적어+원형부정사 또는 to부정사

11 their는 people who are older or weaker를 가리킨다.

12 in safety = safely: 안전하게, 전치사+추상명사 = 부사

13 so+형용사/부사+that+주어+can't ... = very ~, so+주어+can't ...

영역별 핵심문제　　　　　p.93~97

01 tight　　02 ③　　03 ④　　04 ②
05 jumps rope　　06 ①
07 There are some people who can't see.
08 ④　　09 ③　　10 ⑤　　11 ③
12 ④　　13 ⑤　　14 help, open
15 (1) This question is so difficult that I can't solve it.
　(2) The big panel was so light that it floated on the water.
　(3) He held her by the sleeve so tightly that she couldn't ran away.
　(4) The bus is so noisy that I can't hear the music.
　(5) He took a taxi so that he wouldn't be late.
16 ③　　17 ③　　18 taken　　19 ③
20 ④　　21 ④
22 (A) During　(B) anybody　(C) is
23 Patricia felt the difficulties that[which] old people go through.　　24 ②
25 (1) 그녀는 잘 보거나 잘 들을 수 없었다.
　(2) 그녀는 지팡이 없이는 잘 걸을 수 없었다.
26 used → use　　27 ①, ④　　28 ②, ③
29 ⑤　　30 ②　　31 ④

01 반의어 관계. 편안한 : 불편한 = 느슨한 : 꽉 조이는

02 여러분의 주위를 둘러보고, 더 나이 들거나 더 약한 사람들의 어려움을 느껴 보고, 그들의 관점에서 해결책을 찾으려고 노력해 봐라.

03 많은 사람들 또는 너무 많은 사람들이 있는

04 • 나는 숙제를 거의 끝마쳤다. 'almost'는 부사로 동사를 수식한다. 'most'는 형용사로 명사를 수식한다. • 그 개는 맹인 남자를 돕는다. 의미상 'old'도 가능하다. • 길을 건널 때는 조심해라. 'across'는 전치사로 '~을 가로질러'의 뜻이다.

05 '줄넘기를 하다'는 'jump rope'이고, 주어가 3인칭 단수이므로 jumps를 사용한다.

06 product'는 '제품'이고, '생산적인'은 'productive'이다.

07 '…가 있다'는 'There is[are] ...'를 사용한다. 주어가 복수 명사인 'some people'이므로 'There are some people'로 문장을 시작한다. '볼 수 없는'은 people을 수식하는 역할을 하므로 관계대명사 who를 이용한 문장을 사용해서, people뒤에 'who can't see'를 쓴다..

08 (C) 전등에 대한 불평에 대해 → (B) 이유와 무엇이 문제인지 묻는다 → (A) 문제점을 언급하자 → (D) 알겠다고 말하며 대안을 제시한다.

09 'What do you think?'는 '어떻게 생각하니?'의 뜻으로 상대방의 의견을 물어보는 표현이다. G의 대답 'Looks great' 앞에 오는 것이 자연스럽다.

10 '…할까 생각 중이야'라는 미래 계획이나 의도를 나타내는 말이 적절하다.

11 부정문에서 '또한, 역시'는 too 대신 either를 사용한다.

12 ④ step box(디딤대)에 무슨 문제가 있는지는 알 수 없다. ⑤번은 '누가 더 큰 스위치에 대한 아이디어를 생각해 냈는가?'라는 뜻이다.

13 ⑤ I was so thirsty that I drank a bottle of water.

14 주어진 문장을 영어로 옮기면 'It'll help my grandma open the door more comfortably.'이다.

15 (1), (3), (4) too ~ to ... = so+형용사[부사]+that+주어+can't ... = very ~, so+주어+can't ... = 주어+can't ..., because+주어+동사+very ~ (2) ~ enough to ... = so+형용사[부사]+that+주어+can ... (5) 'so that+주어+동사'는 목적을 나타내어 '~하기 위해서' 혹은 '~하도록'이라는 의미로 쓰인다. 'so ~ that ...'과 혼동하지 않도록 유의한다.

16 사역동사의 목적격보어로 수동의 의미가 필요하므로 과거분사가 적절하다.

17 'so+형용사[부사]+that+주어+can't ...'의 형태로 '너무 ~해서 …할 수 없다'는 뜻을 나타낼 수 있다.

18 사역동사의 목적격보어로 '병원으로 데려가지는' 수동의 의미가 필요하므로 과거분사가 적절하다.

19 첫 문장에서 get이 '~하게 하다'라는 사역동사의 뜻으로 쓰일 때 목적격 보어로 to부정사를 쓴다. 두 번째 문장에서 help는 준사

역동사로 목적어와 목적격보어의 관계가 능동일 경우 목적격보어로 원형부정사 또는 to부정사를 쓴다.

20 ① He is tall enough to touch the ceiling. ② She ran fast so that nobody could catch up with her. ③ Ron asked me to have his computer repaired. ⑤ I'll have him copy all the files for the meeting.

21 ⓒ Sarah always lets me use her laptop computer. ⓓ It'll help my grandma (to) eat food more comfortably. ⑧ Charlotte did her best to have the project finished on time.

22 (A) during+기간을 나타내는 명사, for+숫자, (B) '누구나'라고 해야 하므로 anybody가 적절하다. 긍정문의 any: 어떤 ~이라도, (C) 주어가 'One example'이므로 is가 적절하다.

23 old 앞에 목적격 관계대명사 which[that]가 생략되어 있다.

24 주어진 문장의 This에 주목한다. ②번 앞 문장의 내용을 받고 있으므로 ②번이 적절하다.

25 앞 문단에서 찾아 쓰는 것이 적절하다.

26 had to에 걸리는 것이므로, 동사원형으로 고치는 것이 적절하다.

27 tired of = sick of = bored with: ~에 싫증 난, ②와 ⑤: tired with[from]: ~으로 피곤한, ③ worn out: (특히 힘든 노동·운동으로) 매우 지친, 닳아서 못 쓰게 된

28 ⓑ는 '동사(make)+목적어(her hearing)+목적격보어(bad)'의 5형식 문장의 어순이다. ②, ③: 5형식, ① 4형식, ④ make = go(1형식), ⑤ 한 재산 벌다(3형식)

29 그녀는 청력을 나쁘게 하려고 일부러 귀에 많은 솜을 넣었다.

30 ⓐ와 ①, ②, ④: 명사적 용법, ③ 부사적 용법, ⑤ 형용사적 용법

31 이 글은 '주위를 둘러보고, 더 나이 들거나 더 약한 사람들의 어려움을 느껴 보고, 그들의 관점에서 해결책을 찾으려고 노력하라'는 내용의 글이므로, 제목으로는 '다른 사람들의 관점에서 해결책을 찾으라'가 적절하다.

단원별 예상문제
p.98~101

01 stick **02** (A) flat (B) handle **03** ③
04 ⑤ **05** ② **06** ④ **07** ④
08 ③ **09** ⑤
10 I'm thinking of adding Braille on the sign.
11 She was so kind that she told me the way to the station.
12 very → so / riding → (to) ride **13** ①, ⑤
14 ③, ④ **15** ② **16** ①, ③, ④ / ②, ⑤
17 They have no steps and have such a low floor
18 ③
19 (A) universal design (B) design for all

20 ③ **21** trip **22** (A)difficulties (B) 115 cities **23** ⓐ flat ⓑ handles ⓒ touch
24 your → their

01 그녀는 지팡이가 없이는 잘 걸을 수 없었다.

02 (A) flat: 평평한 (B) handle: 손잡이

03 빈칸 다음의 말에서 '아이들과 휠체어를 탄 사람들이 닿을 수 없다'고 했으므로 버튼이 너무 높다는 말이 적절하다.

04 소유물을 보관할 수 있고 일정 기간 동안 남겨둘 수 있는 금속으로 만들어진 종종 큰 벽장

05 '나도 그것이 마음에 안 들어.'라고 앞에 말한 내용에 대해 동의하는 표현으로 (②)가 적절하다.

06 여동생 Miso를 위해 스위치 아래에 디딤대를 놓고, 할머니를 위해 스위치를 더 큰 것으로 교체할 것이라는 말로 미루어 보아 제목은 '가족을 위한 좋은 아이디어'가 적절하다.

07 할머니가 혼자서 스위치를 켤 수 없는지는 대화에서 언급되어 있지 않다.

08 G의 마지막 말에 '그건 할머니가 쉽게 전등을 켤 수 있도록 도와줄 거야.'라는 말로 보아 스위치가 마음에 들지 않는다는 것을 알 수 있다.

09 G의 두 번째 말에서 그것이 너무 작다고 했기 때문에 문제점에 대한 해결책으로 더 큰 것으로 바꾸는 것이 적절하다.

10 표지판이 마음에 들지 않는 이유가 볼 수 없는 사람들이 있기 때문이라고 했다. 이 문제에 대한 해결책으로는 표지판에 점자를 추가하는 것이 적절하다.

11 'so+형용사[부사]+that+주어+동사'의 형태로 '매우 ~해서 …하다'라는 의미를 나타낸다..

12 help는 목적격보어로 동사원형이나 to부정사가 나온다.

13 ② Ms. Han made her son go to bed immediately. ③ It gave him such a shock that he couldn't say a word. ④ I am so tired that I can't walk any more.

14 ① I'm too tired to go there. ② The man is so rich that he can buy the big house. 또는 The man is rich enough to buy the big house. ⑤ Mom made me clean my room.

15 사역동사(made)+목적어+원형부정사

16 ⓑ와 ①, ③, ④: 명사적 용법, ⓒ와 ②, ⑤: 부사적 용법

17 such+a+형용사+명사

18 이 글은 '유니버설 디자인'에 관한 글이다.

19 Patricia는 그녀가 직접 겪은 경험으로부터 '유니버설 디자인'을 만들었고, 저상 버스의 사례에서 볼 수 있듯이 그것은 '모두를 위한 디자인'이 될 수 있었다. in person: 직접[몸소]

20 주어진 문장의 all these difficulties에 주목한다. ③번 앞 문장의 내용들을 받고 있으므로 ③번이 적절하다.

21 journey = trip: 여행

22 비록 많은 '어려움'이 있었지만, 그 여성은 미국과 캐나다에 있는

‘115개’ 이상의 ‘도시’를 방문하였으며 1982년에 여행을 끝마쳤다.

23 ⓐ 크고 ‘평평한’ 전등 스위치, ⓑ 편한 ‘손잡이’를 가진 문, ⓒ ‘터치’ 버튼을 가진 전화기

24 ‘너의’ 관점이 아니라 ‘그들의’ 관점에서 해결책을 찾으려고 노력해야 한다.

서술형 실전문제 p.102~103

01 The traffic lights look the same to some people who are blind to colors.

02 I'm not happy about, too low / I'm thinking of / comfortably

03 by herself, high, a step box below, change, bigger, more easily

04 (1) Mom made me throw away the trash.
　(2) The teacher made the students do homework.
　(3) Anna made her daughter come home early at night.

05 (1) Betty was too busy to come to the party.
　(2) This food is delicious enough for me to eat all.
　(3) This problem is easy enough to solve.

06 (1) This ice cream is too cold for me to eat.
　(2) It rained too hard for us to play soccer.

07 why　　　　08 (1) What　(2) Why　(3) Shall

09 the, the

10 나이 든 사람들이 겪는 어려움에 대해 Patricia가 그녀의 여행 동안 겪었던 경험

11 low-floor buses　　　　12 so

01 주어는 ‘The traffic lights’로 시작하고 ‘look the same to ...’(…에게 똑같이 보이다)를 주어 뒤에 위치시킨다. 관계대명사 who를 이용하여 ‘some people’을 수식하는 절을 만든다. ‘be blind to …’는 ‘…을 못보다’라는 의미이다.

03 스위치가 너무 높기 때문에 미소는 혼자 전등을 켤 수가 없다. 그래서 그녀의 오빠는 스위치 아래에 디딤대를 놓기로 결심한다. 아빠도 스위치를 더 큰 것으로 바꿀 것이다. 미소와 할머니는 더 쉽게 전등을 켤 수 있을 것이다.

04 사역동사 make의 목적격보어로 동사원형이 적절하다.

05 ‘so+형용사[부사]+that+주어+can't ...’ = ‘too+형용사[부사]+to 동사원형’, ‘so+형용사[부사]+that+주어+can ...’ = ‘형용사[부사]+enough+to 동사원형’ 주절의 주어와 that절의 주어가 다를 경우 의미상의 주어(for+목적격)를 빠뜨리지 않도록 주의한다. 의미상의 주어가 for anyone과 같이 일반인일 경우 생략할 수 있다. 또한 that절의 목적어와 문장의 주어가 같을 경우 to부정사의 목적어를 쓰지 않는 것에 주의한다.

06 so+형용사[부사]+that+주어+can't ... = too ~ to ...

07 무엇이 그녀로 하여금 이 모든 것을 하게 만들었을까?(물주구문) = 그녀는 ‘왜’ 이 모든 것을 했을까?

08 How about ~ing? = What about ~ing? = Why don't we 동사원형? = Shall we 동사원형? = Let's 동사원형.: ~하는 게 어때? 지금의 경우, Let's 동사원형은 마침표를 찍어야 하므로 ⓑ 대신 쓰기에 부적절하다.

09 the+형용사 = 복수 보통명사

10 첫 문장의 내용을 가리킨다.

11 ‘저상 버스’가 ‘유니버설 디자인’의 예에 해당한다.

12 so+형용사, such+a+형용사+명사

창의사고력 서술형 문제 p.104

|모범답안|

01 A: I'm not happy about the locker. It's too old.
　B: I think so, too. Do you have any ideas?
　A: I'm thinking of decorating its door.
　B: That's a good idea.

02 (1) Amy made her brother fix her computer.
　(2) She let her daughter go to the K-pop concert.
　(3) The baby cried so loudly that I covered my ears.
　(4) He spoke so fast that I could not understand him.

03 (A) so　(B) that　(C) can't　(D) special legs

단원별 모의고사 p.105~108

01 ②　　　　02 point of view　　　　03 ④

04 (A) thinking　(B) doesn't have to hold　05 ⑤

06 ①　　　　07 I intend to put some pads on it.

08 ④　　　　09 I'm not happy about it, either.

10 ③　　　　11 ③

12 I'm thinking of changing it with a bigger one.

13 (1) The noise was so loud that I couldn't sleep.
　(2) The steps are so high that I can't get on the bus.

14 ①　　　　15 (1) it → 삭제　(2) to carry → carry

16 (A) better lives　(B) solutions　　　17 their

18 저상 버스는 계단이 없고 낮은 바닥을 가지고 있어서 휠체어를 탄 사람도 아무 도움 없이 이용할 수 있는 것

19 ⑤　　　　20 ②, ③

21 ⓑ with → without　ⓒ without → with

22 ①　　　　23 her → herself

01 ②번은 'switch'에 대한 영어 설명이다. 'pad'는 'a piece of soft, thick cloth or rubber, used to protect a part of the body, give shape to something'(신체의 일부를 보호하고, 어떤 것에 모양을 부여하기 위해 사용되는 부드럽고 두꺼운 천이나 고무 조각)

02 point of view: 관점

03 사람들이 타고 내릴 수 있도록 버스나 기차가 멈춰서는 건물이나 장소

04 (A) '…할까 생각 중이다'는 계획을 말하는 표현으로 'I'm thinking of ...'를 사용한다. (B)는 그림에 'Don't hold it. Just wear it'이라고 적혀 있는 걸로 보아 '손가락으로 그것을 잡을 필요가 없다'는 'doesn't have to'가 적절하다.

05 불만을 나타내는 표현이 아닌 것은 ⑤번으로 '이 장소에 대해 불평하고 싶지 않다'는 뜻이다.

06 버튼이 너무 높다고 말하고 있으므로 아이들이나 휠체어를 탄 사람들이 버튼에 닿을 수 없다는 'reach'가 적절하다.

07 책상이 너무 낮다는 불만에 어울리는 해결책으로 그 위에 몇 장의 패드를 놓는다는 말이 자연스럽다. 'intend to+동사원형'을 이용한다.

08 스위치가 너무 높다는 불만의 말에 대해 알맞은 해결책으로 '스위치 아래에 디딤대를 둘 생각이야.'라는 ④가 적절하다.

09 '나도 그렇다'는 의미로 부정문에서는 'either'를 사용한다.

10 G가 계단이 높다고 불만을 말하고 있고, B가 계단이 없는 새로운 길을 만들까 생각 중이라는 말로 보아 ③이 적절하다.

11 표지판에 점자(Braille)를 추가할까 생각 중이라고 말하는 것은 볼 수 없는 사람들에 대한 해결책이다.

12 '나는 …할까 생각 중이다'는 "I'm thinking of ..."로 문장을 시작하고 전치사 of 뒤에는 동명사 changing을 사용한다. 'change A with B'는 'A를 B로 바꾸다'라는 의미이다.

13 'so+형용사[부사]+that+주어+can't ...' 구문을 이용하여 원인과 결과를 나타낸다.

14 사역동사의 목적어와 목적격보어가 능동의 관계에 있을 경우 목적격보어로 원형 부정사를 쓴다.

15 (1) 'so+형용사[부사]+that+주어+can't …' 구문을 'too+형용사[부사]+to 동사원형' 구문으로 바꿀 때, that절 내의 동사의 목적어와 문장의 주어가 같으면 목적어를 쓰지 않는 것이 적절하다. (2) 사역동사의 목적어와 목적격보어가 능동의 관계에 있을 경우 목적격보어로 원형부정사를 쓴다.

16 그것은 더 나이 들거나 더 약한 사람들의 어려움을 느껴 보고, 그들의 관점에서 '해결책'을 찾으려고 노력함으로써 사람들이 '더 나은 삶'을 살도록 도와주는 방법이다.

17 put oneself in another's shoes: 상대편의 처지나 입장에서 생각하다(역지사지)

18 앞 문장의 내용을 가리킨다.

19 저상 버스는 다른 사람들도 버스를 '더 편안하게 탈 수 있도록' 도와준다.

20 ⓐ와 나머지들: 마침내, ② 실제로, 정말로, ③ 특히

21 ⓑ 지팡이 '없이'는 잘 걸을 수 없었다고 하는 것이 적절하다. ⓒ 안경을 '쓰고'는 잘 볼 수 없었다고 하는 것이 적절하다.

22 get on: (버스 따위에) 오르다 / be difficult for: ~에게 어렵다

23 목적어가 주어 자신이므로 재귀대명사를 써야 한다.

Teens' Magazine

Reading

확인문제 p.112

1 T 2 T

확인문제 p.113

1 F 2 T 3 F

확인문제 p.114

1 F 2 T

확인문제 p.115

1 T 2 F 3 T

교과서 확인학습 A p.116~119

01 Teens'
02 in Shapes
03 Like
04 like, because
05 Snowman
06 outside
07 go out, play
08 have to
09 to snow, be cold
10 on days like these
11 a second, the most wonderful
12 cover myself up, hide here
13 Looking Back
14 art
15 yours
16 UNTIL, OVER
17 slow walker
18 little things
19 Follow
20 My Bike
21 take, To any place, home, enjoy riding
22 Giving
23 there
24 here
25 umbrella
26 Between
27 Selfies
28 Though
29 robots
30 cute
31 a big cake
32 made him happy
33 Have you ever seen

34 What, Life
35 moment
36 take tests
37 have nothing
38 before, after
39 sleepy
40 after, rings
41 lovely time
42 lunch
43 favorite
44 last class
45 during break time
46 myself
47 awesome
48 than before
49 finishes earlier
50 because, rains, snows
51 for dessert
52 same class
53 most difficult
54 trash
55 Studying
56 Making a presentation
57 on time
59 Places, Village
60 Traditional
61 something delicious
62 make, full
63 choose, add, to
64 Youth
65 in the middle of
66 such as
67 take a break
69 near
70 after, because
71 to enjoy
72 Have Fun
73 Shape
74 cut, into, from
75 Five Lines
76 in such a way
77 Eating
78 are thrown away
79 breaks down into
80 go, fish
81 Up to
82 Let's
83 universal design
84 winners' works
85 come close
86 pull, away
87 need to
88 save lots of water
89 between
90 up, down easily
91 get some rest
92 special
93 together, for
94 LAUGH
95 Jokes
96 hopeful
97 full of
98 How, friendly
100 Why
101 To get

교과서 확인학습 B p.120~123

1 Teens' Magazine
2 Works of Art in Shapes
3 Like a Circle
4 I love you like a circle because a circle never ends.
5 Snowman
6 It's cold outside.
7 I don't want to go out and play.
8 But Mom says I have to.
9 It's starting to snow and I'm going to be cold.
10 I don't like playing outside on days like these.

21

11 But wait a second, I have the most wonderful idea!

12 I'll cover myself up with snow and I'll hide here!

13 Looking Back with Your Handwriting

14 Life is art.

15 Live yours in COLOR.

16 IT ISN'T OVER UNTIL IT'S OVER.

17 I am a slow walker, but I never walk back.

18 I love the little things you do.

19 Follow your dream.

20 My Bike

21 Two wheels take me / To any place / To school / Back home / To the mountain / To the river / I love my bike / I enjoy riding it every day

22 Giving Tree

23 Out there – wet

24 In here – dry

25 Pretty big umbrella

26 Between me and the sky.

27 Selfies of This Year

28 Though we lost the game, we had a lot of fun.

29 Look at the robots we made.

30 Aren't they cute?

31 We made a big cake for Mr. Han.

32 It made him happy.

33 Have you ever seen a handsome Peter Pan like me?

34 What Do You Think of Your School Life?

35 The most uncomfortable moment

36 1. When I take tests

37 2. When I am really hungry and have nothing to eat

38 3. When I change clothes before and after P.E. class

39 4. others: When I am sleepy in class

40 When the teacher doesn't finish classes after the bell rings

41 The most lovely time

42 1. lunch time

43 2. class with my favorite teacher

44 3. the last class on Friday

45 4. others: when I am sleeping during break time

46 when I see myself in the mirror

47 The most awesome news

48 1. I got better grades than before

49 2. School finishes earlier today

50 3. I don't go to school because it rains or snows a lot

51 4. others: We eat delicious sweets for dessert

52 My best friend and I are in the same class

53 The most difficult work to do

54 1. Washing trash cans

55 2. Studying

56 3. Making a presentation in front of friends

57 4. others: Being on time every day

58 Group work

59 Places We Love in Our Village

60 Daehan Traditional Market

61 If you want to eat something delicious, visit Daehan Market.

62 You can buy "*yeopjeon*" and use it to make your lunch box full.

63 You can choose many kinds of food and add them to your lunch box.

64 Saebom Youth Center

65 This is Saebom Youth Center in the middle of our town.

66 We like this place because we can learn many things, such as dance and music.

67 We can also play board games and take a break here.

68 Mr. Kim's Bakery

69 This is a small bakery near the school.

70 We like to go there after school because we're always hungry!

71 It is good to enjoy delicious bread with friends.

72 Let's Have Fun with Puzzles!

73 Shape Puzzles

74 If you cut the shape A into two same pieces, you can then make all the other shapes(B, C, D, E, F, G) from those two pieces.

75 Ten Balls in Five Lines

76 Place 10 balls in 5 lines in such a way that each line has exactly 4 balls on it.

77 You Are Eating Plastic Spoons!

78 1. A lot of plastic spoons are thrown away every year.

79 2. Most plastic breaks down into smaller pieces in the ocean.

80 3. Very small pieces of plastic go into fish.

81 4. If you eat the fish, you eat the plastic, too. Up to 11,000 pieces each year!

82 Let's Make a Dream School!

83 We had a universal design contest for our school last month.

84 Here are the winners' works.

85 1. When your hands come close, water comes out.

86 When you pull your hands away, the water stops.

87 You don't need to turn or touch any parts.

88 We can save lots of water with this. — by O Juyeon(1-3)

89 2. This is our school park between two buildings.

90 Anybody can go up and down easily here.

91 Also we can sit and get some rest here. — by Gim Jimin(3-5)

92 3. These are special desks and chairs for the classroom.

93 For group activities, you can get them together and make a wonderful group table for three, four, or five students. — by Choi Yumi(2-1)

94 LET'S LAUGH

95 Funny Earth Day Jokes Ha! Ha!

96 Why are recycle bins hopeful?

97 Because they're full of cans.

98 How can you tell the ocean is friendly?

99 It waves.

100 Why did the sun go to school?

101 To get brighter.

서술형 실전문제 p.124~125

01 Though[Although]

02 (1) such as (2) are thrown away (3) friendly

03 (1) wheel, 바퀴 (2) circle, 원 (3) grade, 성적
(4) bread, 빵

04 (1) works (2) special

05 (1) I'll cover myself up with snow and I'll hide here!
(2) A cloth doll was made for her daughter by her.
(3) When did you go to Seoul?

06 (1) Though he is young, he has much gray hair.
(2) It is good to have friends.

07 like   08 go out and play

09 I'll cover myself up with snow and I'll hide here!

10 People throw away a lot of plastic spoons every year. 또는 People throw a lot of plastic spoons away every year.

11 but also   12 eleven thousand

13 깡통, 할 수 있다   14 일렁이다, 손을 흔들다

15 더 밝은, 더 똑똑한

01 양보의 부사절 though[although]가 적절하다. (1) 우리는 경기에서 졌지만, 아주 즐거웠다. (2) Anne은 Tim이 자신을 자

주 짜증스럽게 했는데도 그를 좋아했다.

02 (1) 춤과 음악 같은 많은 것을 배울 수 있어서 우리는 이곳을 좋아한다. (2) 해마다 많은 플라스틱 숟가락이 버려진다. throw away는 '버리다'는 뜻으로 숟가락이 버려지는 수동의 의미이기 때문에 be thrown away로 수동태가 적절하다. (3) 바다가 다정하다는 것을 어떻게 알 수 있는가? '다정한'의 의미로 명사 friend에 ly를 사용해서 형용사로 바꾸어 준다.

03 (1) 중심에서 막대기에 연결되어 차량 또는 기계 부품을 이동시키기 위해 사용되는 원형 물체 (2) 고정된 중심점으로부터 항상 동일한 거리인 점들의 연속된 곡선 (3) 누군가의 일이나 수행이 얼마나 좋은지 보여주는 숫자나 글자 (4) 밀가루, 물 및 보통 효모로 만들어지고 함께 섞여서 구워진 음식

05 (1) '동사+대명사 목적어+부사'의 어순이다. (2) make는 직접 목적어를 주어로 한 수동태만 가능하다. (3) when으로 시작하는 의문문이므로 현재완료 시제를 쓸 수 없다.

07 (A) don't like playing: 놀고 싶지 않다 (B) days like these: 이런 날

08 '내가 노는 것'이 생략되어 있다.

09 '눈으로 몸을 덮고 여기에 숨는 것'을 가리킨다.

10 People을 주어로 해서 고치는 것이 적절하다.

11 여러분이 물고기를 먹을 때, 물고기'뿐만 아니라' 그 물고기가 먹었던 아주 작은 플라스틱 조각들'도' 먹게 되기 때문이다.

12 'eleven thousands'처럼, 복수 형태로 쓰지 않도록 조심해야 한다.

13 재활용 통은 '깡통[할 수 있다]'으로 가득 차 있기 때문에 희망적이다.

14 바다가 '일렁이기[손을 흔들기]' 때문에 다정하다는 것을 알 수 있다.

15 태양은 '더 밝아지기[똑똑해지기]'를 위해서 학교에 간다.

단원별 예상문제 p.126~130

01 ③   02 like   03 ③

04 (1) breaks down (2) Up to (3) lots of

05 (1) cut, into, shapes (2) take, to

06 ①   07 ④   08 up   09 ③

10 ②   11 so we like this place

12 (1) We had a universal design contest for our school last month.
(2) It is good to enjoy delicious bread with friends.

13 ⓐ ②, ⑤ ⓑ ①, ③, ④   14 눈이 오는 날

15 me → myself   16 ④

17 that[which]   18 ②   19 ②

20 your life[lives]   21 ②, ④, ⑤

22 (A) last (B) during (C) myself   23 ⑤

24 ③   25 ⓐ yeopjeon ⓒ many kinds of food

26 ①, ⑤　　　27 *yeopjeon*　　28 time, ourselves

29 the robots (we made)　　30 happily → happy

31 (A) awesome　(B) dessert　(C) the same

32 because of

33 school finishes earlier than usual → they got
better grades than before 또는 the most wonderful
→ the second most wonderful

34 ②　　　　35 like　　　36 ④

01 ③번은 'wave'에 대한 설명이다. 'shake hands'는 'to greet each other or say goodbye by briefly joining hands and moving them slightly up and down(짧게 손을 맞잡고 가볍게 아래위로 손을 움직임으로써 인사하거나 작별인사하다)'

02 유의어 관계다. 정확하게 : ~와 같은

03 '1. 시험을 칠 때 2. 정말 배가 고픈데 먹을 것이 없을 때 3. 체육 시간 전후에 옷을 갈아입을 때'는 모두 '불편한' 순간이다.

04 (1) break down: 분해되다 (2) up to: ~까지 (3) lots of: 많은

05 • cut A into B: A를 B로 자르다. 'all the other+복수 명사' 형태로 shapes가 맞다. • take A to B: A를 B로 데려 가다

06 '식사 끝에 먹는 단 음식'으로 '후식'이 맞다.

07 모두 반의어 관계이고, ④번은 '졸리는'의 뜻을 가진 유의어 관계다.

08 • cover A up with B: B로 A를 덮다 • up and down 위아래로

09 ① a such way → such a way ② is the ocean → the ocean is ④ either → too ⑤ little → lot[few]

10 ②번은 비인칭 주어이고 나머지는 모두 가주어이다.

11 '결과+because절(이유)' = '이유+so절(결과)'

12 (1) last month라는 과거를 나타내는 부사구가 있으므로 현재완료 시제를 쓸 수 없다. (2) 가주어로 That이 아니라 It이 적절하다.

13 ⓐ와 ②, ⑤: 현재분사, ⓑ와 ①, ③, ④: 동명사

14 '눈이 오는 날'을 의미한다.

15 주어와 목적어가 같으므로 재귀대명사로 고치는 것이 적절하다.

16 우리는 게임에 '졌지만', 아주 즐거웠다라고 해야 하므로, Though(비록 …이긴 하지만)가 적절하다.

17 목적격 관계대명사 that[which]이 생략되어 있다.

18 ⓒ와 ①, ④번: 경험 용법, ② 결과 용법, ③ 완료 용법, ⑤ 계속 용법

19 ⓐ 손 글씨 ② 캘리그래피: 붓이나 특별한 펜을 사용하여 아름다운 손 글씨를 만드는 예술, ① (컴퓨터 자료를 출력한) 인쇄(물), ③ 광고, ④ 생산물, 상품, ⑤ (물품·책 등의) 목록, 카탈로그

20 '너의 삶'을 가리킨다.는 entire와 같은 의미이다.

21 ⓒ와 ②, ④, ⑤: (형상·규모가) 작은(opp. big, large), ⓒ '작은' 일들, ① [추상명사·물질명사와 함께] (a little+명사) 《긍정적으로》 조금은 있는(some), 다소간의, 어느 정도의, ③ a little: 《긍정적으로》 조금은, 조금

22 (A) '마지막' 수업이라고 해야 하므로 last가 적절하다. last: 마지막의, latest: 최근의 (B) '쉬는 시간에'라고 해야 하므로 during이 적절하다. 'during+기간을 나타내는 명사', 'for+숫자' (C) 주어와 목적어가 같으므로 myself가　　적절하다.

23 위 글은 'survey(설문조사)'이다. ① (책·연극·영화 등에 대한) 논평[비평], 감상문, ② 요약, 개요, ③ 수필, ④ (신문·잡지의) 글, 기사

24 ③ 학생들은 '쉬는 시간에 잠잘 때'보다 '점심 먹는 것'을 더 좋아한다.

25 ⓐ 엽전, ⓒ '많은 종류의 음식'을 가리킨다.

26 ⓑ와 ②, ③, ④는 부사적 용법, ① 명사적 용법, ⑤ 형용사적 용법

27 대한 전통 시장에서 여러분의 점심 도시락을 가득 채우고 싶다면, '엽전'을 쓸 수 있다.

28 have a lot of fun = have a good[great] time = enjoy oneself: 재미있게 놀다, 즐겁게 보내다

29 '우리가 만든 로봇들'을 가리킨다.

30 목적격보어 자리에 부사를 쓸 수 없으므로 형용사로 바꾸는 것이 적절하다.

31 (A) 가장 '멋진' 뉴스라고 해야 하므로 awesome이 적절하다. awesome: 기막히게 좋은, 굉장한, awful: 끔찍한, 지독한 (B) '후식'으로 맞있는 단것을 먹는다고 해야 하므로 dessert가 적절하다. dessert: 후식, desert: 사막 (C) '같은' 반이 되었다고 해야 하므로 'the same'이 적절하다.

32 because+주어+동사, because of+명사구

33 학생들에게는 '전보다 좋은 성적을 받았다'는 뉴스가 가장 멋진 뉴스이다.

34 이 글은 장소를 소개하는 글이므로, 제목으로는 '우리 마을에서 우리가 좋아하는 곳들'이 적절하다.

35 such as = like: ~와 같은

36 '하이킹을 갈 수 있다.'는 말은 언급되어 있지 않다.

교과서 파헤치기

Lesson **7**

p.02

단어 TEST Step 1

01 멋있는, 대단한, 굉장한	02 ~의 아래에
03 고전의	04 실제로, 사실 05 예, 사례
06 계절	07 독특한, 특별한 08 널리
09 훌륭한, 뛰어난 10 차이	11 표현하다
12 판타지, 환상, 공상 13 포함하다	14 왕조, 왕가
15 마법사 16 이야기	17 탐정; 탐정의
18 공예 19 (사람, 동물의) 상, 모형	
20 예술의, 예술적인 21 공연	22 시
23 외국의 24 창의적인	25 인기 있는
26 괴물 27 둘 다	28 완벽한
29 도구, 수단 30 상상하다	31 손 글씨, 필적
32 번개 33 모으다	34 날카로운
35 ~로 만들어지다 36 ~로 이끌다, ~로 이어지다	
37 만들다 38 ~처럼 보이다	39 수업을 듣다
40 ~하는 데 시간이 걸리다	41 무료로
42 ~에 맞춰 춤추다 43 처음에	

단어 TEST Step 2

p.03

01 below	02 detective	03 craft
04 actually	05 perfect	06 character
07 performance	08 fantasy	09 creative
10 awesome	11 handwriting	12 hold
13 excellent	14 figure	15 poem
16 dynasty	17 difference	18 artistic
19 tale	20 horror	21 widely
22 popular	23 tail	24 foreign
25 learn	26 lightning	27 example
28 between	29 collect	30 monster
31 wizard	32 sharp	33 express
34 unique	35 dance to	36 at first
37 build up	38 for free	39 be interested in
40 lead to	41 be made of	42 take a class
43 look like+명사		

단어 TEST Step 3

p.04

1 artistic, 예술의   2 below, ~의 아래에   3 unique, 독특한
4 wizard, 마법사   5 dynasty, 왕조   6 express, 표현하다
7 include, 포함하다   8 lightning, 번개
9 nowadays, 요즘음에는, 오늘날   10 autumn, 가을
11 popular, 인기 있는   12 tale, 이야기   13 season, 계절

---

14 title, 제목   15 tool, 도구   16 poem, 시

대화문 TEST Step 1

p.05~06

Get Ready 2

(1) enjoy listening, dance to / Great
(2) Are, interested in cooking / sometimes, for
(3) Are you interested in learning, Actually, calligraphy class, work / Excellent

Start Off Listen & Talk A

(1) Good job, holding, How creative / interested in taking pictures / taking, online class for free / good for
(2) Good, expresses, feeling, autumn / Are, interested / taking, on weekends / didn't that

Start Off Listen & Talk B

did, job, awesome / made of / Are, interested in glass art / How long, take to make / It took

Speak Up Look and talk

enjoyed, performance, a good job / interested, playing the / Can you / problem

Speak Up Mission

interested in watching horror / am, I'm not, interested in reading detective

Real-life Scene

are, doing / practicing calligraphy / writing, looks fun / interested, calligraphy / What, think / looks like, dancing, open / got, means / did, job, try / Why not, brush

Your Turn

writing something / art homework / did, good

Express Yourself

(1) learning / interested in / join, learn
(2) interested in / Not / what, interested / interested, traditional, awesome
(3) Look at, learning / interested / sound, want to learn

Learning Diary Listen & Speak

interested / good at taking care of / How about, interested, too / can't grow

대화문 TEST Step 2

p.07~08

Get Ready 2

(1) B: Do you like K-pop?
   G: Yes. I enjoy listening to SJ's songs. I can dance to his songs.

B: Great!

(2) B: Are you interested in cooking Korean dishes?

W: Yes. I sometimes cook bulgogi for my family and they love it.

(3) B: Are you interested in learning *Hangeul*?

G: Yes. Actually, I'm learning it in my calligraphy class. Look! This is my work.

B: Excellent!

Start Off Listen & Talk A

(1) B: Good job! Someone is holding a cloud? How creative!

G: Thank you. Are you interested in taking pictures?

B: Yes, I am. Actually, I'm taking an online class for free.

G: Oh, good for you.

(2) G: Good work! I think your painting expresses the feeling of autumn well.

B: Thank you. Are you interested in painting?

G: Yes, I am. I started taking a class on weekends.

B: Oh, I didn't know that.

Start Off Listen & Talk B

B: You did a good job! It's awesome.

G: Thanks.

B: What is it made of? Glass?

G: Yes, it is. Are you interested in glass art?

B: Yes, very much. How long did it take to make it?

G: It took one month.

Speak Up Look and talk

B: I enjoyed your performance. You did a good job.

G: Thank you. Are you interested in playing the ukulele?

B: Sure. Can you teach me?

G: No problem.

Speak Up Mission

A: Are you interested in watching horror movies?

B: Yes, I am. I watch horror movies very often. / No, I'm not. I'm interested in reading detective stories.

Real-life Scene

James: What are you doing, Mina?

Mina: I'm practicing calligraphy.

James: You're writing with a brush. It looks fun.

Mina: Are you interested in calligraphy?

James: Yes, very much.

Mina: Look at this! I just wrote it. What do you think?

James: It looks like a person dancing with open arms.

Mina: You got it. This Korean word means "dance."

James: You did a good job! Can I try it?

Mina: Why not? Take this brush.

Your Turn

A: You're writing something. What's this?

B: It's my art homework. Do you like it?

A: Sure. I think you did a good job!

Express Yourself

(1) B: Look! Two girls are learning Hangeul.

G: Are you interested in *Hangeul*, Kevin?

B: Yes, very much. I want to join them and learn it.

(2) B: Julie, are you interested in *hanbok*?

G: Not really.

B: Then, what are you interested in?

G: Well, I'm interested in taekwondo. It is a traditional Korean sport. It's awesome.

(3) G: Look at the two men learning *pansori*.

B: Are you interested in pansori, Nancy?

G: Sure. I like the sound of it. I want to learn it.

Learning Diary Listen & Speak

B: Minji, are you interested in animals?

G: Yes, I am. I'm good at taking care of them.

B: How about plants? Are you interested in them, too?

G: No, I'm not. I can't grow them well.

본문 TEST Step 1   p.09~10

01 Write, Feelings A

02 How, express, feelings

03 sing, dance   04 write, poem, draw

05 Nowadays, express, through

06 at, works, art

07 includes, image, delicious

08 autumn, season, fruit

09 work, word, Chinese character

10 looks like, walking down

11 Both, express, feeling, through

12 kind, called calligraphy

13 not new

14 kinds, works, be found

15 at, examples, below   16 tell, difference

17 created by, period

18 painted with, brush

19 created by, in, late   20 was written with

21 Different, tools, styles

22 Of, practice hard, unique

23 widely used around

24 artistic touches, clothes

25 Below, examples   26 at, title, poster

27 How, feel

28 imagine, sharp, ugly, tail

29 How about, fantasy

30 lightning, wizard hats   31 Anyone, writing

32 by hand, practice, perfect

33 Keep trying, part, everyday

34 with, feelings, gifts   35 build up, own

01 Write, Feelings

02 How, express. feelings

03 sing, dance

04 poem, draw a picture

05 Nowadays, popular, through handwriting

06 Let's look at, works of art

07 work of art, includes an image

08 a season of fruit

09 Korean word, Chinese character

10 looks like, walking, autumn leaves

11 express the feeling, through beautiful handwriting

12 called calligraphy   13 not new

14 can be found, around the world

15 examples from, below   16 tell the difference

17 was created by, period   18 were painted with

19 was created by, in the late 1400s

20 was written with

21 Different writing tools, different styles

22 Of course, practice hard, unique styles

23 is widely used around

24 designers' artistic touches, clothes

25 are some examples   26 the title

27 How, feel

28 sharp teeth, ugly, long tail

29 How about, fantasy novel

30 lightning, wizard hats

31 Anyone, writing calligraphy

32 to write by hand, practice makes perfect

33 Keep trying, part, everyday

34 with your feelings, bookmarks, gifts

35 build up

1 여러분의 느낌을 써라

2 여러분은 자신의 느낌을 어떻게 표현하는가?

3 노래를 부르거나 춤을 추는가?

4 시를 쓰거나 그림을 그리는가?

5 요즈음에는 손 글씨를 통해 감정을 표현하는 것이 인기다.

6 몇몇 작품을 살펴보자.

7 오른쪽 예술 작품에서는 단어가 맛있는 과일인 홍시의 이미지를 포함하고 있다.

8 그것은 가을이 결실의 계절임을 보여 준다.

9 왼쪽에 있는 예술 작품은 한글 단어와 한자를 보여 주고 있다.

10 그것은 마치 단풍잎이 깔린 길을 따라 걷고 있는 행복한 여인처럼 보인다.

11 이 두 작품은 아름다운 손 글씨를 통해 가을의 느낌을 표현한다.

12 이런 종류의 예술은 '캘리그래피'라고 불린다.

13 캘리그래피는 새로운 것이 아니다.

14 오래전의 다양한 종류의 많은 캘리그래피 작품들이 세계 곳곳에서 발견되고 있다.

15 아래에 있는 한국과 영국의 두 사례를 보라.

16 여러분은 그 차이를 구별할 수 있는가?

17 왼쪽 작품은 조선 왕조 시대에 추사에 의해 창작되었다.

18 그 글자들은 부드러운 붓으로 그려졌다.

19 오른쪽의 '캔터베리 이야기'는 1400년대 후반 영국에서 Chaucer에 의해 창작되었다.

20 그것은 펜으로 쓰였다.

21 각기 다른 필기구가 각기 다른 캘리그래피의 스타일을 이끌었다.

22 물론, 모든 캘리그래피 작가들은 자신의 독특한 스타일을 만들어 내기 위해 열심히 연습해야 했다.

23 캘리그래피는 요즘음 우리 주변에서 널리 쓰이고 있다.

24 여러분은 영화 포스터, 책 표지, 음악 CD, 그리고 의류에서 디자이너들의 예술적인 손길을 발견할 수 있다.

25 아래에 몇 가지 예가 있다.

26 영화 포스터의 제목을 보라.

27 어떤 느낌이 드는가?

28 괴물의 커다란 입, 날카로운 이빨, 그리고 추하고 긴 꼬리를 상상할 수 있는가?

29 공상 소설의 제목은 어떠한가?

30 Harry의 번개와 마술사 모자가 보이는가?

31 누구든지 캘리그래피를 쓰기 시작할 수 있다.

32 처음부터 손으로 글씨를 잘 쓰기는 쉽지 않지만, 연습하면 완벽해진다.

33 계속해서 노력하고 자신의 일상의 한 부분이 되게 하라.

34 생일 카드, 책갈피, 또는 선물에 느낌을 담아 써 보라.

35 곧 자신만의 캘리그래피 세계를 만들게 될 것이다.

1 Write Your Feelings

2 How do you express your feelings?

3 Do you sing or dance?

4 Do you write a poem or draw a picture?

5 Nowadays, it is popular to express feelings through handwriting.

6 Let's look at some works of art.

7 In the work of art on the right, the word includes an image of a delicious fruit, *hongsi*.

8 It shows that autumn is a season of fruit.

9 The work of art on the left shows a Korean word and a Chinese character.

10 It looks like a happy woman walking down a road with autumn leaves.

11 Both of these works express the feeling of autumn through beautiful handwriting.

12 This kind of art is called calligraphy.

13 Calligraphy is not new.

14 Many different kinds of calligraphy works from long ago can be found all around the world.

15 Look at the two examples from Korea and the UK below.

16 Can you tell the difference?

17 The left one was created by Chusa in the period of the Joseon Dynasty.

18 The characters were painted with a soft brush.

19 The right one, *The Canterbury Tales*, was created by Chaucer in England in the late 1400s.

20 It was written with a pen.

21 Different writing tools led to different styles of calligraphy.

22 Of course, all calligraphers had to practice hard to make their unique styles.

23 Today calligraphy is widely used around us.

24 You can find designers' artistic touches on movie posters, book covers, music CDs, and clothes.

25 Below are some examples.

26 Look at the title on the movie poster.

27 How do you feel?

28 Can you imagine the monster's big mouth, sharp teeth, and ugly, long tail?

29 How about the title on the fantasy novel?

30 Do you see Harry's lightning and the wizard hats?

31 Anyone can start writing calligraphy.

32 It's not easy to write by hand well at first, but practice makes perfect.

33 Keep trying and make it part of your everyday life.

34 Write with your feelings on birthday cards, bookmarks, or gifts.

35 Soon you will build up your own world of calligraphy.

After You Read B

1. Korean characters

2. laughing out loud

3. characters mean

4. growing in a pot

Express Yourself C

1. Look at, learning[doing]

2. traditional Korean, wear, to do

3. It, to learn

4. Are, interested

5. come, try

6. Look at, playing

7. traditional Korea, to play

8. It, to play

9. Are, interested

10. come, try

Link to the World

1. Russian dolls, is called

2. When, keep coming

3. It, to see, inside each doll

4. The first set, with six children

5. many new styles, are created, loved

After You Read B

1. These Korean characters mean "Let's laugh."

2. This calligraphy shows two people laughing out loud .

3. These Korean characters mean "tree."

4. This calligraphy shows a tree growing in a pot .

Express Yourself C

1. Look at the two girls learning[doing] *taekwondo*.

2. Taekwondo is a traditional Korean sport, and we wear dobok to do it.

3. It is exciting to learn *taekwondo*.

4. Are you interested?

5. Please come and try.

6. Look at the two boys playing *yunnori*.

7. *Yunnori* is a traditional Korean board game, and we use yuts and mals to play it.

8. It is exciting to play *yunnori.*

9. Are you interested?

10. Please come and try.

Link to the World

1. This is a set of Russian dolls . It is called matryoshka.

2. When you open it, smaller dolls keep coming out of it.

3. It is interesting to see a smaller doll inside each doll.

4. The first set of matryoshka dolls was a mother doll with six children.

5. Today, many new styles of matryoshkas are created and loved by many people.

Lesson 8

단어 TEST Step 1   p.21

01 책꽂이	02 또 하나의, 또 다른	
03 불편한	04 더러운	05 보편적인
06 눈이 먼	07 솜	08 꽉 조이는, 딱 붙는
09 청력	10 해결책	11 결심하다
12 쉽게	13 장식하다	14 더하다, 추가하다
15 어려움	16 자리, 좌석	17 마침내
18 거의	19 분수, 원천	20 손잡이
21 상품, 제품	22 낮은	23 붐비는
24 매달다, 걸다	25 여행, 여정	26 회사
27 욕조	28 순간	29 사물함
30 두꺼운	31 견해, 관점	32 교통
33 평평한	34 목욕	35 ~을 겪다
36 ~을 입다	37 조심하다	38 혼자서
39 위험에 처한	40 ~에 지친, ~에 싫증 난	
41 너무 ~해서 …할 수 없다		42 ~에 들어가다
43 점점 더 많은		

단어 TEST Step 2   p.22

01 almost	02 hang	03 dirty
04 stick	05 solution	06 cushion
07 decide	08 hearing	09 decorate
10 difficulty	11 easily	12 flat
13 bath	14 bathtub	15 fountain
16 handle	17 journey	18 cross
19 crowded	20 way	21 blind
22 bookshelf	23 locker	24 view
25 uncomfortable	26 low	27 thick
28 product	29 seat	30 company
31 tight	32 universal	33 traffic
34 another	35 get on	36 in danger
37 by oneself	38 more and more	
39 go through	40 put on	41 tired of
42 be thinking of	43 watch out	

단어 TEST Step 3   p.23

1 blind, 눈이 먼   2 crowded, 붐비는

3 below, ~의 아래에   4 solution, 해결책

5 cross, 건너다   6 stick, 지팡이   7 flat, 평평한

8 handle, 손잡이   9 journey, 여행, 여정

10 low, 낮은   11 product, 제품

12 uncomfortable, 불편한   13 view, 관점. 견해

14 decorate, 장식하다   15 company, 회사

16 locker, 사물함

Get Ready 2

(1) not happy about, fountain, too high / m planning to put lower / good idea

(2) don't like, in wheelchairs, get in / thinking of building, with, steps

(3) happy, in wheelchairs, get on, easily / planning to hang, safer seat

Start Off Listen & Talk A

(1) not happy about / wrong with / reach, I'm thinking of, another

(2) happy about, There are, who / any / thinking, adding Braille / good idea

Start Off Listen & draw

I'm not happy about / What's wrong with / traffic lights, the same, who, blind to colors / How about putting / walking, standing

Speak Up Look and talk

I'm not happy about, too low / thinking of putting

Speak Up Mission

not happy about, bookshelf / too, any ideas / thinking of putting another bookshelf / good idea

Speak Up Real-life Scene

are, doing / thinking, ways, help / wrong / turn on, by herself, too high / happy about, either, about that / thinking of putting, step box, below / change, bigger one / turn on, more easily

Express Yourself A

(1) I'm not happy about, too low, too hard / I'm thinking of buying, What, think / Looks great, for so long, after, grows taller

(2) not happy about, handles, easy to use / How about, easily

(3) I'm thinking of, help, eat / doesn't have to

Learning Diary Check Yourself

not happy, light switch / wrong / too small / any ideas / I'm thinking of changing, with, bigger, turn on

Get Ready 2

(1) B: I'm not happy about this fountain. It's too high for some kids.

G: Well, I'm planning to put lower fountains together with it.

B: That's a good idea.

(2) G: I don't like the high steps here. People in wheelchairs can't get in.

B: Right. I'm thinking of building a new way with no steps.

(3) G: I'm not happy about this swing. People in wheelchairs can't get on it easily.

B: Right. I'm planning to hang a bigger and safer seat for them.

G: Good idea.

Start Off Listen & Talk A

(1) G: I'm not happy about the button.

B: Why? What's wrong with it?

G: It's too high. Children or people in wheelchairs can't reach it. I'm thinking of putting another switch for them.

(2) G: I'm not happy about the sign. There are some people who can't see.

B: Right. Do you have any ideas?

G: Well, I'm thinking of adding Braille on the sign.

B: That's a good idea.

Start Off Listen & draw

B: I'm not happy about the lights.

G: What's wrong with them?

B: The traffic lights look the same to some people who are blind to colors.

G: Oh, I see. How about putting an image on each light?

B: A walking man on the green light and a standing man on the red light? Good idea!

Speak Up Look and talk

B: I'm not happy about the desk. It's too low.

G: Right. I'm thinking of putting some pads on it.

B: Good idea.

Speak Up Mission

A: I'm not happy about the bookshelf. It's too small.

B: I think so, too. Do you have any ideas?

A: I'm thinking of putting another bookshelf on it.

B: That's a good idea.

Speak Up Real-life Scene

Dad: What are you doing here?

Son: I'm thinking of ways to help Miso.

Dad: What's wrong?

Son: She can't turn on the light by herself. This switch is too high for her.

Dad: That's right. I'm not happy about it, either. Do you have any good ideas about that?

Son: I'm thinking of putting a step box here below the switch.

Dad: Good idea. And I'll change the switch to a bigger one.

Son: Great. Grandma will like it, too. She can turn on the light more easily.

Express Yourself A

(1) G: I'm not happy about my brother's chair. It's too low and too hard.

B: Right. I'm thinking of buying this one. What do you think?

G: Looks great. I think he can use it for so long, even after he grows taller.

(2) B: I'm not happy about the door handles in my house. They are not easy to use for my grandma.

G: How about this one? She will pull it and open the door easily.

B: That's good.

(3) G: I'm thinking of buying this spoon. It will help my grandma eat soup easily.

B: Right. She doesn't have to hold it with her fingers.

Learning Diary Check Yourself

G: I'm not happy about this light switch.

B: Why? What's wrong?

G: It's too small. Grandma can't use it easily.

B: Do you have any ideas?

G: I'm thinking of changing it with a bigger one. That'll help her turn on the light easily.

B: Good idea.

본문 TEST Step 1   p.28~29

01 Mother, Universal Design

02 woman, journey, cities

03 looked over   04 couldn't see, hear

05 walk, without, stick

06 With, difficulties, climb, crowded

07 heavy, with, weak   08 got, found, in danger

09 moment, difficult, than, trip

10 Who, what, do

11 a 26-year-old designer

12 During, worked, company

13 meetings, designing, weak

14 other, design, those   15 became tired, same

16 Finally, around, understand, difficulties

17 clothes, uncomfortable, thick glasses

18 so, that, couldn't, without

19 thick, couldn't, with   20 put, of, make hearing

21 During, felt, go through

22 From, products, safely, easily

23 beginning, universal design

24 example, universal, low-floor

25 steps, such, without, help

26 course, other, get, comfortably

27 more, following, way   28 flat, easy, touch lives

29 around, weaker, point, view

30 next, better place, everybody

본문 TEST Step 2   p.30~31

01 Universal Design

02 started a journey to cities

03 looked over 80   04 couldn't see or hear

05 couldn't walk, without a stick

06 With all these difficulties, get on crowded

07 heavy doors, with her weak hands

08 found herself in danger

09 very difficult for her, more than

10 what made her do   11 a 26-year-old designer

12 During the 1970's, worked for

13 How about designing, weak people

14 for those people

15 became tired of, cold answer

16 Finally, to understand their difficulties

17 For this, put on, uncomfortable, thick glasses

18 so, that, couldn't, without a stick

19 so, that, couldn't, with them

20 lots of cotton, to make her hearing bad

21 During, felt, difficulties, go through

22 From this experience, safely, easily

23 beginning, universal design, design for all

24 One example, low-floor , buses

25 no steps, such a low floor, in a wheelchair, without any help

26 helps, get on, more comfortably

27 following Patricia's way

28 like, with, with, live better lives

29 Look around, from their point of view

30 next, a better place for everybody

31

1 Patricia Moore – 유니버설 디자인의 어머니

2 1979년에, 한 여성이 미국과 캐나다의 도시로 여행을 시작했다.

3 그녀는 80세가 넘어 보였다.

4 그녀는 잘 보거나 잘 들을 수 없었다.

5 그녀는 지팡이 없이는 잘 걸을 수 없었다.

6 이 모든 어려움을 가진 채, 그 여성은 지하철역에서 계단을 올라가거나 붐비는 버스에 올라타야 했다.

7 그녀는 무거운 문을 열거나 그녀의 약한 손으로 깡통 따개를 사용해야 했다.

8 때때로 그녀는 다치거나 위험에 처하기도 했다.

9 모든 순간이 그녀에게 매우 어려웠으나, 그녀는 115개 이상의 도시를 방문하였으며 1982년에 여행을 끝마쳤다.

10 그 여성은 누구였고 무엇이 그녀로 하여금 이 모든 것을 하게 만들었을까?

11 그녀는 26살의 디자이너인 Patricia Moore였다.

12 1970년대 동안, 그녀는 큰 디자인 회사에서 일했다.

13 그녀는 종종 회의에서 물었다. "나이 들거나 약한 사람들을 위해 디자인하는 게 어떨까요?"

14 다른 디자이너들은 항상 대답했다. "우리는 그런 사람들을 위해 디자인하지 않습니다."

15 그녀는 똑같은 냉담한 대답에 지쳤다.

16 마침내, 그녀는 '그런 사람들' 중의 하나가 되어 그들의 어려움을 더 잘 이해하기 위해 많은 도시를 여행하기로 결심했다.

17 이를 위해, 그녀는 자신의 할머니 옷을 입고, 불편한 신발을 신고, 두꺼운 안경을 썼다.

18 신발은 너무 불편해서 그녀는 지팡이 없이는 잘 걸을 수 없었다.

19 안경은 너무 두꺼워서 그녀는 안경을 쓰고는 잘 볼 수 없었다.

20 그녀는 또한 그녀의 청력을 나쁘게 하려고 귀에 많은 솜을 넣었다.

21 여행 동안, Patricia는 나이 든 사람들이 겪는 어려움을 느꼈다.

22 이 경험으로부터, 그녀는 누구나 안전하고 쉽게 사용할 수 있는 제품들을 고안했다.

23 이것이 '유니버설 디자인' 또는 '모두를 위한 디자인'의 시작이었다.

24 그녀의 유니버설 디자인 아이디어의 한 가지 예는 저상 버스이다.

25 그것은 계단이 없고 낮은 바닥을 가지고 있어서 휠체어를 탄 사람조차 아무 도움 없이 이용할 수 있다.

26 물론, 이것은 다른 사람들도 버스를 더 편안하게 탈 수 있도록 도와준다.

27 오늘날 점점 더 많은 디자이너가 Patricia의 방식을 따르고 있다.

28 크고 평평한 조명 스위치, 편한 손잡이를 가진 문, 터치 버튼을 가진 전화기와 같은 제품들은 사람들이 더 나은 삶을 살도록 도와주고 있다.

29 여러분의 주위를 둘러보고, 더 나이 들거나 더 약한 사람들의 어려움을 느껴 보고, 그들의 관점에서 해결책을 찾으려 고 노력해 봐라.

30 여러분은 다음의 Patricia Moore가 되어 세상을 모두에게 더 나은 곳으로 만들 수 있을 것이다.

1 Patricia Moore – Mother of Universal Design

2 In 1979, a woman started a journey to cities in the U.S. and Canada.

3 She looked over 80.

4 She couldn't see or hear well.

5 She couldn't walk well without a stick.

6 With all these difficulties, the woman had to climb stairs in subway stations and get on crowded buses.

7 She had to open heavy doors and use can openers with her weak hands.

8 Sometimes she got hurt or found herself in danger.

9 Every moment was very difficult for her, but she visited more than 115 cities and ended her trip in 1982.

10 Who was the woman and what made her do all this?

11 She was Patricia Moore, a 26-year-old designer.

12 During the 1970's, she worked for a big design company.

13 She often asked at meetings, "How about designing for old or weak people?"

14 The other designers always answered, "We don't design for those people."

15 She became tired of the same cold answer.

16 Finally, she decided to become one of "those people" and travel around many cities to understand their difficulties better.

17 For this, she put on her grandmother's clothes, uncomfortable shoes, and thick glasses.

18 The shoes were so uncomfortable that she couldn't walk well without a stick.

19 The glasses were so thick that she couldn't see well with them.

20 She also put lots of cotton in her ears to make her hearing bad.

21 During her journey, Patricia felt the difficulties old people go through.

22 From this experience, she designed products anybody could use safely and easily.

23 This was the beginning of "universal design," or "design for all."

24 One example of her universal design ideas is low-floor buses.

25 They have no steps and have such a low floor that even a person in a wheelchair can use them without any help.

26 Of course, this helps other people get on the bus more comfortably, too.

27 Today more and more designers are following Patricia's way.

28 Products like big flat light switches, doors with easy handles, and phones with touch buttons are helping people live better lives.

29 Look around you, feel the difficulties of people who are older or weaker, and try to find solutions from their point of view.

30 You could be the next Patricia Moore and make the world a better place for everybody.

Project Step 3

1. The hole cover was so dangerous that I couldn't ride my bike on it.

2. So I want to change the cover like this.

3. The new cover will help people ride a bike safely.

Link to the World

1. Kim Mandeok was born to a poor family in Jeju.

2. She worked hard and became rich.

3. In 1794, lots of people in Jeju were dying of hunger because of bad weather.

4. She spent almost all she had and saved a lot of people.

5. King Jeongjo let her take a trip to Mountain Geumgang.

구석구석지문 TEST Step 1   p.38

Express Yourself C1

1. washing machine, so, that, can't put, easily

2. However, side door

3. help, put, more easily

Project Step 3

1. so dangerous that, couldn't

2. to change, like

3. help, ride, safely

Link to the World

1. was born to

2. worked hard, became rich

3. were dying of, because of

4. spent almost all, saved

5. let her take a trip

구석구석지문 TEST Step 2   p.39

Express Yourself C1

1. The washing machine door in my house is so high that my little brother can't put clothes easily into it.

2. However, this machine has a side door.

3. It'll help my brother put clothes in more easily.

단어 TEST Step 1 p.40

01 활동	02 느린	03 승자
04 맛있는	05 초, 짧은 시간, 두 번째	
06 바퀴	07 젊음, 청춘	08 정확하게
09 끝나다, 끝내다	10 쉬는 시간	11 밝은, 똑똑한
12 단것, 단 음식	13 친근한, 다정한	14 비록 ~일지라도
15 옷	16 특별한	17 성적
18 손 글씨	19 희망적인	20 쓰레기 통
21 파도치다, 손을 흔들다		22 밖에
23 젖은	24 고르다	25 바다, 대양
26 가까이; 닫다	27 장소; 놓다, 두다	28 절약하다
29 결코 ~하지 않다	30 갈아입다, 바꾸다	31 동그라미, 원
32 귀여운	33 거울	34 체육 수업
35 A를 B로 자르다	36 잠깐만	37 B로 A를 덮다
38 ~할 필요가 없다	39 위아래로	40 휴식을 취하다
41 ~와 같은	42 A를 B에 더하다	43 ~로 가득 차다

단어 TEST Step 2 p.41

01 slow	02 most	03 never
04 activity	05 circle	06 finish
07 friendly	08 close	09 outside
10 save	11 delicious	12 wet
13 shape	14 change	15 grade
16 handwriting	17 hopeful	18 second
19 break time	20 winner	21 choose
22 exactly	23 ocean	24 bright
25 trash can	26 special	27 P.E. class
28 place	29 wheel	30 clothes
31 though	32 wave	33 sweet
34 youth	35 take a break	36 up to
37 don't need to	38 cut A into B	39 walk back
40 add A to B	41 cover A up with B	
42 be full of	43 wait a second	

단어 TEST Step 3 p.42

1 sweet, 단것 2 friendly, 친절한 3 bread, 빵

4 choose, 고르다 5 ocean, 바다, 대양

6 handwriting, 손 글씨 7 wet, 젖은 8 save, 절약하다

9 winner, 승자 10 grade, 성적 11 wave, 손을 흔들다

12 youth, 젊음 13 place, 장소 14 mirror, 거울

15 circle, 원 16 wheel, 바퀴

본문 TEST Step 1 p.43~48

01 Teens' Magazine	
02 Works, Art, Shapes	
03 Like, Circle	
04 like, because, ends	
06 cold outside	07 want, out, play
08 says, have to	
09 starting, going, cold	10 outside, days like
11 wait, second, most	12 cover, up, hide
13 Looking Back with	14 Life, art
15 Live yours	16 UNTIL, OVER
17 slow, never, back	18 little things, do
19 Follow, dream	20 My Bike
21 take, place, Back, riding	
22 Giving Tree	23 Out, wet
24 In, dry	25 Pretty big
26 Between, and	27 Selfies, Year
28 Though, lost, lot	29 Look at, made
30 Aren't, cute	31 made, big, for
32 made him happy	33 Have, seen, like
34 What, Think, Life	35 most, moment
36 take tests	
37 When, hungry, nothing	
38 change, before, class	
39 When, sleepy , class	
40 When, classes, rings	41 lovely time
42 lunch time	43 class with, favorite
44 last class	
45 when, during break	
46 when, myself, mirror	47 most awesome
48 got, grades, before	49 finishes earlier
50 because it, lot	51 delicious, for
52 best, in, same	53 most difficult, do
54 Washing, cans	
56 Making, presentation, front	
57 on, every	58 Group work
59 Places, Love, Village	60 Traditional Market
61 something delicious, visit	
62 buy, use, make, full	
63 choose, add, to	64 Youth Center
65 middle of, town	
66 because, learn, such as	67 play, take, break
68 Mr, Bakery	69 small bakery near
70 after, because, hungry	71 It, to, with
72 Let's Have Fun	73 Shape Puzzles
74 cut, into, shapes, from	75 Balls, Lines
76 such, way, exactly	
77 Eating Plastic Spoons	78 lot, thrown away

79 breaks down, pieces | 80 pieces, go, into

81 If, too, to, each | 82 Let's Make

83 universal, contest, last | 84 winners' works

85 come close, out | 86 pull, away, stops

87 need, turn, touch | 88 save lots, with

89 our, between, buildings | 90 Anybody, up, easily

91 can, get, rest

92 special, chairs, classroom

93 activities, together, wonderful

94 LET'S LAUGH | 95 Funny, Jokes

96 recycle, hopeful | 97 Because, full of

98 How, tell, friendly | 99 It waves

100 Why, sun, to | 101 get brighter

---

01 Teens' Magazine | 02 Works, in Shapes

03 Like, Circle

04 like, because, never ends

05 Snowman | 06 cold outside

07 go out, play | 08 have to

09 to snow, going to be cold | 10 on days like these

11 wait a second, the most wonderful

12 cover myself up, hide here

13 Looking Back with, Handwriting | 14 Life, art

15 yours | 16 UNTIL, OVER

17 slow walker, walk back | 18 little things

19 Follow | 20 My Bike

21 take, To any place, home, enjoy riding, every day

22 Giving | 23 there, wet

24 here, dry | 25 umbrella

26 Between, and | 27 Selfies, This

28 Though, lost, lot | 29 Look at, robots

30 Aren't cute | 31 a big cake

32 made him happy

33 Have you ever seen

34 What, Think of, Life

35 uncomfortable moment

36 take tests | 37 have nothing

38 change, before, after | 39 sleepy in class

40 after, rings | 41 most lovely time

42 lunch | 43 class, favorite

44 last class

45 sleeping during break time

46 myself, mirror | 47 most awesome

48 better grades than before | 49 finishes earlier

50 because, rains, snows

51 delicious, for dessert

---

52 in the same class | 53 most difficult, to do

54 trash cans | 55 Studying

56 Making a presentation, front

57 on time | 58 Group work

59 Places, Village | 60 Traditional Market

61 something delicious | 62 to make, full

63 choose, kind of, add, to | 64 Youth Center

65 in the middle of | 66 because, such as

67 take a break | 68 Bakery

69 near

70 after, because, always hungry

71 It, to enjoy | 72 Let's Have Fun

73 Shape Puzzles

74 cut, into, other shapes, from

75 Five Lines

76 in such a way, each line | 77 Are Eating

78 are thrown away | 79 breaks down into

80 go into fish, pieces | 81 Up to, each year

82 Let's Make | 83 universal design

84 winners' works | 85 come close, out

86 pull, away | 87 don't need to

88 save lots of water | 89 between, buildings

90 up, down easily | 91 get some rest

92 special, for

93 group activities, together, for

94 LET'S LAUGH | 95 Jokes

96 Why, recycle, hopeful | 97 Because, full of

98 How, tell, friendly | 99 waves

100 Why | 101 To get

---

1 십대들의 잡지

2 모양으로 표현된 예술 작품

3 동그라미처럼

4 나는 동그라미처럼 너를 사랑해. 왜냐하면 동그라미는 절대 끝나지 않기에.

5 눈사람

6 바깥은 추워.

7 나는 밖으로 나가 놀고 싶지 않네.

8 하지만 엄마는 그래야 한다고 하시네.

9 눈이 오기 시작하고 나는 추워질 거야.

10 나는 이런 날에는 나가서 놀고 싶지 않아.

11 하지만 잠깐만, 나는 최고로 멋진 생각이 났어!

12 나는 눈으로 내 몸을 완전히 덮고 여기에 숨어야지!

13 손 글씨로 돌아보기

14 인생은 예술이다.

15 다양한 색깔로 살아라.

16 끝날 때까지 끝난 게 아니다.

17 나는 느리게 걷는 사람이지만 절대 물러서지는 않는다.

18 나는 네가 하는 작은 일들을 사랑해.

19 네 꿈을 좇아라.

20 나의 자전거

21 바퀴 두 개가 나를 데려가네 / 어느 곳으로든지 / 학교로 / 다시 집으로 / 산으로 / 강으로 / 나는 내 자전거가 아주 좋아 / 나는 그걸 매일 즐겨 타네

22 아낌없이 주는 나무

23 저곳 바깥은 – 젖어 있고

24 이곳 안쪽은 – 말라 있네

25 엄청 큰 우산이네

26 나와 하늘 사이에 있는

27 올해의 셀피들

28 우리는 게임에 졌지만, 아주 즐거웠다.

29 우리가 만든 로봇들을 봐.

30 귀엽지 않니?

31 우리는 한 씨 할아버지께 드릴 큰 케이크를 만들었다.

32 그것은 할아버지를 행복하게 해 주었다.

33 나처럼 잘생긴 피터 팬을 본 적이 있니?

34 학교생활에 대해 어떻게 생각하니?

35 가장 불편한 순간

36 1. 시험을 칠 때

37 2. 정말 배가 고픈데 먹을 것이 없을 때

38 3. 체육 시간 전후에 옷을 갈아입을 때

39 4. 기타: 수업 중에 졸릴 때

40 종이 울렸는데 선생님이 수업을 끝내지 않을 때

41 가장 사랑스러운 시간

42 1. 점심시간

43 2. 가장 좋아하는 선생님의 수업 시간

44 3. 금요일의 마지막 수업 시간

45 4. 기타: 쉬는 시간에 잠잘 때

46 거울 속의 나를 볼 때

47 가장 멋진 뉴스

48 1. 전보다 좋은 성적을 받았다

49 2. 오늘 수업이 일찍 끝난다

50 3. 비나 눈이 많이 와서 학교에 가지 않는다

51 4. 기타: 후식으로 맛있는 단것을 먹는다

52 가장 친한 친구와 내가 같은 반이 되었다

53 가장 하기 힘든 일

54 1. 쓰레기통 씻기

55 2. 공부하기

56 3. 친구들 앞에서 발표하기

57 4. 기타: 매일 제시간에 등교하기

58 모둠 활동

59 우리 마을에서 우리가 좋아하는 곳

60 대한 전통 시장

61 맛있는 것이 먹고 싶으면, 대한 시장을 방문하세요.

62 엽전을 사면 여러분의 점심 도시락을 가득 채우는 데 그걸 쓸 수 있어요.

63 많은 종류의 음식을 골라서 점심 도시락에 담을 수 있답니다.

64 새봄 청소년 센터

65 이곳은 우리 마을 한가운데에 있는 새봄 청소년 센터입니다.

66 춤과 음악 같은 많은 것을 배울 수 있어서 우리는 이곳을 좋아한답니다.

67 우리는 또한 이곳에서 보드게임도 하고 휴식도 취할 수 있어요.

68 김 씨네 빵집

69 이곳은 학교 근처의 작은 빵집입니다.

70 우리는 항상 배가 고파서 방과 후에 거기에 가는 것을 좋아해요!

71 친구들과 맛있는 빵을 즐기는 것이 좋아요.

72 퍼즐로 즐거운 시간을 보내자!

73 도형 퍼즐

74 A를 똑같은 두 개의 조각으로 자르면, 그 두 조각으로 다른 모든 형태(B, C, D, E, F, G)를 만들 수 있다.

75 5개의 선에 놓인 10개의 공

76 각각의 선 위에 정확하게 4개의 공이 놓이도록 10개의 공을 5개의 선에 놓아라.

77 너는 플라스틱 숟가락을 먹고 있다!

78 1. 해마다 많은 플라스틱 숟가락이 버려진다.

79 2. 대부분의 플라스틱 숟가락은 바닷속에서 더 작은 조각으로 부서진다.

80 3. 아주 작은 플라스틱 조각들이 물고기의 몸속으로 들어간다.

81 4. 여러분이 그 물고기를 먹으면 여러분도 플라스틱을 먹게 되는 것이다. 해마다 11,000개의 조각까지!

82 꿈의 학교를 만들어 보자!

83 지난달에 우리는 우리 학교를 위한 유니버설 디자인 경시대회를 열었습니다.

84 여기 우승자들의 작품이 있습니다.

85 1. 손을 가까이 가져가면 물이 나옵니다.

86 손을 멀리 떨어뜨리면 물이 멈춥니다.

87 어떤 부분도 돌리거나 만질 필요가 없습니다.

88 우리는 이것으로 많은 물을 절약할 수 있습니다. — 오주연(1-3)

89 2. 이것은 두 개의 건물 사이에 있는 학교 정원입니다.

90 여기서는 누구라도 쉽게 위아래로 이동할 수 있습니다.

91 또한, 우리는 이곳에 앉아 휴식을 취할 수 있습니다. — 김지민 (3-5)

92 3. 교실용의 특별한 책상과 의자가 있습니다.

93 모둠 활동을 하기 위해 그것들을 함께 모아 3명, 4명, 또는 5명이 활동할 훌륭한 모둠 책상을 만들 수 있습니다. — 최유미 (2-1)

94 웃읍시다

95 재미있는 지구의 날 농담들 하! 하! 하!

96 재활용 통은 왜 희망적인가?

97 왜냐하면 '깡통[할 수 있다]'으로 가득 차 있기 때문이지.

98 바다가 다정하다는 것을 어떻게 알 수 있는가?

99 그것이 일렁이기[손을 흔들기] 때문이지.

100 태양은 왜 학교에 가는가?

101 더 밝아지기[똑똑해지기] 위해서지.

본문 TEST Step 4~Step 5　　　　p.57~64

1 Teens' Magazine

2 Works of Art in Shapes

3 Like a Circle

4 I love you like a circle because a circle never ends.

5 Snowman

6 It's cold outside.

7 I don't want to go out and play.

8 But Mom says I have to.

9 It's starting to snow and I'm going to be cold.

10 I don't like playing outside on days like these.

11 But wait a second, I have the most wonderful idea!

12 I'll cover myself up with snow and I'll hide here!

13 Looking Back with Your Handwriting

14 Life is art.

15 Live yours in COLOR.

16 IT ISN'T OVER UNTIL IT'S OVER.

17 I am a slow walker, but I never walk back.

18 I love the little things you do.

19 Follow your dream.

20 My Bike

21 Two wheels take me / To any place / To school / Back home / To the mountain / To the river / I love my bike / I enjoy riding it every day

22 Giving Tree

23 Out there – wet

24 In here – dry

25 Pretty big umbrella

26 Between me and the sky.

27 Selfies of This Year

28 Though we lost the game, we had a lot of fun.

29 Look at the robots we made.

30 Aren't they cute?

31 We made a big cake for Mr. Han.

32 It made him happy.

33 Have you ever seen a handsome Peter Pan like me?

34 What Do You Think of Your School Life?

35 The most uncomfortable moment

36 1. When I take tests

37 2. When I am really hungry and have nothing to eat

38 3. When I change clothes before and after P.E. class

39 4. others: When I am sleepy in class

40 When the teacher doesn't finish classes after the bell rings

41 The most lovely time

42 1. lunch time

43 2. class with my favorite teacher

44 3. the last class on Friday

45 4. others: when I am sleeping during break time

46 when I see myself in the mirror

47 The most awesome news

48 1. I got better grades than before

49 2. School finishes earlier today

50 3. I don't go to school because it rains or snows a lot

51 4. others: We eat delicious sweets for dessert

52 My best friend and I are in the same class

53 The most difficult work to do

54 1. Washing trash cans

55 2. Studying

56 3. Making a presentation in front of friends

57 4. others: Being on time every day

58 Group work

59 Places We Love in Our Village

60 Daehan Traditional Market

61 If you want to eat something delicious, visit Daehan Market.

62 You can buy "*yeopjeon*" and use it to make your lunch box full.

63 You can choose many kinds of food and add them to your lunch box.

64 Saebom Youth Center

65 This is Saebom Youth Center in the middle of our town.

66 We like this place because we can learn many things, such as dance and music.

67 We can also play board games and take a break here.

68 Mr. Kim's Bakery

69 This is a small bakery near the school.

70 We like to go there after school because we're always hungry!

71 It is good to enjoy delicious bread with friends.

72 Let's Have Fun with Puzzles!

73 Shape Puzzles

73 Shape Puzzles

74 If you cut the shape A into two same pieces, you can then make all the other shapes(B, C, D, E, F, G) from those two pieces.

75 Ten Balls in Five Lines

76 Place 10 balls in 5 lines in such a way that each line has exactly 4 balls on it.

77 You Are Eating Plastic Spoons!

78 1. A lot of plastic spoons are thrown away every year.

79 2. Most plastic breaks down into smaller pieces in the ocean.

80 3. Very small pieces of plastic go into fish.

81 4. If you eat the fish, you eat the plastic, too. Up to 11,000 pieces each year!

82 Let's Make a Dream School!

83 We had a universal design contest for our school last month.

84 Here are the winners' works.

85 1. When your hands come close, water comes out.

86 When you pull your hands away, the water stops.

87 You don't need to turn or touch any parts.

88 We can save lots of water with this. — by O Juyeon(1–3)

89 2. This is our school park between two buildings.

90 Anybody can go up and down easily here.

91 Also we can sit and get some rest here. — by Gim Jimin(3-5)

92 3. These are special desks and chairs for the classroom.

93 For group activities, you can get them together and make a wonderful group table for three, four, or five students. — by Choi Yumi(2–1)

94 LET'S LAUGH

95 Funny Earth Day Jokes Ha! Ha! Ha!

96 Why are recycle bins hopeful?

97 Because they're full of cans.

98 How can you tell the ocean is friendly?

99 It waves.

100 Why did the sun go to school?

101 To get brighter.